Memory in Shakespeare's Histories

Routledge Studies in Shakespeare

1 **Shakespeare and Philosophy**
Stanley Stewart

2 **Re-playing Shakespeare in Asia**
Edited by Poonam Trivedi and Minami Ryuta

3 **Crossing Gender in Shakespeare**
Feminist Psychoanalysis and the Difference Within
James W. Stone

4 **Shakespeare, Trauma and Contemporary Performance**
Catherine Silverman

5 **Shakespeare, the Bible, and the Form of the Book**
Contested Scriptures
Travis DeCook and Alan Galey

6 **Radical Shakespeare**
Politics and Stagecraft in the Early Career
Christopher Fitter

7 **Retheorizing Shakespeare through Presentist Readings**
James O'Rourke

8 **Memory in Shakespeare's Histories**
Stages of Forgetting in Early Modern England
Jonathan Baldo

Memory in Shakespeare's Histories

Stages of Forgetting in Early Modern England

Jonathan Baldo

NEW YORK LONDON

First published 2012
by Routledge
711 Third Avenue, New York, NY 10017

Simultaneously published in the UK
by Routledge
2 Park Square, Milton Park, Abingdon, Oxon OX14 4RN

Routledge is an imprint of the Taylor & Francis Group, an informa business

Typeset in Sabon by IBT Global.

Library of Congress Cataloging-in-Publication Data

Baldo, Jonathan.
Memory in Shakespeare's histories : stages of forgetting in early modern England / Jonathan Baldo.
p. cm. — (Routledge studies in Shakespeare ; 8)
Includes bibliographical references and index.
1. Shakespeare, William, 1564–1616—Histories. 2. Historical drama, English—History and criticism. 3. Memory in literature. I. Title.
PR2982.B28 2012
822.3'3—dc22
2011028310

ISBN: 978-0-415-89683-2 (hbk)
ISBN: 978-0-203-14212-7 (ebk)

To Roberta, Nathaniel, and David

and in loving memory of Gaspar and Ebba Baldo
and Rosalind Schwartz

Contents

Acknowledgments

This project began with a paper I delivered at a meeting of the Shakespeare Association of America (SAA) titled "Wars of Memory in *Henry V*." I am grateful to the SAA for the opportunity to present those initial findings at its annual conference and to *Shakespeare Quarterly* for permission to reprint the article of the same name that eventually grew out of that talk. A joint meeting of the SAA and the International Shakespeare Association chose an early version of my chapter on *King John* for a special session of their meeting in Los Angeles. Subsequent meetings of the SAA also helped me to shape individual chapters—most notably, in seminars led by Paul Yachnin, Lloyd Kermode, Brian Walsh, and James Bulman. I would like to thank all those who helped me improve earlier drafts of these chapters with their astute comments and suggestions, particularly William Carroll, James Siemon, and James Bulman. Linda Levy Peck first suggested that I contextualize this study of remembering, forgetting, and nationhood in Shakespeare's histories by acknowledging what was then the elephant in the room of Shakespeare studies: the Reformation. Theorist of history Hans Kellner pointed me toward recent scholarship on Hayden White's category of the historical sublime. Though it has only an indirect bearing on the subject of this study, the brilliant and suggestive work of Patricia Parker has been a constant source of inspiration and influence on my own thinking about Shakespeare. Specialists will no doubt recognize, from my title onward, the considerable debt I owe to Phyllis Rackin's celebrated study of Shakespeare's history plays, *Stages of History: Shakespeare's English Chronicles* (Cornell University Press, 1990). To the Department of English at the Ludwig-Maximilians-Universität München, especially Isabel Karremann and Tobias Döring, I am grateful for their invitation to present a portion of Chapter 1 at their stimulating, cross-disciplinary conference "Forgetting Faith? Negotiating Confessional Conflict in Early Modern Europe" in July, 2010.

The American Council of Learned Societies (ACLS) helped advance this project immeasurably with an ACLS Senior Fellowship, and I want to express my profound gratitude to that organization.

Our secretarial staff provided invaluable service following a fatal hard drive crash, resulting in a sudden and massive memory loss that brought the meaning of my research topic home to me in unexpected ways. The staff of Rush Rhees Library of the University of Rochester has been unfailingly helpful in securing research materials I needed for this project.

My colleagues and students at the Eastman School of Music, the University of Rochester, have been a steady source of stimulating thought and conversation. I thank all of my colleagues in the vigorous Department of Humanities—Jean Pedersen, Ernestine McHugh Piskáčková, Tim Scheie, Reinhild Steingröver, Tom Donnan, Caterina Falli, Rachel Remmel, and Glenn Mackin—for collectively producing an environment that has been so hospitable to interdisciplinary intellectual inquiry.

Finally, to Roberta, Nathaniel, and David, who make memory such a joyous and affirmative part of my life and whose love and support give meaning to everything I do, I affectionately dedicate this book.

Introduction
Be Our Ghost

This is the most obvious thing in the world: man is separated from the past (even from the past only a few seconds old) by two forces that go instantly to work and cooperate: the force of forgetting (which erases) and the force of memory (which transforms).

It is the most obvious thing, but it is hard to accept, for when one thinks it all the way through, what becomes of all the testimonies that historiography relies on? What becomes of our certainties about the past, and what becomes of History itself, to which we refer every day in good faith, naively, spontaneously? Beyond the slender margin of the incontestable (there is no doubt that Napoleon lost the battle of Waterloo), stretches an infinite realm: the realm of the approximate, the invented, the deformed, the simplistic, the exaggerated, the misconstrued, an infinite realm of nontruths that copulate, multiply like rats, and become immortal.

—Milan Kundera, *The Curtain*[1]

Michel Foucault commented on the power of film to shape perceptions of the past, "Memory is actually a very important factor in struggle . . . if one controls people's memory, one controls their dynamism."[2] Or as George Orwell memorably wrote in *1984*, "'Who controls the past,' ran the Party slogan, 'controls the future: who controls the present controls the past.'"[3] Nearly four hundred years earlier, a different sort of popular entertainment, Shakespeare's plays, dramatized this idea with unmatched complexity and power. Not merely particular ways of shaping and recollecting late medieval English history from less memorable sources, namely, printed chronicles, Shakespeare's history plays also stage vigorous explorations of the shifting and tenuous partnerships between historical memory and forgetting, changing religious practices and doctrine, social stability, the power of the English state, and nationhood. A distinguishing feature of Shakespeare's later histories, beginning with *King John*, is the prominent role he assigns to the need to forget and the opportunities that issue from forgetting. For plays ostensibly designed to recover the past and make it available to the present, they devote remarkable attention to the ways in which states and individuals alike passively neglect or actively suppress the past and rewrite history. Nearly every prominent feature of Shakespeare's second tetralogy—for instance, *Richard II*'s strangely occluded opening and its marginalizing of Ireland to the bizarre treatment of the Lollard martyr Oldcastle, the side trip to the English countryside to witness its climate of unrelieved nostalgia, and even Henry V's apparent triumph over the unruly forces of memory in the last play in the cycle—bears testimony to the growing accent on erasure and on rewriting in Shakespeare's staging of English history.

Two broad and related historical developments caused remembering and forgetting to occupy increasingly equivocal positions in Shakespeare's history plays: an emergent nationalism and the Protestant Reformation. Due to a growth in England's sense of national identity, constructed largely in opposition to international Catholicism, historical memory increasingly appeared to be a threat as well as a support to the cause of unity. Because of the ongoing, transformative process known as the Reformation, many Elizabethans felt themselves to be irreparably divided from their recent past, a condition that is reflected in the fluidity and uncertainty of the values the history plays attach to remembering and forgetting.

Shakespeare's historical imagination seems to have been drawn to material that could be conceived and represented in terms of rupture rather than continuous development: the outbreak of the Wars of the Roses in *1 Henry VI*, for example, or the rebellion in *2 Henry VI* whose leader Cade declares, "my mouth shall be the parliament of England" (4.7.11–12).[4] In the plays usually referred to as the first tetralogy—*The Three Parts of Henry VI* and *Richard III*—these ruptures are more often than not to be deplored, and memory is assigned the role of antidote to such breaks with the forms of the past. Efforts at sustaining or reestablishing a sense of historical continuity become an important aspect of the first sequence's conflicts. In the earlier histories, memory plays the role of guardian of history and of the collective identity of the realm against all the forces—time, forgetfulness, conquest—that would erase it. Thus, the English in the plays of the first tetralogy battle not only for political control but for a kind of historical sovereignty as well. Defined by words and by their will to preserve the historical record, Phyllis Rackin has demonstrated, the English contend with a French iconoclasm associated with things, with a "physical reality that Joan invokes to discredit" the written English record[5]:

> The French action—to erase the English record—operates at two levels. Within the represented action, the French fight to drive the English from their country. Moreover, at the rhetorical level, they attack both the English version of history and the values it expresses with an earthy iconoclasm that subverts inherited notions of chivalric glory invoked by the English heroes.[6]

Historical memory itself is the main prize to be won, and possession of it, like England's possession of French territories, remains precarious: a lesson continually reinforced by Shakespeare's translation of chronicle history into the oral and evanescent performance that is a play. Conversely, whereas in the earlier histories the power to erase historical memory plays the role of English history's dangerous and seductive other, usually conceived as French and feminine, as Rackin has argued, in the later plays it becomes an aspect of English monarchal power itself: no longer threatening but constitutive of national and dramatic unity alike; not history's confirmed enemy but to a large extent the hand that writes it.

By contrast with Shakespeare's first forays into English history, *King John* makes it very hard to determine where the national interest lies: with historical memory or with its cancellation, with strengthened memory of the past or with amnesia. Like the first tetralogy, *King John* and the second tetralogy lean toward conceptualizing change—whether of Richard II, Prince Hal, or the English state—in terms of interrupted sequences, ruptures rather than continuous development. But unlike the first sequence, the later plays tend to explore creative uses of forgetting both for answering traumatic loss and for establishing a sense of national unity. The first tetralogy begins by looking back upon a heroic past, embodied by the recently deceased Henry V, whose values and memory it struggles to revive or sustain; *the second tetralogy, by contrast, begins by looking back upon a culture in which looking back—that is, historical memory—held a stable and unequivocal value. Richard II* recalls a time in which remembering itself held a more respected place within the kingdom. In other words, in the second tetralogy, Shakespeare seems to be exploring the differences between his own culture—divided from the past, sharply divided from within by conflicting interpretations of the past, and even divided about the very value of recalling the past—and what Mary Carruthers has characterized as the "profoundly memorial" aspect of cultures of the Middle Ages.[7] *Richard II* is nothing less than Shakespeare's daring revaluation of mnemonic values.

In the plays of the second tetralogy that will be the focus of this study, characters manufacture and adhere to widely varying and sometimes sharply divergent interpretations of the past, not unlike those produced in England by the forces of the Reformation. According to Keith Thomas, "Early modern England had not one myth of the Middle Ages, but two; and they were sharply opposed to each other. One was supportive of the social order, the other potentially subversive." Some looked upon the era as "a dreadful period of brutality and violence"; others viewed it nostalgically as a time of "feasting praying, chivalry, courtly love and charity."[8] Perceptions of the past, however, were not always polarized according to religious affiliation. As Ian Archer writes,

> [T]he intellectual world of Elizabethan England was not rigidly divided between the adherents of a Protestant view of a medieval dark age and a Catholic view of an idealized golden age. Protestants could appreciate the virtue that had existed in former times, and some of [John] Stow's

> characteristic emphases [in his *Survey of London* (1598)] surface in other more obviously godly writers.[9]

But what both views shared was a sense of a breach with the immediate past. England was no longer as it quite recently had been. Elizabethan England experienced a jostling of competing historical memories, very much in evidence in the internal memory wars of the second tetralogy, as various forces strive to produce a more uniform perception of the past that political theorists associate with nationhood.

Other causes, intimately related to both the ongoing process of Reformation and the growth of nationalism, exerted pressures on the relation of the people of early modern England to their personal and collective pasts: for instance, the growth of a mercantile economy and the spread of printing. Regarding the former, the expansion of an economic model of credit, contract, and exchange and the social mobility it produced, particularly as reflected in the two *Henry IV* plays, Nina Levine has written, "By the beginning of the seventeenth century defenses of credit and commerce began to appear in print, as London merchants and tradesmen attempted to justify their place within the changing economy."[10] These justifications had more to do with the reconciliation of private gain and the public good than with anchoring their validations of wealth through reference to the past. As W. H. Auden asserted in connection with *The Merchant of Venice*,

> In a mercantile society, social power is derived from money, the distribution of power is constantly changing, which has the effect of weakening reverence for the past; who one's distant ancestors were soon ceases to be of much social importance. The oath of lifelong loyalty is replaced by the contract which binds its signatories to fulfill certain specific promises by a certain specific future date, after which their commitment to each other is over.[11]

The brisk market in land that emerged in the sixteenth century as a direct consequence of the confiscation of monastic lands resulted in increased disputes between tenants and landlords, inevitably informed by memories of past traditions and practices. According to Adam Fox, "A new breed of landlords who acquired their land not by inheritance but through investment . . . had little knowledge of local customs, little empathy with the traditional mores of neighbourhood, and very often saw such things as inimical to their proprietorial freedoms and commercial interests."[12] In a compelling reading of John Stow's *A Survey of London* (1598), a nostalgic record of London's antiquities, Lawrence Manley shows how Stow registers his "preference for an explicitly integrated urban order, where the articulation of custom, hierarchy, order and degree were visibly and ritually affirmed as a matter of routine" and his corresponding "distaste for a theatricalisation of public life that he associates with the coming of the Reformation, acquisitive individualism and the secular bureaucratic state."[13] Mercantilism, in other words, was part of a nexus of social and economic forces that resulted in weakened attachments to the past.

The rise of both written records and print and the growth of literacy in the vernacular within a largely oral culture constituted another development that helped alter the relationship of the people of early modern England to their past. Like the expansion of mercantilism, the rise of print and written records was tied to the twin tides of nationalism and the Reformation. The spread of print culture has been credited by Benedict Anderson and others with helping to foster the "imagined communities" that are nations, and Richard Helgerson has shown in detail how a literature of the vernacular produced competing and heterogeneous "forms of nationhood" in Elizabethan England.[14] Adam Fox underscores the impact of the Reformation on the "extent to which England had become . . . a society which drew heavily on written forms of communication," as Thomas Cromwell and other reformers exploited the propaganda value of written sources and the "new medium of print" as never before.[15] Shakespeare's age, like our own, witnessed significant changes in the technologies of memory, in the ways in which individuals and societies remember their pasts, and it is this homology between his age and our own, a period of startling transformations in cyber-technologies of preserving and recording, I would suggest, that helps to explain the explosion of interest in memory studies in general and in Shakespeare's chronicle histories in particular over the past two decades. In a recent and provocative book, Viktor Mayer-Schönberger warns about a digital age that has made the storage and retrieval of information so cheap and easy that it has caused the demise of forgetting and its social benefits: forgiveness, for instance, and the ability to reinvent or refashion oneself.[16] A surfeit of memory in the digital realm can be an encumbrance, Mayer-Schönberger argues, an obstacle rather than an aid in making sound decisions. The plays of Shakespeare's second tetralogy, I will argue, mount a surprisingly similar argument. In fictionalized form, they explore both the virtues and the difficulty of forgetting in an era of radical social change, in which the past could seem a lost world and memory of the past a source of suffering. "Heaven and earth,/ Must I remember?" Hamlet asks in anguish of the memory of his father and his loving relationship with his mother (I.2.142–3). Both explicitly, in Richard II's belated discovery of the torments of the past tense, and implicitly, in Shakespeare's rough, comic treatment of the Protestant martyr Oldcastle, Shakespeare's second tetralogy poses Hamlet's rhetorical question in an astonishing variety of ways. It is a question that must have resonated intimately with audiences for whom remembrance of the pre-Reformation past produced responses ranging from disquieting nostalgia to a traumatic sense of loss, "the difficult engagement of a mournful present with a hardly retrievable past," as Zenon Luis-Martinez writes of *Richard II*.[17] The first of Shakespeare's histories to contend with the memory of a Reformation hero, *King John*, I will argue, inaugurates a series of plays in which Shakespeare explores the virtues of forgetting in a print age, to adapt Mayer-Schönberger's title to the exigencies of early modern England.

In this study of conflicts over the function of historical memory and forgetting in Shakespeare's later histories, the last two factors I have named—the rise of mercantilism and of print—will arise only tangentially. Although they will not be entirely forgotten, they will not receive the attention they no doubt deserve as part of a complete explanation as to why various forms and functions of forgetting receive so much attention in plays ostensibly designed to recover the past. Instead, these chapters will focus their attention more directly on the sense of historical rupture and the experience of trauma associated with the ongoing process of the Protestant Reformation and on a shift in the way the plays construe English political identity: from medieval dynastic realm to early modern nation.

In Shakespeare's earlier history plays, England is represented primarily as a dynastic realm whose identity is based on historical continuity. The "sanctity of medieval kingship," in Tillyard's phrase,[18] appears to derive from history itself. Royal power derives its authority from historical continuity (which is constantly under siege in the first tetralogy), at least until Shakespeare's Richard II severs the connection between present power and past authority, thereby altering the implicit alliance between the chronicle history play and historical memory. Once history ceases to function as a means of authorizing royal power, it is free to be waylaid by the rebel powers, as it is in *1 Henry* IV amidst a flurry of other robberies. Hotspur is eventually "robbed" of his youth (5.4.76). The "squires of the night's body" and "thieves of the day's beauty" (body and booty), led by Falstaff, steal both gold and honor, as Falstaff will outrageously claim to have killed Hotspur in hand-to-hand combat. Having stolen from the court, the prince steals hours (which he vows to "redeem" or pay back, 1.2.177) and borrows identities in the taverns of England, all beneath the unwitting tutelage of England's chief robber, the King himself, who in some eyes has stolen the crown with relative impunity. In the play's heady atmosphere of "borrowed title[s]" (5.3.23) and grotesquely extended credit, the rebels make off with the cause of historical memory itself, charging the King with forgetfulness and repeating at every opportunity, like a "popinjay" or parrot (Hotspur, 1.3.50), their favorite history lesson about the King's ingratitude toward the kingmaking Percies. Shakespeare's second tetralogy of chronicle plays, in other words, enact vigorous, internal history wars. They increasingly reflect divisive attitudes toward the past in Elizabethan England, and even sharper conflicts between the obligation to remember and the need to forget, the state's interest in forming and controlling a national narrative, and the challenges such a project met from the counter-memories of various communities like England's Catholics, church papists, and Puritans.

By contrast with the modern idea of the nation, writes Anderson, "in the older imagining" of the "dynastic realm," "states were defined by centers, borders were porous and indistinct, and sovereigns faded imperceptibly into one another."[19] In her comparative study *Nationalism: Five Roads to Modernity*, Liah Greenfeld argues that the modern Western construct of the nation first took shape in sixteenth-century England: "[B]y 1600, the existence in England of a national consciousness and identity, and as a result, of a new geo-political entity, a nation, was a fact."[20] John Guy makes a similar point when discussing "the shift from 'realm' to 'state'" in the Tudor period. The concept of a "state," a "defined territory" with "a sovereign government which recognized no superior in political, ecclesiastical, and legal matters," was well established by the 1590s.[21] Both Greenfeld and Guy point toward terminological shifts—largely from "realm" and "kingdom" to "state" and "nation"—that register the conceptual shift from dynastic realm to unitary nation whose identity and stability do not depend entirely on a principle of legitimate succession.[22] A similar shift is discernible over the course of Shakespeare's chronicle histories. "Nation" and "state" appear with increasing frequency in the later histories, gradually supplanting "realm," which predominates in the early *Henry VI* plays.[23]

The social anthropologist Ernest Gellner identifies two paths whereby European nation-states grew out of and replaced dynastic-religious ones. Nations "could roll their own culture out of existing folk traditions, and then form a state around such a newly created normative great tradition": the path of "created memory" and ethnographic exploration. Or else they could "grow around pre-existing states and/or High Cultures": the path of "induced oblivion," of consigning folk traditions to the dustbin.[24] The latter path was famously mapped by the historian Ernest Renan in the late nineteenth century in his lecture "What Is a Nation?" delivered at the Sorbonne in 1882, in which he urged the French "to abjure the political use of ethnography and ethnology."[25] For the most part, according to Gellner, Western European nation-building has followed the path advocated by Renan: "Western nationalism ignores and does not explore folk diversity."[26] By contrast, the Eastern European theory and practice of nation-building has a strong ethnographic component, stressing folk cultures and ethnic origins: "In the East they remember what never occurred, in the West they forget that which did occur."[27] As a result, historical memory can counteract or impede rather than foster national unity. In Renan's famous declaration, "Forgetting, I would even go so far as to say historical error, is a crucial factor in the creation of a nation, which is why progress in historical studies often constitutes a danger for [the principle of] nationality."[28] Arguing against attempts to base the nation on ethnographic analysis, Renan saw nations as the products of human will and "convergent facts,"[29] not as deterministic products of race and geography. Above all, nations are produced by the contingencies of what their citizens collectively remember and forget.

Shakespeare wrote his English chronicle histories, especially those from *King John* to *Henry VIII*, with a growing awareness that, as Ernest Gellner paraphrases Renan, "the basis of national identity is not memory but amnesia"[30]—or, at least, a complicated partnership of the two.[31] Shakespeare's histories both reflect, help construct, and critically examine a growing sense of national identity in early modern England on what Gellner identifies as the Western model. One of the most intriguing ways in which they do so is by casting remembering and forgetting in increasingly equivocal roles. In a cultural milieu that was sharply divided in its perceptions of the past and in its ideas of how the past ought to be remembered, Shakespeare's histories stage battles over memory and the uses of forgetting, and they expose the degree to which national unity is produced by selective erasure of the past. The power to manipulate the memories of others and particularly to erase the past and make others forget becomes a critical aspect of state power, culminating in the charismatic Henry V, with reprises of the type in Prospero and Henry VIII.[32] Standing at the beginning of the era of European nationalism, his plays empower us to see the "imagined community" of the nation as in large part a forgery or imposture, founded on a forgetting that frequently masquerades as remembrance. Even as Shakespeare's histories help to fashion the early modern nation, they subject that construct to critical exposure and scrutiny. To be sure, they help recollect the nation's past, but they also foreground acts of forgetting and explore memory as a source of conflict and a site at once dangerous and opportune for political power. It is intriguing to speculate that the author most frequently employed, long after his death, as an instrument of English nationalism and expansionism might already have exposed, in the early stages of the formation of the modern English nation-state, the ironies, the fragilities, and the masks of a political formation based largely on forgetting.

In the later history plays that are the focus of this study, historical memory becomes increasingly dangerous: not a prize but a problem, a threat to English political identity as well as its foundation. The second sequence of history plays reflects early Tudor England's experience in Wales in trying to assimilate that people and region to a dominant national culture as well as Elizabethan campaigns of cultural erasure in Ireland. They also anticipate by a few years King James' argument before his first English parliament on March 19, 1604, of the dangers of historical memory for the sense of national unity. The prospect that fragments of the past will slip into what Thomas Nashe called "the grave of oblivion,"[33] which in the earlier histories is represented as a form of defeat akin to military surrender or conquest, becomes an increasingly important aspect of English power. Furthermore, the second tetralogy explores both the agonies and enticements associated with loosened attachments to the past that frequently resulted from Protestant reforms.[34]

Taken collectively, Shakespeare's second tetralogy of history plays forcefully ask the question posed in the title of Eric Foner's collection of essays *Who Owns History?*[35] Shakespeare represents monarchs struggling to command the popular memory; rebels who wave the banner of memory in the face of a king they deem "forgetful"; commoners who nostalgically recall a world that perhaps never was; an outrageous historical palimpsest, a hedonist bearing the name of a Lollard martyr, Sir John Oldcastle/Falstaff, who over the course of two plays becomes the symbol of a merry world for which there was considerable nostalgia in late Elizabethan England, but which most of Shakespeare's contemporaries associated with the traditional faith and its ritual year, not Lollardy or the reformed religion; and, at the head of all, a king, Richard II, who, through the traumatic loss of his throne, suffers a painful initiation into the past tense and a permanent sense of loss not unlike the one that many Elizabethans experienced as a result of the English Reformation. Ultimately Shakespeare dramatizes a nation whose fragile and threatened sense of unity will hinge on banishing certain disruptive historical memories to the corners of the kingdom, and monarchs who, beginning with Richard II, need to suppress memories of the past in order to maintain or consolidate their own hold on power.

In the chapters that follow I explore the increasingly complex roles assigned to forgetting, demonized as history's "other" in Shakespeare's earlier history plays, in *King John*, *Richard II*, *1 Henry IV*, *2 Henry IV*, and *Henry V* and its critical part in the fashioning of the nation in late Elizabethan England. Following the civil memory wars of *1 Henry IV* and the dispersed, heterogeneous forms of memory in *2 Henry IV*, the final play in the tetralogy, *Henry V*, represents a national narrative-in-the-making, one that seems largely unchallenged by the end of the play, as the viewpoint of even the ferociously historical Welsh Captain Fluellen seems almost too easily incorporated into the English monarchy's master narrative. Even in *Henry V*, however, the apparent triumph of unity—political, artistic, and mnemonic—is qualified by manifold reminders of elements of the past that the forces of consolidation have tried to forget or suppress. To the extent that Shakespeare encourages us to hear those reminders of history's remainders, those ghostly and potentially rebellious mnemonic traces in *Henry V*, the early modern nation remains a work-in-progress, an ongoing fiction whose completion is always destined to lie in the future. My final chapter will sketch the ways in which *King John* accomplishes a remarkable revaluation of the values attached to remembering and forgetting. With the social elevation of Philip the Bastard, Shakespeare enacts nothing less than the renovation of forgetting itself, a kind of bastard muse of the chronicle history play. As Shakespeare seemed increasingly to recognize, especially as he came to work with controversial and divisive historical figures like King John and Sir John Oldcastle, such a play depended for its intelligibility and coherence largely on what its author chose to omit, forget, or suppress in order to produce its own imagined unity as well as the unity of the nation it reflected.

1 Birth of a Nation from the Spirit of Tragedy

The Historical Sublime in *Richard II*

Like the play it treats, this chapter begins with a challenge. *Richard II* is commonly read as marking the passing of a medieval world and its immemorial theory of sacramental kingship.[1] Subscribed to by Richard, this theory proves obsolescent and gives way in the course of the play to modern, Machiavellian ideas of rule embodied by Bolingbroke and associated with personal power, adeptness, and political cunning. The new world of Bolingbroke's sober and practical realism stands in stark contrast to the extravagant, elegiac poeticism of Richard.

The following reading seeks to revise this paradigm by focusing on the complex interplay of remembering and forgetting, the subjects of plots and counterplots in *Richard II*. Such an approach reveals that Richard himself represents a new approach to kingship based upon a novel orientation toward the past; that he eventually bequeaths a modified version of this orientation to his Lancastrian successors, who do not so much represent a new beginning as a continuation of the dynasty of the "forgetful" established by Richard; and that his casual relation to and limited attention to the past are closely related to the new construct of the early modern nation and to what were to many English the traumatic effects of the ongoing Reformation. Focusing attention on the politics of amnesia helps make sense of the strangely occluded beginning of the play and illuminates how that beginning sets the stage for all that follows, including the marginalizing of Ireland and especially the play's sense of history as rupture rather than a linear succession of causes and effects.

Habitually regarded by critics as having a stubborn, atavistic attachment to medieval rites and cultural forms that guarantee his identity, Richard breaks with the medieval past as much as Bolingbroke does. Specifically, he discards what Mary Carruthers characterizes as the "profoundly memorial" aspect of medieval culture. The Middle Ages, Carruthers argues, identified "memory with the formation of moral virtues."[2] The development of the memory arts in that period, the aim of well-developed pedagogical methods, served not dialectic and rhetoric, as they had in ancient Greece and Rome, but ethics: "it was in trained memory that one built character, judgment, citizenship, and piety."[3] Eamon Duffy has shown at length how in the pre-Reformation Church "the language of memory pervaded the cult of the dead."[4] In neglecting a medieval discourse of memory and ostentatiously rejecting the values associated with a memory culture, Richard lays the foundation for the Lancastrian monarchs' project of legitimating their rule by means other than continuity with the past.[5] In other words, this apparent relic of an England from which we have become forever separated is the play's first innovator or modernist, preparing the ground for the early modern nation.

After his deposition, however, Richard will recover a semblance of medievalism in the form of an immersion in memory, a self-representation that borrows heavily from medieval hagiography,[6] and a habit of thinking of the present in terms of biblical history, but only after a traumatic loss that will produce a painful birth of historical consciousness. From a wholesale disinterest in the past, Richard is plunged into one of the more harrowing ways of experiencing the past, one that may be summarized by the term "the historical sublime," introduced by Hayden White and developed more recently by theorists of history Frank Ankersmit and Hans Kellner. Belatedly transformed into a creature of memory (Richard is too late in everything he does), Richard regards the past in ways that are less medieval than Elizabethan. As his attention shifts from the present to the past, the types of forgetting he practices are transformed, from those associated with casual or pedestrian neglect in the first half of the play to those associated with trauma. What changes utterly and irrevocably in the course of the play, besides the institution of kingship and the grounds for legitimating power, is the relation of both Richard and Bolingbroke to what now appears to be England's irrecoverable past. *Richard II* enacts a birth of historical consciousness and shows such consciousness to originate in traumatic loss. Over the course of the play, Richard is transformed from a monarch who is defined largely by his studied neglect of the past to an embodiment of painful historical awareness. It is a transformation with which Elizabethans would have been all too familiar. A trauma in five acts, *Richard II* held up a mirror to its original audiences in which they might have regarded their own detachment from a medieval past as a result of the Protestant Reformation.[7]

"FAIR SEQUENCE AND SUCCESSION"

In the first twenty-three lines of the play, we witness the deposition of a political construct that augurs the later deposition of a monarch. These same lines present the linguistic equivalent of a trial by combat. The matter in question, only slightly hidden, is the proper attitude one ought to hold towards the past: an apt question, certainly, with which to begin a history play.

Richard II begins with the careful orchestration of continuity in time, a model for political continuity and a means for making such continuity appear a natural form rather than a contingent social construct, as a later speech by the Duke of York makes clear: "Take Herford's rights away and take from time/ His charters and his customary rights./ Let not tomorrow then ensue today" (2.1.195–7). By marking orderly transitions from past to present to future, the play's opening rehearses the traditional grounds for political stability that will seem obsolescent by the second half of the play, where historical rupture, dislocation of identities, and traumatic loss prevail. The first twenty-three lines mimic the outlook of the play's elder statesmen, Gaunt and York, sons of Edward III: specifically, their desire to keep the present connected with the past in a steady line of historical development, even as they are aware of the rupture produced by Richard's profligate and ineffectual reign that drifts unanchored by proper attention to his predecessors.

But before we learn of Richard's habitual dismissal of the past, we hear in his misleading opening line, "Old John of Gaunt, time-honored Lancaster," a reverential attitude toward predecessors and apparent respect for precedent.[8] A few lines later, he commands that the complainants be called "to our presence. Face to face/And frowning brow to brow ourselves will hear/The accuser and the accusèd freely speak" (1.1.15–7). This presentist language yields to unctuous forecasts as Bolingbroke and Mowbray compete to flatter the king. Bolingbroke wishes Richard "Many years of happy days," which Mowbray expands to, "Each day still better other's happiness,/ Until the heavens, envying earth's good hap,/ Add an immortal title to your crown" (1.1.20, 22–4). Within the play's first twenty-three lines, therefore, we have spanned past, present, and future in orderly succession. The play's beginning seems to establish, in grammatical miniature, the ideal of what York terms "fair sequence and succession" (2.1.199), a principle of order that will be repeatedly violated in the course of the play.

A closer look at these lines, however, reveals evidence of corruption within the very principle of orderly succession as each temporal phase—past, present, and future—is riddled with doubt, contradiction, or the suspicion of dissembling. The epithets "old" and "time-honoured" to describe John of Gaunt suggest an attitude of obligation toward the past that is confirmed by Gaunt's use of the feudal term in his reply, "I have, my liege" (1.1.7). But in his next speech Richard asks whether Bolingbroke has accused Mowbray "on ancient malice,/ Or worthily as a good subject should/ On some known ground of treachery in him?" (1.1.9–11). Richard's "ancient malice" throws down the gauntlet, as it were, to "time-honoured." It invites us to reconsider the reverential status tacitly accorded to acts of remembering by the play's opening line, and looks ahead to revelations about Richard's mixture of inattention toward and denigration of the past. Does memory yield continuity and protect social order, or does it fuel conflict? The opening tilts toward the latter, as evidenced by Richard's command that the antagonists "forget" (1.1.156).

Shifting from past to present, Richard commands that the opponents be called "to our presence" (1.1.15), thereby fusing the spatial to the temporal and both to royal power.[9] In Richard's presence, however, nothing is illuminated, nor can it be, because Mowbray is constrained to speak obliquely, having taken part in Gloucester's murder at Richard's behest. The very phrase "our presence" seems strange in a scene in which the King himself is an exercise in concealment, characterized largely by absences or omissions. Images of the future turn out to be just as tarnished as those of past and present. Mowbray's and Bolingbroke's flattery produces nothing but corrupt images of future happiness, prefiguring the downfall of a monarch surrounded by sycophants. The play's opening slyly reveals a taint within a paradigmatic form of lineal succession, the orderly sequence of past, present, and future, hinting at a Gaunt-like debility within time's "charters and his customary rights," the basis for political stability. It is precisely this debility, however, that will liberate England from its older identity as dynastic realm and prepare the way for the emerging conception of the early modern nation.

Violations of lineal succession are embedded in the deep structure of the play itself: the non-sequential opening disrupts a causal chain of events, just as the lineal succession of England's crown will soon be disrupted by Richard's deposition. Crimes against rightful inheritance and dynastic continuity lie at the center of the play's action. The murder of Gloucester by his nephews Richard and Aumerle, the alleged plot against John of Gaunt by Thomas Mowbray (1.1.137),[10] Richard's denying Bolingbroke his inheritance, and the latter's usurpation of the English throne all belong in this class. Richard denies Bolingbroke his patrimony, and Bolingbroke will in turn deny Mortimer his superior claim to the English crown.[11] Richard's repeated pattern of treating a future condition as if it were past and irrevocable—for example, his behaving as if he has already been deposed in the deposition scene—and his lack of interest in history, the very thing that his audiences have come to see reenacted, may be counted among his crimes against what York calls "fair sequence and succession" (2.1.199). He figuratively disinherits English audiences of their past, just as he disinherits Bolingbroke of his title and property. As an anti-historical figure, Shakespeare's Richard closely resembles his historical counterpart, who regularly elevated royal prerogative over custom and law. As articles from the Assembly of 1399 put it, Richard "refused to keep and defend the just laws and customs of his kingdom, but [wished] at his own arbitrary will to do whatever appealed to his desires" and claimed "that his laws were in his own mouth, or occasionally in his own breast; and that he alone could establish and change the laws of his realm."[12]

One consequence of Richard's disregard for the rule of succession is his deepening isolation. Through his inattention to a specifically English past, Richard isolates himself historically from his predecessors, a dynastic succession of legitimate rulers. This self-imposed isolation in time in turn reflects his political detachment from his contemporaries, both nobles and commons. Mirroring these, Richard embodies what I would call a theatrical solitude, a figurative isolation from audiences who have come to the playhouse to collectively witness the revival of their collective past. All these dimensions of Richard's isolation issue from violations of blood inheritance. The play as a whole may be considered one such violation, for the play surreptitiously challenges dynastic inheritance as the fundamental principle of English political identity and the grounds for political stability. In fact, it might be argued that as blood inheritance drifts from the center of English identity in the play, it is imposed on England's other: it lands, with Richard, in Ireland as the basis of what Clare Carroll, in commenting on John Derricke's verses with engravings, *The Image of Ireland* (1581), refers to as a "proto-racialist discourse," in which intersect "the early modern notion of race as family lineage or genealogy and as inherited disposition imposed on a whole group of people."[13] As England becomes freed from a discourse of blood inheritance, Ireland becomes its questionable heir, even its victim.

"That I could forget what I have been,/ Or not remember what I must be now!" Richard wails at the prospect of his deposition (3.3.138–9). Following the deposition, experienced as a sudden break with his recent past and his prior identity as king, the simulation of temporal, political, and historical continuity will give way to repetition, the endless, compulsive retelling of his tale that he projects as his nation's future. As Judith Butler writes in an essay on author and Holocaust survivor Primo Levi, a traumatic experience can produce

> a repetition of storytelling that belongs to a traumatic compulsion to repeat . . . As we know, trauma takes on the character of repetition. It breaks into the present and reabsorbs the very possibility of the present into the past, maintaining those who are traumatized in an uncertain historical time in which the agents who inflict traumatic suffering repopulate one's world and foreclose upon the possibility of opening to a different future.[14]

Butler could very well have been describing Shakespeare's Richard II as well as Levi in this passage. A Richard traumatized, it seems, by his own imaginings indeed proves incapable of projecting a future different from the one that he imagines to have already come to pass. He attempts to "people" or repopulate the little world of his cell in Pomfret Castle, but conjures only a multitude of discontented thoughts. Furthermore, he uses language that universalizes rather than historicizes his own loss, thereby expressing a medieval sense of universal mutability but also, as Butler notes, the characteristic response of a victim of trauma, which maintains "those who are traumatized in an uncertain historical time."

The troubled and illusory continuity of past, present, and future at the beginning of the play yields in the second half to a present without a future, one that has also been evacuated by its relation to the past. One is tempted in this case to use the play's own metaphor: for Richard in the second half of the play, the past has usurped his present. All that remains is the traumatized compulsion to repeat and to attempt to "fully control the discursive uses of [his] story,"[15] what Richard himself calls the "lamentable tale of me" (5.1.44). Lacking a kingdom to rule, he attempts to govern his story, and, more ambitiously, to use his story to reign (and rain) over England's past: to be crowned prince of stories and therefore of history. As Shakespeare will remind us repeatedly in the sequence of play to which *Richard II* belongs, however, and as the example of Holinshed's *Chronicles* attests, nothing is more difficult to control, more unruly and more prone to riot and rebellion, than the kingdom of the dead.

"ONE DAY TOO LATE"

The opening is deceptive and unsound, like England under Richard's rule, in quite another way. The references to Gloucester's murder in the opening scene, as well as hints of Richard's involvement, make us aware that something critical has been omitted or perhaps suppressed, whether or not we can recite the sequence of events leading up to the murder. Just as Richard urges the antagonists Mowbray and Bolingbroke to "forget" (1.1.156) the grounds for their quarrel, we might feel as if we have been enjoined to forget events that cast their shadow over the beginning. Shakespeare seems to conspire with his leading character in a cover-up. He makes no reference to the arrest of several of Richard's closest advisors by the five Lords Appellant (among these were Bolingbroke, Mowbray, and Gloucester) and the conviction and execution of those advisors by the so-called "Merciless Parliament" in 1388, events whose aftermath reverberates in the opening scene of *Richard II*. Nor does he make it clear that the banishments of Mowbray and Bolingbroke, like the murder of Gloucester, were retaliatory measures against the Lords Appellant. Shakespeare's early history play *I Henry VI* begins with the staging of a memorable event, the funeral procession of the great medieval warrior-king, Henry V, and a vivid demonstration of the heroic role memory will play in that history. The assembled court occupies a painful moment of transition that greatly enhances the importance of living memory: "Henry the Fifth, thy ghost I invocate," Henry's uncle, the Duke of Bedford, implores (1.1.52). By contrast, *Richard II* marks its oblique beginning with a scene of forgetting, a sense of memory's pathways having been occluded. Indirectly, the play announces that it is forgetting that will play a leading role in this history play, whereas advocacy of memory is confined to the supporting cast.

It is possible to argue that reasons of dramatic economy, frugal management of theatrical time, or a desire to begin in the manner of an epic, *in medias res*, caused Shakespeare to truncate the history. There are other important events of Richard's reign to which Shakespeare makes no reference, notably the Peasants' Revolt of 1381, which a fourteen-year-old Richard handled capably, calming the rebels and causing them to disperse peaceably. But the opening of *Richard II* does not merely omit: it also telegraphs its omissions to audiences and readers alike.[16] A theatrical palimpsest, it compels us to see that crucial events remain unaccounted for. In keeping with this calculated sense of something important having been obscured, Richard's line to Mowbray and Bolingbroke, "Forget, forgive, conclude and be agreed" (1.1.156), strikes a curious and unexpected note, because those who came to the playhouse presumably expected a play steeped in memory of England's past, not an explicit invitation to forget elements of that same past. As Richard urges the antagonists Mowbray and Bolingbroke to forget, we might sense that we have been enjoined to take part in a conspiracy of silence. The opening projects an atmosphere of concealment. No one dares utter in the King's presence what Gaunt says in private—"correction lieth in those hands/ Which made the fault that we cannot correct" (1.2.4–5). But even the private conversations in *Richard II* do little to clear the air of uncertainties. Only hushed whispers among theatergoers might fill in some of the gaps: the identity and grievances of the Lords Appellant; the King's involvement with his favorite, chamberlain Robert de Vere; Richard's retaliation against the Lords for the dismissing and executing of many of his friends; Mowbray's and Richard's parts in Gloucester's death; or the reasons for Richard's apparent partiality toward Mowbray, only thinly disguised by what Mowbray protests must be Richard's partiality toward his cousin Bolingbroke.

In sum, the opening of *Richard II* serves as a powerful reminder that nearly any play based on chronicle histories, necessarily highly selective and truncated in its treatment, may easily assume the qualities of a cover-up as much as a rescue of memorable, heroic acts from the "grave of oblivion," as Thomas Nashe colorfully described the patriotic and commemorative function of plays based on English history.[17] Above all, it is an opening thoroughly consistent with the character of Richard himself: Richard's weakness as a ruler mirrors what appears to be his weak control of England's collective memory, which appears on the verge of rebellion against royalty at the beginning of the play. The Bishops' Order of 1599 illustrates Elizabeth's government attempt to take control of implied analogies between times past and present, specifying that "noe English historyes be printed excepte they bee allowed by some of her maiesties privie Counsell."[18] By contrast, Richard at the beginning of the play seems to have left such comparisons between the present and the past to others and to have already abdicated any rule he might have claimed over the kingdom of the dead.

Richard returns "one day too late" from Ireland (3.2.67), rebellion having hatched in his absence.[19] All his Welsh supporters have fled to Bolingbroke. The Earl of Salisbury advises in desperate, vaunting rhetoric, "Oh call back yesterday, bid time return/ And thou shalt have twelve thousand fighting men" (3.2.69–70). Richard's strange deposition is consistent with this larger pattern. Even before Bolingbroke insists that he has returned only to recover his patrimony, his "lineal royalties" (3.3.113), Richard behaves as if it were one day too late, as if he had already been deposed. "Too late" proves an apt description of both historical and dramatic time in *Richard II*. The opening of the play can make audiences feel that they have arrived at the theater late and thereby missed crucial elements of the exposition. Of course, audiences in the 1590s might have recalled the murder of Gloucester and Richard's complicity in that action from the probably earlier, anonymous play *Thomas of Woodstock: or, Richard the Second, Part I* (1592?).[20] Shakespeare's play picks up where the earlier play leaves off, and it is possible that Shakespeare chose not to repeat events that were already widely known from the Woodstock play. What editor Nick de Somogyi refers to as the "puzzlingly incomplete" nature of Shakespeare's account of Woodstock's murder and Richard's complicity has lead some scholars to suppose that the two plays were two parts of a single whole. Like Arden editor Charles R. Forker, de Somogyi notes, "[D]espite some scholars' best efforts . . . and a series of shared themes and imagery, the two plays are incompatible as two parts of a single whole . . . [Shakespeare] seems, in any case, to have trusted more than usually to a common reservoir of historical knowledge in his audiences."[21] Rather than a sign of Shakespeare's trust in his audience's command of history or retention of events from the Woodstock play, however, I would argue that his opening seems to match too closely the play's larger pattern of arriving "too late" to be accidental. The sketchy beginning seems an overture to a play that will prove to be deeply elegiac and rehearse for its audiences the many registers of the feeling that we arrive always already "too late" for history. Indeed, the whole play is suffused with the fear that it is too late to call back yesterday, to rescue the medieval world whose passing it enacts.[22]

In a comic reprise of the heretofore tragic theme of lateness, the Duke and Duchess of York, together with their son Aumerle, race against time at the end of the play, driven by a fear of being "too late." The episode seems to repeat the play's beginning in its concern with opposed loyalties—here, Aumerle's allegiance to Richard and York's altered allegiance to Bolingbroke. The Duke of York leaves first to inform the King of the conspiracy against his life. At his mother's urging to "[s]pur post, and get before him to the king/ And beg thy pardon ere he do accuse thee" (5.2.111–2), Aumerle leaves next, followed by the Duchess herself: "Though I be old,/ I doubt not but to ride as fast as York" (5.2.113–4). This family drama undoes all the tragic implications of being "one day too late" throughout the play. In a race to be the first to reach the King's palace, Aumerle arrives moments before his father. The larger pattern of being an epoch too late (medieval England is irretrievably lost) or one day too late (Richard's reign lies in ruins) is compressed into the prospect of being moments too late. This time, however, because the Duke of York arrives moments too late, something is not lost (a crown, a kingdom, an era) but preserved: the life of his son. The effect of this comic reversal is powerful: it is as if the spell cast by the allure of the past, the very wish to "call back yesterday," has been broken.[23]

FORGETTING AND FORGIVING

Allow me to call back several lines that deserve closer inspection. Ostensibly trying to avoid bloodshed, and covertly deflecting suspicions of his own part in Gloucester's murder, Richard urges, "Let's purge this choler without letting blood./ This we prescribe though no physician./ Deep malice makes too deep incision./ Forget, forgive, conclude and be agreed./ Our doctors say this is no month to bleed" (1.1.153–7). In his 1723–1725 edition of Shakespeare's plays, Alexander Pope regarded these couplets as "excessively bad." Suspecting them (together with many of the play's rhymes) to be the product of a hand other than Shakespeare's, he relegated them to a footnote.[24] Pope, eager to perform a kind of textual bloodletting, may have been right in his characterization but nevertheless have missed the point. They are patently bad—deliberately awkward, if you will—because they attempt to resolve the present crisis by inadequate means, by distracting the antagonists rather than addressing their charges and complaints directly. By means of the second line, Richard reduces the issue between Mowbray and Bolingbroke to a joke about doctors and the practice of bleeding, and simultaneously places the whole quarrel within an astrological context that diminishes individual responsibility[25]: not a bad line's work for a king who wishes to deflect responsibility for Gloucester's murder from his own person. The rhyme, like the proverbial aspect of "Forget, forgive,"[26] curiously serves to aid the memory in ways that contradict the meaning of the lines, its injunction to "forget." Other tensions and contradictions inform this line. It is odd indeed for the king to urge a conclusion at the beginning of a play. And it is curious that a king admonish others to forget within a history play that is ostensibly designed to rescue him and others from the jaws of oblivion. Richard's "forget" reflects the indirectness of Shakespeare's opening, with its hushed, barely audible, half remembered and half forgotten betrayal of Richard's own part in the murder. Furthermore, although "forgive" and "forget" are proverbial partners ("Forgive and forget"), there remains a tension between them, one that the philosopher Avishai Margalit has recently explored in *The Ethics of Memory*. From a certain ethical perspective, Margalit writes, "Forgiveness, which is voluntary, should not be tied to forgetting, which is involuntary."[27] Richard's line seems designed to cancel the difference between voluntary forgiving and involuntary forgetting, and to blithely suggest that forgetting can be as willful an act as forgiving.

Margalit identifies four major models of forgiveness in the Bible, the two most important of which are the opposed ideas of forgiveness as blotting out and forgiveness as covering up: "[T]he metaphor of blotting out depicts forgiving as absolutely forgetting the sinful act . . . The metaphor of covering up, in contrast, suggests disregarding the offence without forgetting it. Traces of the sinful offense remain, but the offended party does not retaliate by taking revenge against the one who wronged him."[28] Margalit regards the covering up model as preferable to that of blotting out, both psychologically and morally, because "it is better to cross out than delete memories of an offense . . . Forgiveness is based on disregarding the sin rather than forgetting it."[29] Forgetting cannot be the *basis* for real forgiveness, but a partial forgetting—a wrong "covered up" rather than "blotted out"—can be the *end result* of forgiveness. Forgetting can be voluntary, the result of a conscious decision, only in the limited sense that a decision to begin a process of forgiveness may lead to partial forgetting. [30]

The blotting-out model for forgiveness is ethically dubious for two reasons. If the overcoming of anger and vengefulness "occurs through simple forgetfulness, it is not real forgiveness." Also, the injunction to forget contradicts our common belief that forgetting may erode the foundation of our very identities: "The role of memory in constituting who we are and what we are is in tension with the ideal of successful forgiveness as that which ends in forgetting the wrong done to us." He therefore downplays the role of forgetting, or at least the idea of forgetting as a complete erasure, in the process of forgiveness, which involves "not forgetting the wrong done but rather overcoming the resentment that accompanies it."[31]

Margalit's observation that the idea of forgetting as a blotting out stands opposed to the important role of memory in fashioning and sustaining our identities speaks directly to the example of Richard II. Distracting the combatants Mowbay and Bolingbroke with a jest, Richard practices the model Margalit rejects, namely, the idea of forgiving as a blotting out. Furthermore, he covertly asks for forgiveness for himself with this same line: in other words, he wishes others to perform this same type of forgiving—forgiving that entails absolute forgetting and that therefore cannot constitute real forgiving at all—toward his own crime against the Duke of Gloucester. The tension between this type of forgiving, and our very identities, which require perpetual nourishment from our memories in order to sustain them, is revealed in the middle of the play by Richard's self-forgetting on his return from Ireland: "I had forgot myself. Am I not king?" (3.2.83). He appears to be justly punished for his own crimes against memory. He begins by forgetting the example of noble Edward and by blotting out his own crimes; he ends by forgetting himself. Urging others to "[f]orget, forgive, conclude," Richard begins a process that "conclude[s]" in his cancelling his own identity as king.

Although Richard calls for a forgiving as blotting out, Shakespeare, I would contend, works by adhering to Margalit's preferred model for forgiveness, namely, forgiving as covering up. Shakespeare does not so much blot out as he covers up Richard's role in the murder of Thomas Woodstock, Duke of Gloucester in the opening scene. The crime peeks through the subsequent dialogue between Gaunt and Woodstock's widow, although not in the form of open accusation, and continues to be hinted at in the third scene, the dueling scene between Bolingbroke and Mowbray. Part of the drama of the opening scene derives from the tension between what Margalit identifies as rival biblical models for forgiveness, forgiveness as blotting out and forgiveness as covering up, Richard's model and Shakespeare's. Shakespeare's model extends even to his oblique treatment of incendiary historical material, namely, the Peasants' Revolt, which, I shall argue in the next section, he treats in a manner similar to the way he handles Richard's culpability in the opening scene.

THE PEASANTS' REVOLT BETWEEN THE LINES

Richard II is a mnemonic paradox: a history play whose eponymous hero has little or no interest in the past, at least until he is deposed, and in which active and passive forms of forgetting—that is, deliberate erasure and careless neglect of the past—seem as prominent as the acts of memory that presumably form the foundation of any history play. Its opening serves as a reminder that a play based on chronicle histories is bound to be shaped at least as much by what it omits as by what it includes, by what it forgets as much as by what it remembers.

One of the best-known events of Ricardian England omitted from the play is the Peasants' Revolt of 1381.[32] Like the murder of Woodstock, it was the subject of an earlier play, the rough-hewn and anonymous *The Life and Death of Jack Straw* (1593), a play that shows Richard as a strong, resolute young ruler. Although the revolt is nowhere mentioned in *Richard II*, Holinshed's account of that decisive event does inform Shakespeare's representation of the Jack Cade rebellion in *2 Henry VI*.[33] Nevertheless, there is a way in which the revolt shades not only *Richard II* but also the sequence of history plays that follows. In the course of discussing what he refers to as the "time of those hellish troubles," Holinshed writes,

> Could they have a more mischievous meaning than to burn and destroy all old and ancient monuments and to murder and dispatch out of the way all such as were able to commit to memory either any new or old records? For it was dangerous among them to be known for one that was learned, and more dangerous if any men were found with a penner and inkhorn at his side; for such seldom or never escaped from them with life.[34]

The horror of one who must have written these sentences with pen and inkhorn is palpable. The commons' binge of book and document burning (they "purposed to burn and destroy all records, evidences, courtrolls, and other monuments"[35]) and their sudden hostility toward "their landlords that demanded of them their ancient customs and services"[36] read in Holinshed like an insurrection against all inherited rights and responsibilities, a heady riot against the past: "that the remembrance of ancient matters being removed out of mind, their landlords might not have whereby to challenge any right at their hands."[37] Even though, as Annabel Patterson argues, Holinshed's account of the rebellion as a whole is far more "evenhanded" than those of his sources, moving between "a guarded sympathy and a shocked antipathy" toward the rebels[38] as he discusses various aspects of the revolt, he is particularly harsh on the revolt as an act of vandalism against England's legal and cultural memory.

According to Holinshed, one of the two rebel leaders, Wat Tyler, was called upon to discuss with one Sir John Newton, an emissary from the king, the substance of certain "articles" to have been inserted in "divers forms of charters" demanded by the Essex rebels,

> of the which one was to have had a commission to put to death all lawyers, escheators, and other which by any office had anything to do with the law; for his meaning was that, having made all those away that understood the laws, all things should then be ordered according to the will and disposition of the common people. It was reported indeed that he should say with great pride the day before these things chanced, putting his hands to his lips, that within four days all the laws of England should come forth of his mouth.[39]

This passage is extraordinary for its vision of a complete overhaul of "the documentary culture of feudal tenure and royal government," in Steven Justice's phrase.[40] In Holinshed's account, this overhaul takes the specific form of a reversion from a written to an oral culture. The rebel Wat Tyler, in Holinshed, embodies the fantasy of a legal and cultural memory that, no longer constructed and guarded by an educated elite armed "with penner (pencase) and inkhorn" (like the chroniclers themselves), might issue directly from the *mouth* of the rebels' spokesman.[41]

In his analysis of the rebellion, Justice shows that, in fact, the rebels did not seek to destroy the culture of writing that upheld feudal England but rather to "re-create it." Theirs was an "insurgent literacy":

> [T]hey recognized the written document as something powerful but also malleable, something that, once written, could be *re*written. When they successfully demanded charters of manumission from Richard II—their most significant and public attempt to rewrite the government of Britain—they showed a precise understanding of the forms

> and procedures of document and archive. That they demanded them at all demonstrates their respect for the forms of official writing, and also their knowledge of these forms.[42]

Nevertheless, the account Shakespeare read as preparation for *his* semi-oral rewriting of one aspect of England's documentary culture, namely, the chronicle tradition, did pit a threateningly oral rebel leader against the stability and orthodoxy of a potentially tyrannical documentary culture.[43] Shakespeare's extraordinary innovation is this: in *Richard II*, it is Richard himself, not England's disgruntled commoners, who represents the force of a powerful and potentially distracting orality, the replacement of documents ("charters") with a charismatic theatricality. Something like Holinshed's account of the Peasants' Revolt does indeed occur in Shakespeare's play, although in a clandestine way, with the King cast as England's chief rebel, a Wat Tyler figure in robes. Even Richard's behavior during his deposition supports this analogy. As Naomi Conn Liebler has written, "In denying his acts, decrees, and statutes he erases all record of his existence and occupation of the throne. This is more than the passage of control; it widens the hole in the historical record, the breach in 'the fair sequence and succession' of the Plantagenet dynasty that began with the death of Edward III."[44]

Laboring with pen and ink and precariously poised between oral performance and written playscript, Shakespeare also "recognized the written document as something powerful but also malleable, something that, once written, could be *re*written" (Justice). Reshaping the chronicles he read, using the chronicler's tools but for the purpose of shaping a decidedly oral performance, Shakespeare must have felt divided as he read Holinshed's account of the oral upstart Wat Tyler's rebellion against the documentary culture that in Tyler's view helped keep the commons in thrall. Like Holinshed's Wat Tyler, Shakespeare was an oral upstart. He apparently knew the power of his own pen to re-create the written chronicles that, alongside more oral and popular means of recalling England's past, stood as imperfect and contested guardians of England's historical memory.

USURPATION AT THE COURT OF MEMORY: RICHARD'S DEPOSITION OF EDWARD III

Like Shakespeare's *Henry VI* plays, *Richard II* features a deceased, heroic monarch who acts as a polestar of collective memory. *1 Henry VI* opens with the funeral procession of Henry V, bearing him to a place in history just beyond the reach of the play's re-presentational powers. By contrast, *Richard II*, set in the last two years of Richard's reign, begins a full twenty years after the death of Edward III, the monarch who first broke England's feudal connection to France. In *1 Henry VI*, muddled, diminished present and heroic past are tantalizingly close; in *Richard* II they are divided by a generation, so that memory of Edward and his eldest son the Black Prince, Richard's grandfather and father respectively, tends to be more variable. The older generation—the sons of Edward III, John of Gaunt, Duke of Lancaster and Edmund Langley, Duke of York—strains to keep Edward in its sights, whereas the younger generation seems content to forget him. The second tetralogy begins with a mnemonic generation gap, a division between those guided by a living memory of Edward (Edward's sons) and the historically neglectful attitudes of the young: an incipient rift, in other words, between memory and history.[45] Gaunt and York possess a vivid memory of Edward's reign; we, the audience of *Richard II*, know Edward III through historical reconstruction: chronicles and oral history in Shakespeare's time, certainly, but also through references in the play itself. If the play *Edward III*, widely thought to be partly authored by Shakespeare,[46] preceded *Richard II* on stage (it was published anonymously in 1596, its title page declaring, "As it hath bin sundrie times plaied about the Citie of London"), audiences would have possessed the simulacrum of Gaunt's and York's living memories of their father. Theatrical enactment serves as a cultural form that mediates history and memory, the means of access to the past of the younger and older generations, respectively, in *Richard II*. If many in Shakespeare's audience knew Edward through theatrical reenactment, then these might have identified more with Gaunt and York than with the youth of Shakespeare's play. Otherwise, *Richard II*'s younger generation, who know of Edward III's reign largely through the reports of others (Richard was ten years old when he succeeded Edward), acts as a pivot between Gaunt, York, and ourselves. This generation represents a vanishing point of memory as it gives way to history. Memory in *Richard II* is as vulnerable and feeble as the dying Gaunt—and at times just as forcefully eloquent.

At the beginning of *1 Henry VI* there is no question as to who holds sway in the kingdom of memory, namely, the recently deceased Henry V; in *Richard II*, the more remotely deceased Edward III holds a more tenuous command of that realm. As Phyllis Rackin has shown so vividly and persuasively, the *Henry VI* plays document English struggles to establish and retain its historical record against the French forces that threaten to erode or obliterate it[47]; in *Richard II* the forces hostile to memory are internal to the kingdom, a situation that will persist in every subsequent play in the series. A monarch who is neglectful toward the past, Richard II spawns a line of the "forgetful," including Henry IV (denounced by Hotspur as "this forgetful man," *1 Henry IV*, 1.3.159) and Henry V, as I will argue in subsequent chapters. Without heirs, Richard stands as figurative progenitor to a sequence of monarchs whose histories explore the manifold dangers of historical memory for the principle of national unity and identity.

Richard is continually distracted by the "new," as York complains: "Where doth the world thrust forth a vanity—/So it be new there's no respect how vile—/That is not quickly buzzed into his ears?" (2.1.24–6).

Richard's taste for novelty reflects his willingness to "take from time/ His charters and his customary rights" (2.1.195–6), which defines all his crimes: the murder of one duke, the erasure of another's legacy, even the dispossession of the Irish.[48] A common gardener, close in rank to the actors who, through their enactments of English history, similarly served as a link to England's past, demonstrates more interest in history than its monarch. He lends the royal garden a monumental quality when he vows to "set a bank of rue . . . / In the remembrance of a weeping queen" (3.4.105,107). The only story Richard wishes to memorialize, by contrast, is his own, "the lamentable tale of me" (5.1.44).[49]

Gloucester's murder has already demonstrated Richard's indifference toward the past, because the generation to which the Duke belonged becomes almost an allegory of the obligation to remember. By appropriating Gaunt's lands following his death, Richard annihilates the very principle by which he wears the crown. Fiscally, too, he obliterates what "his ancestors achieved with blows" through his profligate spending (2.1.254). Richard's supporters Bushy and Green have obliterated all signs of Bolingbroke's patrimony: they have "From my own windows torn my household coat,/ Razed out my imprese, leaving me no sign/ Save men's opinions and my living blood/ To show the world I am a gentleman" (3.1.24–7). Conversely, opposition to Richard seems to promote continuity by restoring the generational links he has sundered: "Both young and old rebel," from "boys with women's voices" to "whitebeards," "beadsmen," and "distaff women" (3.2.112–9).

Isabel is an apt partner for Richard, in that her emotional life, like Richard's political one, seems independent of causes or "forefathers." Her premonition of woe, she asserts, issues from no known source. "Conceit is still derived/ From some forefather grief. Mine is not so,/ For nothing hath begot my something grief,/ Or something hath the nothing that I grieve" (2.2.34–7). It is appropriate, therefore, that when Green, "midwife to [her] woe," informs her of the rebellion, her language of begetting issues in a figure of monstrous birth (2.2.62–6). A similar figure applies to Bolingbroke, whom Berkeley accuses of "frighting our native peace with self-born arms," which Andrew Gurr glosses as "carried for self and not for country. With a pun on birth, presumably monstrous as at 2.2.64."[50] The pun links Bolingbroke with Richard's queen and with Richard himself. It insinuates that Bolingbroke cannot legitimate his authority by reference to the past, specifically to his grandsire Edward, because any such reference bears the potential to revive the memory of Edmund Mortimer's counter-claim. In the absence of historical means of legitimation, he must deploy theatrical strategies for self-legitimation, as he will reveal to his son in *1 Henry IV*. Harry Berger, Jr. writes,

> Of Richard we might say, with Lady Macduff, "fathered he is and fatherless." The ideal relationship which York describes as having existed

between Edward III and the Black Prince fails to repeat itself because either Richard did not assume or his dead father did not renounce the phallic patrimony.[51]

"Self-born," therefore, seems an apt motto for both antagonists, Richard and Bolingbroke.[52]

Following Richard's murder, Bolingbroke inherits an antipathy toward the past that defined Richard at the beginning of the play, haunted as he was by the specter of Woodstock's murder and hounded by unflattering comparisons with his grandfather Edward III. The past becomes a threat to Bolingbroke as it was for Richard, and largely for the same reason: the need to cover up complicity in a murder. In this play of mirrors, Richard meets the fate of his former enemy Gloucester. Bolingbroke inherits Richard's antagonism toward the past, as Richard also takes on the pale hue of his old nemesis, John of Gaunt, whose swansong is perhaps the classic expression of nostalgia in Shakespeare. Richard drowns in nostalgia for a self, and Gaunt for a realm, that are no longer themselves. For his part, although he despises the memory of "the skipping King" in *1 Henry IV* (3.2.60), Bolingbroke must reprise Richard's role as prince of forgetting. His contentious relation with the past, however, will play out very differently than Richard's. Whereas Richard experiences a traumatic rupture leading to nostalgia, Bolingbroke will battle the aristocratic opposition for the right to control the nation's past over the course of the next play: not for "rights of memory in this kingdom," as Fortinbras calls his doubtful claim to Denmark's throne (*Hamlet*, 5.2.373), but for the right to forget.

The deposing of a king, the disinheriting of a duke, and the dispossession of a people, the Irish: on top of these crimes, one might venture to add Richard's uprooting of English history. He disrupts the continuity of English memory by ignoring the legacies of his grandfather Edward III and his father the Black Prince, and also by repeatedly placing his story in a biblical rather than a national context, which is of a piece with his apparent disregard for a specifically English historical memory.[53] Of course, stresses on national history and biblical history need not be incompatible. Biblical history was often used to interpret English history, either to aggrandize the latter, to admonish congregants, or both. Rival comparisons between England and Israel and between England and Assyria rained down from English pulpits, as preachers built, in Michael McGiffert's words, a "towering scaffold of moral nationalism."[54] But in *Richard II*, biblical history plays a different role: not as a parallel history, a means of instructing the English and warning them of their own possible futures, but as a rival to a specifically English historical memory, or to call on the play's governing metaphor, as a means to usurp a national memory. In this respect, Shakespeare's Richard is very like his historical counterpart, who closely identified not with Edward III but with the saintly Edward the Confessor, and his apparent possession of spiritual powers beyond the regal and temporal. The historical Richard aspired to a greater role on the stage of European politics, prodded by a prophecy that he would become Holy Roman Emperor. Among other things, he had ambitions to undertake a crusade to the Holy Land. Elevation to the largely ceremonial post of Holy Roman Emperor promised to lift him beyond the merely national sphere and above the considerable criticism he was receiving at home.

A dethroned Richard paradoxically usurps a privileged place in the very collective memory that he chose to ignore while he was king. He allows Bolingbroke to deprive him of England's throne so that he may depose Edward in England's historical memory. Both Richard and his Queen implicitly trump English memory of Edward with their biblical responses to the deposition. The Queen chides the Gardener on hearing him report Richard's having been deposed, "What Eve, what serpent hath suggested thee/ To make a second fall of cursèd man?" (3.4.75–6). Casting Richard as a second Adam reenacting the expulsion from Eden, the Queen already bestows on him the narrative precedence, the priority in the collective memory of his people, that he craves in the play's final act. In response to his Queen's reproofs, Richard urges,

> In winter's tedious nights sit by the fire
> With good old folks, and let them tell thee tales
> Of woeful ages long ago betid,
> And ere thou bid good night, to 'quite their griefs
> Tell thou the lamentable tale of me
> And send the hearers weeping to their beds. (5.1.40–5)

Memories of Richard, this king of little memory, will take their place, Richard hopes, among "tales/ Of woeful ages long ago." By casting him as a second Adam, however, his Queen had already crowned him prince of stories,[55] claiming for him a priority in the collective memory that far exceeds any possible competition from English chronicle histories. John of Gaunt had already placed Richard in the context of biblical history by professing to have seen England degenerate from "other Eden" to "tenement or pelting farm" (2.1.42,60). Isabella re-places Richard in that history, returning him to the original garden where he now plays the role of victim rather than despoiler. Her accusatory speech to the Gardener, "old Adam's likeness," strategically divides the Adamic role by implicating the Gardener in the part of the story in which Adam was most culpable, the fall, reserving the more passive and pitiable part, the expulsion from Eden, for Richard. In addition to a second Adam, Richard becomes a type of "the humbled Christ," thanks to the Bishop of Carlisle, who as Richard's mind disintegrates, resurrects his former king in biblical comparisons. Richard himself casts his enemies as Judas and Pilate,[56] and himself as a Christ figure in his own Passion Play, as John Joughin has argued: "Richard eventually settles for casting himself in terms of those future commemorative practices that will canonize his memory and by which his anonymity will simultaneously guarantee his legacy."[57] Isabel Karremann perceptively describes his abdication speech as a "rite of oblivion," a Eucharistic transformation through ceremony into "the sacrificial flesh and blood of Christ" that "performs complementary acts of obliterating his memory as subjected worldly king and of re-membering him as heavenly king, subject to no one."[58] Both comparisons, of Richard to the Old Testament's Adam and to the New Testament's Christ, help convey a sense that although he has been unseated politically, he has mnemonically unseated Edward, who had seemed as effective at governing the collective memory at the beginning of the play as Richard was ineffectual at ruling present-day England.

Richard's success in deposing Edward, as it were, is confirmed in *Henry V*, where Edward's claim to the throne of France and his victories at Crécy (1346), like his son Edward, the Black Prince's triumph at Poitiers (1356), are publicly cited as inspirational precedents for Henry's invasion of Normandy. Toward the end of the later play, however, on the eve of the battle of Agincourt, it is a private remembrance of Richard that comes back to forcefully haunt the contrite King. At the end of *Richard II* the deposed king expresses his craving to be remembered as an archetypal pattern of sadness, which I have characterized as the play's second usurpation. Act 4, scene 1 of *Henry V* reveals how successful he has been, although not exactly in the way he imagined. In a very specific sense, Richard has indeed wrested the past from Edward, who at the beginning of *Henry V* seems a convenient precedent, as easily manipulated by King Henry as his living subjects, rather than the living, burning memory that Richard has become.

What is most striking about the deposing of Richard is the way it transforms him from an anti-historical figure who shows no interest in the past to a virtual emblem of historical consciousness. Of course, by contrast with Edward's sons, who long for England as it had been under the rule of their father, Richard longs only for his prior identity, now irretrievably lost. Still, the transformation is sudden and striking: a king who is neglectful of the past becomes a figure for a painful historical awareness, one whose present has become evacuated and whose entire being points backward, yearning for what lies beyond recall. From utter neglect of the past, Richard becomes an example for all those in the audience who wish to "call back yesterday," and who, by virtue of the Reformation, have found themselves, like Richard, divided from their prior selves.

(SUP)PLANTATION SCHEMES

Numerous commentators have noted the ways in which Ireland is silenced or made invisible by the play.[59] The play refuses to offer up a scene that dramatizes Richard's campaign in Ireland. Andrew Murphy notes Ireland's peculiar status as "unseen realm to which Richard ventures."[60] Ireland's invisibility in the text reflects Gaunt's simplified nationalist construction of England as "this scepter'd isle," a representation that many commentators, including Philip Edwards and Michael Neill, have shown to effectively obliterate "Scotland and Wales as distinct political and cultural entities" as well as to marginalize Ireland.[61] Christopher Highley refers to Ireland as "an absent presence in the dramatic action" of *Richard II*.[62] Building on Highley's account, Stephen O'Neill refers to Ireland as "simultaneously invisible and also in view" and suggests that this double aspect of Ireland "registers conflicting Elizabethan desires towards Ireland: on the one hand, the desire to engage with and reform it; on the other, the desire to occlude it."[63] Its substantial invisibility may reflect "an unconscious movement in the text to efface Ireland and the contemporary problem it presents."[64] The absent presence of Ireland in *Richard II* may reflect a persistent trend in early modern English drama. As Michael Neill has observed, given the pressing nature of the Nine Years' War, and "given the amount of political, military, and intellectual energy it absorbed, and the moneys it consumed, Ireland can seem to constitute . . . one of the great and unexplained lacunae in the drama of the period."[65]

I want to enlarge upon the substantial body of commentary on Ireland's marginal position in *Richard II* by stressing its relation to larger patterns in the play. Its "absent presence" recalls the curious treatment of Woodstock's murder at the beginning of the play. In other words, Ireland functions as a spatial and geographical counterpart to the similarly marginalized and forgotten historical materials in the play. As Edmund Spenser, who lived in Ireland for most of the years from about 1580 to shortly before his death in 1599, represents Ireland in *A View of the Present State of Ireland* (1596, publ. 1633), it is a space of oblivion where the loss of English and even human identity were constant threats to English who took up residence there. Clare Carroll writes of early modern Ireland, "Both Old and New English writers used the metaphor of 'Circe's cup' to conjure up the bewitching, sexually seductive, and morally debilitating influence that they attributed to Irish culture."[66] In a play that explores the manifold roles that forgetting plays in the production of historical narrative, it is no wonder that Ireland, the modern equivalent of Circe's island to many English, plays a pivotal role, and further, that its role, like Woodstock's murder, be prominently, even ostentatiously, marginalized or suppressed.

Furthermore, Ireland belongs to a general pattern of dispossession and displacement that links both individual and collective antagonists: Richard and Bolingbroke, England and Ireland. After his deposition, Richard becomes Bolingbroke's Ireland, just as the dispossessed Bolingbroke performed the role of Ireland to Richard earlier in the play. Finally, Ireland serves as a pivot point between England's past and future, between its medieval legacy and the modern world of policy that Bolingbroke ushers in. Not only does Ireland serve as a caesura in the play's action, between Richard's reign and Henry's, but it also served as a point of connection between the play and the contemporary world of its Elizabethan audiences. References to Ireland in the play call up the Elizabethan present and its anxieties regarding the ongoing war. Richard himself becomes redefined for us in the process, as Phyllis Rackin has shown. Increasingly separated from the idealized medieval past expressed by the dying Gaunt's speech, Richard becomes associated with "objects of present anxiety."[67] In a reading of the play from the perspective of an audience's "role" in the action, Rackin shows how the play's audience "must shift its perspective during the course of the play, sometimes taking a long, historical view of the action and sometimes seeing it as insistent, present reality."[68] Given Ireland's status as a pressing concern of the 1590s as well as the 1390s, the absent presence of Ireland in Shakespeare's playtext produces a feeling of historical or temporal as well as spatial elision.[69] It is just such a gap, I would venture to say, and as I will attempt to demonstrate in a later section of this chapter, that characterizes the play's bold conception of history. For this play, the telling of history is marked by an aesthetic not of the beautiful—history is not a connected narrative exhibiting the "fair sequence and succession" of causes and effects—but rather of the sublime. Historical consciousness comes about in this play largely because of disorienting rupture and traumatic loss. The elided present helps convey the sense of the past as beyond recovery, and separated from the modern, practical world of Bolingbroke by a gap that cannot be traversed. In such a telling of history, it is no wonder that Richard's pivotal affairs in Ireland should be elided, or that one of the play's major lacunae should be set in a place of oblivion.

In a way that duplicates the curiously forgetful memory of the opening, the play reminds audiences of contemporary problems in Ireland, but in so fleeting a manner that it would be more accurate to say that it recalls such problems only to forget them. The brief intervention in Ireland returns us to Richard's injunction to the combatants at the beginning of the play to "forget." The episode makes Richards of us all. As we struggle to hold Ireland in our memories, we witness Richard, immediately on returning from Ireland, forgetting himself. As always, it is Richard's dazzling, distracting theatricality that is the primary agent of oblivion.

The Irish in *Richard II* are targets of twin campaigns of socioeconomic and mnemonic supplanting. Referring to the legend of St. Patrick and his legacy of a viper-less Ireland, Richard declares, "We must supplant those rough rug-headed kern,/ Which live like venom where no venom else/ But only they have privilege to live" (2.1.156–8), an endeavor that makes him seem like a second Patrick, although an ironic one, to be sure, not savior but enemy of the Irish people. St. Patrick performed his miracle by luring a snake into a box that the snake declared was too small for him. To prove his point, the snake entered the box, on which Patrick slammed the lid, subsequently throwing it into the sea. Richard seems to surrender the crown and enter "this little world" with "flinty ribs" (5.5.9,20), his prison, as willingly as St. Patrick's snake, and with the same sense of helpless entrapment.

The character of Richard, who strikes some readers and spectators as saintly, fuses both sides of this foundational myth of Ireland that Richard invokes only to scoff at the Irish and justify his Irish wars. Richard plays both saint and serpent in a self-authored Irish pageant. Whether Richard's Irish campaign is designed to "save" Ireland, in the manner of Patrick, by purging it of "venom," or to destroy it depends, of course, on point of view. But because the Irish campaign fits the larger pattern of dispossession that includes the appropriation of Bolingbroke's legacy for the crown and Bolingbroke's deposing of Richard, it is not a stretch to say that the play invites sympathy for the Irish, even while the English were engaged in a fierce campaign against Ireland that would later be known as the Nine Years' War.

If Richard is a would-be saint who, like Patrick's snake, gets lured into the box that is Flint Castle, he is also a "supplanter" of the Irish who ironically returns home only to find himself supplanted. As playgoers we have a similar experience of "supplanting": our very brief attention to the Irish question is quickly displaced by England's brewing civil conflict. Andrew Hadfield, in a study of what he sees as a pattern of excluding Ireland in Shakespeare's British plays, refers to Richard's Irish expedition "as a deliberate attempt to avoid solving problems at home."[70] Certainly this is partly right, but the evasion has ironic results: the problems abroad become duplicated at home. Dispossession becomes the order of the day in both domestic and foreign affairs.

The Irish wars are referred to in so glancing a manner that it is all too easy for audiences and readers to forget them altogether. Forgetting Ireland would have been more difficult, however, in 1595, the date usually ascribed to *Richard II*, when the Irish rebellion led by Hugh O'Neill, Earl of Tyrone was a pressing concern. Shakespeare made it perhaps inevitable that his Elizabethan audiences would have connected past to present, Richard's wars with Elizabeth's: perhaps even to the point of connecting specific details, like his strategy of inciting Leinster lords to attack and occupy Gaelic lands farther west and of installing English lords on Leinster lands, to the Queen's own plantation schemes. As a result, tragic protagonist and audience are utterly out of phase: what Richard finds challenging, namely connecting his present to England's past, his audiences would have found irresistible.

Because the whole point of Richard's Irish campaign is to uproot, it is appropriate that the campaign as a whole be represented in such a way that it is easy to forget. In fact, the whole episode is structured by means of reciprocal or mirroring acts of displacement: as we miss the turmoil in Ireland, Richard in Ireland misses the high drama unfolding in his absence on English shores. In so doing, he becomes one of us, and we become Richards. He reprises the audience's sense of arriving too late and missing the origins of the high drama already well underway at the beginning of the play. Richard's verb "supplant," besides echoing the prolific garden imagery of the play, recalls English plantation schemes, which involved the "plantation" of Irish lordships with English settlers, a Tudor program that began under Edward and increased under Mary and Elizabeth.[71] The plantation schemes' aim, to "plant" English settlers in Ireland and thereby grow English customs, manners, laws, and language in that land, was achieved by a kind of dispossession reminiscent of Richard's action against Bolingbroke and his heirs. Mary's Catholic government stripped Irish landholders of two-thirds of their holdings, granting them to English settlers. Under Elizabeth, the division of the lordship of Monaghan in Ulster province by the Lord Deputy Sir William Fitzwilliam was the immediate cause of Tyrone's rebellion. Fitzwilliam's action provoked anxiety in other great Irish lords, who faced the prospect of a similar reduction in their land and power, not unlike the anxiety felt by the English nobility in *Richard II* at the dispossession of Bolingbroke. English pursuit of these schemes eventually led to the Tyrone Rebellion or Nine Years' War, which broke out in April 1593. A costly uprising for the English government, resulting in expenditures of nearly two million pounds, the war continued until the last year of Elizabeth's reign. Its leader, Hugh O'Neill, Earl of Tyrone, surrendered in March 1603, the same month in which Elizabeth died. All four plays of the second tetralogy—*Richard II, 1–2 Henry IV, and Henry V*—date from the years of this conflict.

The costliness of the Nine Years' War was already apparent by 1595, the year in which Shakespeare wrote *Richard II*. In February of that year, the English garrison on the River Blackwater was destroyed. It was an action that revealed Tyrone's true intentions. Until this event, Tyrone misled the English government into thinking that he would help them suppress the Irish rebels, who were secretly acting under Tyrone's direction while Tyrone himself negotiated with Philip II of Spain for assistance in the struggle. Later in 1595, the Irish won another major victory at Clontibret, which would be succeeded three years later by the most disastrous English defeat of the Nine Years' War, the Battle of Yellow Ford (August 14, 1598).

Richard II seems almost a compendium of anxieties and themes drawn from the early years of the Nine Years' War.[72] We catch an echo of the costliness of Elizabeth's government's suppression of the Irish uprising in complaints against Richard's lavish spending and financing schemes. The deviousness of the uprising's leader, his masking of his true intent from the English, might have reminded some audience members in 1595 of Bolingbroke's usurpation, especially as it was handled by Shakespeare. Holinshed represents Bolingbroke as landing with an invasionary force, at the urging of friends, in order to dethrone Richard. By contrast, Shakespeare stages Bolingbroke's return in a way that enhances suspicions of its deviousness and raises questions of motivation. The recent revelation about the Earl of Tyrone, whom the English thought would help suppress rather than lead the rebellion that was later to bear his name, might very well have influenced Shakespeare's decision to give Bolingbroke "such a questionable shape," as Hamlet calls his father's ghost (1.4.22). The implicit parallel between Tudor policy in Ireland, which resulted in the partial dispossession of several great Irish lords, and anxieties produced among the English nobility by the expropriation of a great English lord's properties two centuries earlier by a king grown tyrannical, seems extraordinary for its times, given the urgency of English affairs in Ireland throughout most of the decade. It is as if the play were holding up a cracked looking glass to those Elizabethans seeking to "supplant" Irish lords. Ireland, like the murdered Duke of Gloucester, haunts the margins, the imaginative as well as the geographical borders, of Shakespeare's play.

In *A View of the Present State of Ireland*, written when he was back in London to arrange publication of his national epic *The Fairie Queene*, Edmund Spenser responded to Tyrone's uprising by advocating policies designed to wean Irishmen from loyalty to "the head of theire sept" and "in shorte tyme learne quite to forgette his Irishe nation."[73] Written within a year of *Richard II* (1595), Spenser's text takes the form of a dialogue between Irenius, sometimes regarded as a mouthpiece for Spenser, and the relatively uninformed Eudoxus. One of the policies proposed by Irenius entailed the assigning of new surnames based on "trade or facultie or of some qualltie of his bodye or mynde, or of the place where he dwelte, so as everie one should bee distinguished from other or from the most parte."[74] The "Oes and the mackes which the heades of septes haue taken to theire names" would be forbidden in a calculated attempt to "enfeeble" them by sabotaging their group identity.[75]

Amid anxieties about the ways in which England's first colony, Ireland, made English Protestant identity vulnerable to modification or erasure, Spenser aimed to show England how to curb a resistant population by starving it into submission. A discussion of Irish apparel leads to Eudoxus's speech on the importance of clothing for reminding men who they are, and the likelihood that a change of apparel will lead one to forget oneself: "for the person that is gowned, is by his gowne put in mynde of gravitye, and also restrayned from lightnes by the verie vnaptnes of his weede." He cites Aristotle's account of the formerly warlike Lydians, whose conqueror, Cyrus, wished to make them more peaceable. Cyrus changed their "shorte warlike Coates" for "longe garments like wyves, and in steade of theire warlike musicke, appointed to them certaine lascivyous layes and loose gigges." Soon their minds were "mollyfied, and abated that they forgot theire former feircenes and became most tender, and effeminate."[76]

Schemes to manipulate the cultural memory of the Irish stemmed in part from anxieties about the tenuous cultural memory of the Anglo-Irish. Earlier in the text Irenius and Eudoxus discuss the degeneracy of the English residing in Ireland, especially those dwelling to the west, far from the "Englishe pale," who "are now growne to be almost as lewde as the Irishe . . . and some of them haue quite shaken of theire English names, and putt on Irishe, that they might bee altogether Irishe." When Eudoxus expresses astonishment "that any should so far growe out of frame that they should in so shorte space quite forget theire Countrie and theire owne names," Irenius cites the examples of two ancient English families currently living in Ireland, the Macmaghons and Macswines, who have actively disguised their Englishness by changing their names.[77] Between them, Eudoxus and Irenius articulate passive and active forms of forgetfulness through acculturation.

In *Richard II* it is a monarch and the very supplanter of the Irish who returns from Ireland, a place that the English associated with the risk of forgetting their own identities, to English shores in a state of self-forgetfulness.[78] "Comfort, my liege. Remember who you are," urges Aumerle. "I had forgot myself. Am I not king?" (3.2.82–3). Richard has returned from the place of supplanting only to find himself, like the unseated Irish lords, supplanted. And like the transplanted Anglo-Irish, Richard has wagered and nearly lost his own memory of who he is by visiting what Spenser imagined to be that isle of oblivion on the margins of the English nation.

Structurally, the play enacts for audiences these patterns of displacement by planting the pressing Irish concerns in audience's minds, only to supplant them by having Ireland disappear from the play almost as soon it appears. Like the memories of the Anglo-Irish, whose weakness and vulnerability caused so much anxiety to writers like Spenser, audience's memories are tested as well. The island of forgetfulness is itself remembered and forgotten in ways that echo both Elizabethan schemes for manipulating the social memory of the Irish and English anxieties about losing their own. Our awareness of Ireland is displaced upon Richard's return by the extravagant poeticism accompanying his solemn, sacramental deposition. It is as if Shakespeare were staging Elizabethan anxieties about the deracination of the Anglo-Irish in the play's forgetful memory of the Irish wars.

The whole episode of Richard in Ireland, no sooner remembered than forgotten, serves as a reminder of the link between memory and displacement. Every memory, according to a view that dates back to the ancient Greeks, harbors an element of erasure, because every memory has the effect of displacing other material that must to some extent be marginalized or forgotten. As Edward Casey notes in his phenomenological study of remembering,

> [F]or the early Greeks generally, remembering and forgetting form an indissociable pair; they are given explicit mythical representation in the coeval figures of Lesmosyne and Mnemosyne, who are conceived as equals *requiring* each other. Or, more exactly, the two co-exist, but in this co-existence Mnemosyne, the pole of remembering, incorporates Lesmosyne, the pole of forgetting.[79]

Richard II has always been understood as a play about dispossession and displacement, but the relation of these patterns to the operations of remembering and forgetting has largely eluded criticism of the play. As a play about how kings, subjects, and nations forget and remember, *Richard II* engages questions of displacement and dispossession in psychological as well as geographical and political senses.

Richard II weaves an elaborate pattern of dispossession and displacement. Richard dispossesses Bolingbroke of his patrimony, the English of their past, and the Irish of their lands, only to find himself, on his return from a campaign of displacement and dispossession in Ireland, displaced and dispossessed. Following his own disinheritance, however, Richard will continue to displace in our memories not only the Irish but also the anchor of historical memory at the beginning of the play, Edward III, as he proceeds to usurp all our attention, making himself into the biblical archetype of all loss and dispossession since the beginning of time. I would go so far as to argue that in *Richard II* and his subsequent histories, Shakespeare develops a view of historical memory as a process of displacement that departs from a retrieval or archival understanding of memory implicit in the memory arts of the Middle Ages and Renaissance, in the medieval figure of memory as a library,[80] or in pronouncements like that of Thomas Wilson, privy councilor in Elizabeth's government, in his influential *The Art of Rhetoric* (1553), the first extensive study of rhetoric published in English, on memory as "the Threasure of the minde": "Memorie is the power of the minde that conteineth things receiued, that calleth to minde things past, and renueth of fresh, things forgotten."[81] A model of memory as retrieval similarly informs Thomas Nashe's defense of plays in *Pierce Penniless* as rescuing England's heroic past from the "grave of oblivion," or Edward Hall's description of the didactic ends of historical works like his *Chronicles*, to "enduce vertue, and represse vice: Thus, memorie maketh menne ded many a thousand yere *still to live as though thei were present*."[82]

In theorizing about postmodern culture, John Frow has proposed a distinction between two conceptual models for memory in the west: one based on the concept of "retrieval," the other on "textuality." The retrieval model, with its logic of the archive, operates according to principles of deposit and storage. Memory traces are deposited in an archive of the mind, as it were, and retrieved, like discrete physical objects, from storage. This conceptual model is supported by two dominant metaphors for memory: the wax writing-tablet and the thesaurus or storehouse.[83] As Mary Carruthers demonstrates in her study of the medieval arts of memory, the metaphor of memory as a process of writing on wax tablets persisted from Aristotle through the Middle Ages.[84]

The longstanding retrieval model for memory makes certain dubious assumptions, according to Frow. First, it assumes a "direct relation between space and mental categories," and of the "physical reality of memory traces." Besides its physical realism, this model has two more shortcomings: "its intentionalism (its assumption that meanings taken up are the repetition of meanings laid down)" and "its inability to account for forgetting other than as a fault or decay or as a random failure of access."[85] By contrast with the retrieval model, what Frow calls a textual model assumes that "memory, rather than being the repetition of the physical traces of the past, is a construction of it under conditions and constraints determined by the present." The retrieval model presupposes a "linear, before-and-after, cause-and-effect time"; the textual model, by contrast, a view of time as in some sense reversible and as the product of "a continuous analeptic and proleptic shaping." In the textual model, the past,

> rather than having a meaning and a truth determined once and for all by its status as event, its meaning and its truth are constituted retroactively and repeatedly; if time is reversible then alternative stories are always possible. Data are not stored in already constituted places but are arranged and rearranged at every point in time. Forgetting is thus an integral principle of this model, since the activity of compulsive interpretation that organizes it involves at once selection and rejection. Like a well-censored dream, and subject perhaps to similar mechanisms, memory has the orderliness and the teleological drive of narrative. Its relation to the past is not that of truth but of desire.[86]

In the textual model for memory, forgetting and displacement—a process of "selection and rejection"—are constitutive elements of the process of remembering, not simply faults or lapses in the process of retrieving bits of information from their storage places.

The play's complex pattern of displacements bears an intimate relation to its preoccupation with the psychology and politics of remembering and forgetting. It is not merely Bolingbroke, Richard, Irish landowners, and the Irish people who are subject to dispossession and displacement. The dead also figure into this category, as I suggested in the preceding section, as Richard, following his deposition, strives to fashion and govern his own future, projected memory: not unlike Henry V, who in his Crispin's Day speech tries to govern the future memory of the battle as well as ensure its present outcome. Richard does so, I have argued, in biblical terms that aim to displace the national terms in which Edward III had been installed as the anchor of his people's memory. In decided contrast with the heroic image of the deceased Henry V in *1 Henry VI*, to be retrieved by the present as needed and reproduced in more or less the same narrative register, Edward is a counter in "a continuous analeptic and proleptic shaping." Remembering itself is the most common form of supplanting or displacement in *Richard II*.

Both models of memory that Frow identifies, the retrieval model and textual model, operate in Shakespeare's histories. It might be argued, for instance, that the sons of Edward, Gaunt and York, operate within the limits of the former, whereas Richard shifts to a textual model, one in which the dominant "relation to the past is not that of truth but of desire" and in which forgetting is an "integral principle." Shakespeare's second sequence of history plays, I would contend, actively diminish the retrieval model of memory dominant in the Middle Ages and in the Renaissance memory theaters explored by Frances Yates,[87] largely replacing it with a textual model for memory of the kind described by Frow. The transitional play *King John* and the second tetralogy of histories with which this study is largely concerned, by their inclusion of figures who spawned divided and contentious historiographical traditions, tacitly regard the past's meaning and truth as not "determined once and for all by its status as event," but rather as "constituted retroactively and repeatedly." Furthermore, forgetting becomes closely partnered with memory in the second tetralogy, as the next few chapters will confirm. In the earlier histories, as Phyllis Rackin has demonstrated, the threat of oblivion was projected onto the "other"—the French and frequently feminine figures who threatened to erase or undo England's historical record. As Shakespeare's practice of history develops, forgetting becomes gendered differently and takes on a new national identity: absorbed into English and masculine stagings of power and collaborative with rather than simply opposed to the operations of memory.

Remembering often entails displacement in critical or crisis moments in Shakespeare, as when Hamlet apostrophizes to the Ghost of his father,

> Remember thee?
> Yea, from the table of my memory
> I'll wipe away all trivial fond records,
> All saws of books, all forms, all pressures past,
> That youth and observation copied there,
> And thy commandment all alone shall live
> Within the book and volume of my brain,
> Unmixed with baser mater. (1.5.97–104)

Other injunctions to remember may not require a wholesale erasure and full-fledged obeisance like this famous one by the Ghost of Hamlet's father upon his son, but even the most ordinary demands upon memory in Shakespeare's later histories and tragedies inevitably produce some degree of displacement or divestiture within the domain of memory. No play better illustrates the textual model of memory: exploring dispossession on a broad scale, *Richard II* repeatedly confirms how memory, born of dispossession in the case of Richard, itself produces further displacements.

RICHARD'S HISTORICAL SUBLIME?

History in *Richard II* is primarily about decisive, irreversible, and traumatic loss, about becoming aware of what one was and is no longer.[88] In other words, historical consciousness in the play resembles what Hayden White and Frank Ankersmit have characterized as "the historical sublime." In "The Politics of Historical Interpretation," White argues that the formation of history as an academic discipline in the nineteenth century entailed a suppression of the aesthetics of the sublime in historical writing in favor of the beautiful. He takes Edmund Burke's *Reflections on the Revolution in France* "as one of many efforts to exorcise the notion of the sublime from any apprehension of the historical process, so that the 'beauty' of its 'proper' development . . . could be adequately comprehended."[89] For historians on both the left and the right, "this same aesthetics of the beautiful presides over the process in which historical studies are constituted as an autonomous scholarly discipline."[90] How does an aesthetic of the beautiful manifest itself in historical studies? In Richard T. Vann's words, it is "the construction of histories so well emplotted that they give intellectual satisfaction and pleasure to the reader."[91] By contrast, a sublime apprehension of history would, in the words of Friedrich Schiller's 1801 essay "On the Sublime," entail confrontation with the "[u]ncertain anarchy of the moral world."[92] For Schiller it is "tragic art" that imitates "the terrifying spectacle of change which destroys everything and creates it anew, and destroys again—of ruin sometimes accomplished by swift undermining, sometimes by swift incursion."[93] According to White, the suppression of the sublime in favor of the beautiful as the aesthetic dimension for the academic discipline of history has produced a history "that can forgive everything or . . . practice a kind of 'disinterested interest' of the sort that Kant imagined to inform every properly aesthetic perception," thereby removing history from any connection with a visionary or utopian politics.[94] Modern ideologies of both the left and right that suppress the sublime

> impute a meaning to history that renders its manifest confusion comprehensible to either reason, understanding, or aesthetic sensibility. To the extent that they succeed in doing so, these ideologies deprive history of the kind of meaninglessness that alone can goad living human beings to make their lives different for themselves and their children, which is to say, to endow their lives with a meaning for which they alone are fully responsible.[95]

Following Nietzsche's consideration of "why and when the historian should welcome and contribute to a forgetting of the past" and Hayden White's notion of an "historical sublime," the Dutch theorist of history Frank Ankersmit differentiates four types of forgetting. The first consists of details that "are devoid of any relevance to our present or future identity." He gives the examples of "what we had for dinner last Sunday or where we went for a walk with our dog." [96] The first type of forgetting derives from a defensible disinterest or neglect, based upon the perceived unimportance of the material being forgotten; a second type, from a misapprehension about what is needful or important to remember. The latter has as its object details that are apparently insignificant to our lives or to the understanding of history, but, with the help of psychoanalysis for the individual's past or "thematic shifts in the history of historical writing" for a collective past, we become aware of "the unexpected significance of aspects of the past that were hitherto universally disregarded."[97]

A third type of forgetting is more active than either of the first two, and issues from a willed repression of traumatic experience: for instance, "how in the first two decades after World War II the Holocaust was 'forgotten' in Germany and not only there." The repression or deliberate withholding of what has been forgotten from conscious memory results in "the curious paradox that traumatic experience is both forgotten and remembered. It is forgotten in the sense that it can successfully be expelled from conscious memory; it is remembered in the sense that the subject of a traumatic experience will be seriously handicapped by it." This type of forgetting, associated with a traumatic personal or historical experience, results in the "dissociation of the self into a conscious and an unconscious self," which "guarantees the possibility of a not forgetting to forget. By relegating the traumatic experience to the domain of the unconscious, we can, indeed, forget it. But precisely by storing it there, we will *also* retain it as an unconscious memory. And as an unconscious memory it is a constant reminder that there is something that we should or wish to forget."[98]

It is the fourth type of forgetting, linked to the collective trauma that he sees as punctuating Western history, that occupies most of Ankersmit's attention. This fourth type, which he identifies with "the historical sublime" named and identified by White, issues from moments at which western man "entered a wholly new world . . . on the condition of forgetting a previous world and of shedding a former identity." Both the third and fourth types of forgetting are linked to traumatic experience, but the crucial difference is that in the third type, "closure of the trauma is possible, whereas it remains a constant and permanent presence in the fourth type." The former allows for resolution of the tension "between what is present consciously and unconsciously or between remembering and forgetting," usually through being "narrativized" and thereby "subsumed in the history of one's life or one's people." As a result of such narrativizing, the traumatic character of the event disappears: "The traumatic experience has then been adapted to identity, and vice versa. Or, to use the right terminology here, a *reconciliation* of experience and identity has then been achieved."[99] In the fourth type of forgetting, by contrast, instead of a reconciliation of experience and identity, there opens a gap between being and knowledge: one now knows what one once had been. The older, lost identity becomes solely an object of knowledge, not a recoverable state of being. In these cases, according to Ankersmit, no reconciliation between an older identity and the new one that replaces it is possible. In fact, "the new identity is mainly constituted by the trauma of the loss of a former identity—precisely *this* is its main content."[100] Put another way, the third type of forgetting involves the temporary loss of a part of our identity; the fourth type, the permanent and irreversible loss of the "*whole* of a previous identity." The third type allows us "to push traumatic loss for some time into the dark background of the unconscious, for the unconscious is an integral part of our identity that may offer us a kind of shelter that we sometimes need more than anything else"; in the fourth type, not even the unconscious can serve as a temporary storage place for the sense of loss.[101] Ankersmit provides the French Revolution and the rupture between the Middle Ages and the Renaissance as examples of this fourth type.[102] Cultural development for Ankersmit depends on these catastrophic experiences of loss or upheaval. Indeed, he contends that Western historical consciousness is itself largely born from a sense of traumatic loss.

Bearing in mind Ankersmit's typology of forgetting, the arc of Richard's tragedy, I would suggest, may be described as his progression from the first two types of forgetting to the fourth. Before he loses the throne, Richard appears to be a trivial creature of the here and now, defined largely by the neglectful forms of forgetting that are not associated with trauma. As examples of the second type, Ankersmit offers, "Historians sometimes 'forget' what has truly been decisive in the past"; individuals may forget "apparently insignificant details of our lives and of our behavior that psychoanalysis has shown to be of the greatest significance for our personality."[103] Until he is deposed, Richard neglects the very past that, unbeknownst to him, fills his identity. He is an inverted medievalist, one who studies forgetting instead of the memory arts that were so essential to ethical training in the Middle Ages. By contrast, his calling for a mirror in the deposition scene at Westminster Hall illustrates Ankersmit's paradoxical idea of "becoming what one is no longer" that he finds characteristic of those ruptures with the past that produce "the historical sublime" (IV.1.264f.). *Richard II* may be Shakespeare's most perfect expression of the historical sublime, which, we may recall, Schiller saw expressed fully only in "tragic art."

The fourth type of forgetting, as Ankersmit describes it, is a particularly paradoxical one: the old identity is lost or forgotten as a state of being, but remembered as an object of knowledge. "One has discarded (part of the) past from one's identity, and in this sense one has forgotten it. But one has not forgotten *that* one has forgotten it, for that one has forgotten precisely *this* is constitutive of the new identity." Hence, the paradoxical experience of seeing or recognizing oneself in what one is no longer: "*one has become what one is no longer*—with all the emphasis on the 'no longer.' What one used to *be*, one's former identity, is now transformed into the identity of the person who *knows* (and no longer *is*) his former identity."[104] *Richard II*'s exploration of the mechanics of and motives for forgetting would have spoken powerfully to the early modern English, who saw so much of their material and doctrinal past swept away by what J. F. Merritt refers to as "the trauma of the Protestant Reformation."[105] Keith Thomas writes, "The dramatic rupture with the medieval past occasioned by the Reformation created a sense of separateness and of an unbridgeable divide. This made it possible to perceive the recent past, not just as a collection of founding myths and precedents, but as the embodiment of an alternative way of life and set of values."[106] Andrew Borde (?1490–1549), a member of the Carthusian order during the early stages of the English Reformation who acknowledged the royal supremacy but still held to traditional rituals and practices of Catholicism, wrote in *The First Boke of the Introduction of Knowledge* (c. 1549), "I am, as I am, but not as I was."[107] Borde had discarded his past identity, forgotten it, but not forgotten that he had forgotten it. During Elizabeth's reign, the sense of a lost identity, of a split between what one is and what one knows that one was, was arguably widespread, not limited to recusant Catholics. Keith Thomas writes that

> when Elizabethan Catholics made a nostalgic appeal to medieval England they were drawing upon assumptions which were shared by many of their contemporaries; and a heavy weight of literary and intellectual authority underpinned their lament. The notion of a lost medieval age of gold was upheld by many social critics, Protestant no less than Catholic.[108]

Eamon Duffy comments, "Nostalgic idealization of the Catholic past [became] as much the voice of the church papist, and of some backward-looking parish Anglicans, as of conscientiously recusant Catholics."[109] According to Susan Brigden, it was precisely not England's militant papists, but rather those who looked upon material and ritual signs of the traditional religion receding into the past either with regret, acceptance, nostalgia, or a mixture of these, of whom it could be said, "In some places, by 1600, the coming generation could look back upon the Catholic past as a lost world."[110] In a reading of John Stow's nostalgic *A Survey of London* (1598), Ian Archer demonstrates,

> The intellectual world of Elizabethan England was not rigidly divided between the adherents of a Protestant view of a medieval dark age and a Catholic view of an idealized golden age. Protestants could appreciate the virtue that had existed in former times, and some of Stow's characteristic emphases surface in other more obviously godly writers.

The Queen herself seemed concerned to protect commemorative monuments, among other targets of radical reformers during the reign of Edward VI.[111] Just as it produces a historicism of sorts (granted, a highly narcissistic one) in Richard, the trauma of the Reformation helped fuel the antiquarian movement in early modern England. According to Patrick Collinson, "A good case can be made for a strong link between antipathy to the Reformation and all that flowed from it and what might be called the antiquarian bug."[112] Adam Fox writes of "the tremendous growth of antiquarian writings in the form of chronicles, county histories, and itineraries from the sixteenth century."[113] Alison Shell notes that there was "an intimate relationship between England's medieval past and the antiquarian spirit, which drew so many outright Catholics, crypto-Catholics and religious conservatives towards this kind of scholarship during penal times."[114] Recent scholarship has confirmed that there were indeed communities within early modern England that regarded the past with a sense of radical loss or upheaval: especially the mass of more pliant traditionalists who, rather than militantly hold onto it, reluctantly let go of the Catholic past from which they felt unalterably separated. For at least some members of this large community, *Richard II* held up a mirror in which it regarded the evacuation of its former identity in the wake of the Reformation. *Richard II* shows how traumatic loss (Richard's for his throne, and at least some communities in Elizabethan England for their medieval, Catholic past) may indeed fuel historical awareness, and how forgetting may play not an antithetical but a constitutive role in the development of a historical consciousness.

Traumatic events produce historical consciousness, and historical consciousness, for Ankersmit, entails a splitting of the self. As Hans Kellner interprets him, "This split self allows the community . . . to distance itself from what it is painfully leaving behind, while embracing the very lost identity as a historical ground."[115] Historical transitions entail a "kind of cultural suicide," which "have the character of the exchange of a former identity for a new one." As a result, "such transitions can properly be described as seeing the former self as if it were the self of somebody else."[116] The last formulation of Ankersmit's suggests a possible link between trauma and theater. *Richard II*, it may be said, enacts the originating conditions for both theater and history: a traumatic birth into historical consciousness through the splitting of the self and an exchange of a former identity for a new one. It might cause one to speculate that it was the very trauma of historical rupture—in other words the historical sublime—that led to the flourishing of theaters in Elizabethan England: an institution founded and dependent on the exchange of former identities for new ones. In diverse ways, Shakespeare's major tragedies all explore the traumatic effects of seeing oneself as if it were the self of somebody else. *Richard II* explores the split between being (the purgatorial loss of his former self, lost or forgotten as a state of being) and knowledge (memory of that former self) in a tragic register. In the 1590s, it offered its audiences, mixed in their religious identities and allegiances, Richard's lost or forgotten state as the historical ground of its own identity as a post-medieval or reformed nation. *Richard II* is a play about the birth of an acute historical consciousness out of traumatic division and loss, a creation *ex nihilo*, as it were, as a painful and incurable historical outlook replaces a habitual and studied neglect of the past. Shakespeare's first tetralogy also begins with an instance of traumatic loss, the burial of Henry V, England's preeminent warrior king, but the heroic legacy he represents has been lost only temporarily. It resurfaces in figures like Talbot and Richmond. England's provisional loss of Henry V represents a reversible trauma, not the irreversible one that Ankersmit associates with the fourth type of forgetting. For an enactment of that deeper form of trauma, one has to wait for the second tetralogy and *Richard II*.

Richard, I am contending, is a figure for a certain kind of historical consciousness that was widespread in late Elizabethan England, one linked to the sense of irreparable loss, and the nostalgia it was likely to spawn. But I do not want to suggest that audiences would have regarded Richard as a straightforward trope for its lost medieval identity, including its Catholicism, even though there is much in his language that marks his as a medieval mind: his *ubi sunt* formulae suggesting a universal mutability, his self-representation as a beadsman and a pilgrim (III.3.147–54), and his and Isabel's placement of their downfall within a *de casibus* interpretive framework. For Elizabethan audiences, however, a straightforward association of Richard with its own pre-Reformation identity or even with a Catholic memory of such an identity would have been complicated by at least four factors. First, Richard increasingly interiorizes the conditions of kingship following his deposition. In a way, it seems that he "reforms," albeit reluctantly, the institution of kingship in ways that reflect the Reformation of the Church and of religious practices. Ernst Kantorowicz notes that following his deposition, his kingship is "relegated to within": "Over against his lost outward kingship he sets an inner kingship, makes his true kingship to retire to inner man, to soul and mind and 'regal thoughts.'"[117] His stripping away the outer forms of kingship would have evoked for many the stripping away of outer forms of worship.

Second, as one who dissolves generational bonds, Richard bears a connection to one of the most common complaints against the effects of the Reformation: that it threatened or dissolved generational bonds linking parents and children. In his preface to *Britain* (1610), William Camden regularly complained about zealous reformers who "peradventure would have us forget that our ancestours were, as we are, of the Christian profession."[118] Conversely, opposition to Richard, I have already noted, appears to hold the power to restore these bonds. The theme of broken generational bonds is developed most fully in the play in the relationship between the Duke of York and his son Aumerle, one that bears echoes of a common family drama that ensued from the Protestant Reformation. Recusant Catholics often voiced the complaint that Protestantism dissolved the bonds of human community, not only between the living and the dead, but also of "husband and wife, child from parent, dissolving the bonds of memory": one of the themes of Sir Thomas More's *The Supplication of Souls*, as Eamon Duffy notes and a common theme of what he calls the "conservative voice." Public opposition to the Protestant Reformation was strengthened in Marian England, during which time authorities attempted to force Protestants to admit that their parents were doctrinally in error and deceived:

> Protestants did, of course, believe that one could do nothing for dead parents, children and spouses, and that the bonds of prayer were of

> no assistance to the dead. Equally, they believed that the faith of our fathers was not the good old way, but a farrago of error and idolatry: woe to the soul who was indeed gathered to their fathers, since the likelyhood was that, seduced by popish error, the fathers were roasting on the hobs of hell. But it was difficult to say so without forfeiting the sympathy of the great Tudor public.[119]

In the oblique form of drama, however, it is possible to say what it is dangerous to say or what cannot be said in polemical treatises, and to explore in a darkly comic register the dissolution of the parent-child bond that some Catholics associated with the Reformation.[120]

Third, insofar as Richard at the beginning of the play turns his back upon England's recent past, he resembles Elizabethan Protestants and humanists, who similarly "made a self-conscious breach with the immediate past," as Keith Thomas reminds us. "The Reformers claimed to return to the traditions of the primitive church, strenuously disowning those of its medieval successor. The humanists preferred classical antiquity to the degenerate Latin and credulous writings of the monastic era."[121] In an analogous move, Richard ignores his nation's recent past and turns to a kind of antiquity, to biblical rather than national history, as a means of self-rescue and self-legitimation once he is stripped of his authority.[122]

Fourth, as Eamon Duffy has stressed, nostalgia was at least as strong if not stronger among a certain kind of "church papist, and of some backward-looking parish Anglicans" as among militant recusants who were vigorously working toward and hoping for a return of their country to the Catholic fold.[123] The "note of nostalgia," he writes, "was sounded more often than not self-consciously, as the voice of the defeated."[124] As perhaps Shakespeare's greatest elegist[125] and most eloquent nostalgic, Richard does not successfully bridge the gap between England's pre- and post-Reformed identities as much as he stands for the breach that opened up as "one of the most catholic of European countries became one of the least," in Patrick Collinson's words.[126] Richard speaks to the post-Reformation sense of a gulf between England's past and present, as the Reformation, in Huston Diehl's account, "disrupted and transformed established modes of perception and knowledge . . . , affecting the way the English people viewed images, engaged in ritual practices, interpreted the physical world, and experienced theater."[127]

It may seem anachronistic to locate trauma stemming from the English Reformation in the theater of the 1590s, because the more extreme manifestations of reform had taken place at mid-century during the reigns of Henry VIII and Edward VI. How to locate trauma more than a generation after the moderate Elizabethan Settlement, which A. G. Dickens, in his influential study *The English Reformation*, regarded as the concluding chapter of the Reformation?[128] More recent work has stressed the Reformation as a process that lasted well into the reign of Elizabeth and beyond. David Cressy writes in his groundbreaking study *Birth, Marriage, and Death: Ritual, Religion, and the Life-Cycle in Tudor and Stuart England*, that

> parish disagreements and local disputes about the meaning and conduct of life-cycle rituals reflect the unresolved problem of England's adoption of Protestantism. The Reformation, however slow and fitful that may have been in England, had effects that were profoundly traumatic. From the mid-sixteenth century to the mid-seventeenth, the secular and ecclesiastical governments asked men and women, laity and clergy, to abandon long-held beliefs about salvation and to give up traditional modes of devotion, to conform themselves to a national protestant church.[129]

Alexandra Walsham writes in her important study *Church Papists*, England's was "a reformation that generated, at least initially, not rapid conversion but grudging conformity."[130] Because of the Reformation's slow development, Peter Marshall concludes, "the later Elizabethan decades can look more like a point of departure than of culmination."[131] The decade of the 1580s in particular has been regarded as a watershed. Marshall has written of recent scholarship in the field, "There is now a substantial body of opinion which holds that it was precisely from this decade onwards that Protestantism in a more than formal sense began to make substantial inroads on a national scale."[132] The extreme edges of Protestantism in particular gave out the impression that the Reformation was a work in progress, not an accomplished fact. Walsham writes, "It was both the godly's greatest disappointment and gravest embarrassment that a generation after the Reformation's restoration—notwithstanding so much 'painful' preaching—'popery' had yet to be effectively stifled."[133] In 1580 Puritan divine William Fulke asked of its persistent and widespread influence, "who living in Englande can be ignoraunt?"[134] Christopher Haigh has directly challenged the traditional assumption that the Elizabethan Settlement marked the culmination of the English Reformation, arguing instead that "the Protestant Reformation was an Elizabethan (and often mid-Elizabethan) event."[135] For much of the Elizabethan period, according to Haigh, the discrepancy between church and laity—in particular, a reformed liturgy and doctrine on the one hand and a non-Protestant laity on the other—was too great in most regions of England, especially the countryside, for the Reformation to be regarded as having culminated in 1558–1559. A popular oral tradition, according to Adam Fox, kept elements of a pre-Reformation culture alive even after attempts to rewrite hagiography in a widely disseminated text like Foxe's *Actes and Monumentes* and in sermons. In the teeth of written and clerical culture, saints' legends survived for centuries after the Reformation.[136] By the last years of the sixteenth century, Haigh concludes, clergy had created "a Protestant nation, but not a nation of Protestants."[137] Besides recusant Catholics, England had substantial numbers of those he chooses to call "parish Anglicans," whom he characterizes as "the spiritual leftovers of Elizabethan England": those who were "no longer Catholics" but who "had not been moved by the evangelistic fervour of the Protestant Reformation" and who "welcomed as much ceremony as the Church of England would sanction."[138]

Both Haigh and Collinson insist on speaking not of a continuous and unified historical process but of double or plural processes: Reformations, not the Reformation. Collinson has argued that the cultural effects of reform lagged behind legislative acts:

> The timetable for concomitant cultural change runs a little later. For the first two or three decades of Elizabeth's reign, much of the old cultural fabric remained intact . . . But towards 1580 there was a sea change. Scripture plays and scripture songs became equally obnoxious to many religious people. Christ had not lived and died in order to be a spectacle on stage. There were now fewer godly ballads, and no more plays deriving their matter from scripture.[139]

The 1580s, he has argued, witnessed a Second English Reformation, during which most of the cultural effects of iconophobia—"the total repudiation of all images," as opposed to the iconoclasm of the first generation of Protestants, a more limited and targeted attack on "certain unacceptable images"—took place.[140] The more significant cultural shift took place not between England's last generation of traditional Catholics and first generation of "Protestant communicators who . . . were in continuity and communication with the tradition, sharing common cultural ground with their Catholic opponents," but rather "between the first and second generations of Protestants."[141] When Shakespeare's histories were staged in the 1590s, many of the more visible and material aspects of reform, in other words, were indeed of recent memory and coincided roughly with the beginnings of a popular, secular theater in England. Change was also abrupt, according to Collinson, like Richard's fall: "The cultural impact of what looks like a second English Reformation resembles that famous day in Sweden when, at a certain signal, vehicles stopped driving on the left and changed to the right, so relatively sudden and drastic was the change."[142]

Collinson, however, does not see the Second English Reformation and the development of a secular English drama as related in any more than a "negative" sense. Hewing to the traditional argument that radical Protestantism was an enemy to the stage in Elizabethan and Jacobean England, he writes, "No one turns Shakespeare himself into a chapter of the English Reformation."[143] Huston Diehl and others have tacitly challenged this assumption, arguing

> that Elizabethan and Jacobean drama is both a product of the Protestant Reformation—a reformed drama—and a producer of Protestant

> habits of thought—a reforming drama . . . Elizabethan and Jacobean tragedies articulate the anxieties created by Protestant assaults on late medieval piety, but I do not believe that they are hostile to Protestantism or particularly sympathetic to the old religion.[144]

My reading of *Richard II*, a play concerned with history as rupture rather than "fair sequence and succession" of cause and effect, concurs with Diehl's view of early modern drama as highly articulate responses to the English Reformation. However, I see this particular play not as a "reforming drama" or "a producer of Protestant habits of thought" but rather as an attempt to answer trauma with drama, and thereby to express a sympathy for those among Shakespeare's contemporaries who could not regard the recent past without desiring to "call back yesterday." Perhaps it is time, *pace* Collinson, to regard Shakespeare as, among other things, a chapter in the English Reformation.

THE ACT OF OBLIVION

I conclude with another rupture in English history, one that also peered into the historical mirror that was the reign of Richard II: one that, in Adam Fox's words, "was instrumental in creating a new series of battle grounds and symbolic sites which helped to supplant some of the old landmarks in the mental map of the past."[145] In 1660, following the conclusion of the English Civil Wars and the restoration of the monarchy, Parliament, urged by Charles II, passed an Act of Pardon, Indemnity, and Oblivion that granted amnesty to nearly all former enemies of the crown.[146] It was an attempt to say good night to the late conflict by spreading a comforting blanket of forgetfulness over the land. The Act of Oblivion, as it is often called, not only decided the fate of former rebels but also attempted to legislate the nation's recollection of the recent past. In the language of the Act, "[A]ll manner of treasons, misprisions of treason, murders, felonies, offences, crimes, contempts and misdemeanors . . . [shall] be pardoned, released, indemnified, discharged, and put in utter oblivion."[147] Differences of party were to be forgotten, although the flowering of party politics in England was just around the corner.[148] The entire piece of legislation might have been an elaboration on Richard's line to the quarreling Mowbray and Bolingbroke, "Forget, forgive, conclude and be agreed" (1.1.156).

In order to halt prospects of revenge and retribution, Parliament banned for three years language that would evoke memories of the late conflict, imposing penalties on acts of speech or writing that reflected on any man's conduct "since the first day of January in the Year of Our Lord 1637[–8]."[149] The Act provided that "to the intent and purpose that all names and terms be put into utter oblivion, . . . any name or names, or other word of reproach any way tending to revive the memory of the late differences or the occasions thereof" would result in heavy fines ranging from forty shillings to ten pounds, depending less on the nature of the insult than on the rank of the insulted party.[150] In many ways it recalled the Royal Injunctions of 1559, which were similarly addressed to what Alexandra Walsham refers to as a "politics of language" informing the English Reformation.[151] In the wake of the Elizabethan Settlement, these injunctions demanded that subjects refrain from uttering "in despite or rebuke of any person these contentious words: papist, or papistical heretic, schismatic, or sacramentary, or any such like words of reproach."[152]

Insofar as the 1660 Act restored land, goods, and titles,[153] it might also be characterized as an act of manufactured remembrance whose aim was to restore, along with the crown, the illusion of continuity and a stable tradition by means of legislated forgetting. Needless to say, the Act of Oblivion did not immediately succeed in establishing uniformity among English recollections of the past two decades. In fact, there was even some disagreement about who or what the act was designed to forget. Many cavaliers felt that it was they, not republican wrongs or excesses, that were being consigned to the dustbin of history. As Tim Harris writes, "It became a common jest that 'the king had passed an act of oblivion for his friends, and of indemnity for his enemies.'"[154] Although opposed by the cavaliers, tactically the bill proved a masterstroke. It eventually produced just the effect the crown desired. Ostensibly designed to forgive past actions, its true import was to ensure that there would be no vigorous future republican opposition. It effectively sent the opposing parties into oblivion. J. R. Jones writes,

> There can be little doubt that the accelerated decline and early disappearance of the defeated republican and Cromwellian parties were ensured by this avoidance of a harsh and general proscription. Although most regicides died bravely, believing that they were sealing with their blood the good old cause, no cult ever developed around their martyrdom, and later generations forgot them.[155]

A theatrical act of oblivion of sorts followed twenty years later, with Shakespeare's *Richard II*—or, more precisely, Nahum Tate's Royalist version of the play, *The History of King Richard the Second* (1680)—the target. During the Restoration, one of the most controversial elements from the past that needed to be silenced was the example of Richard II, including Shakespeare's theatrical treatment of his foibles and deposition. Even two decades after the Restoration of the monarchy and a little more than three decades after the execution of Charles I, a play about the deposing of a monarch remained a dangerous and contentious property. As Ernst Kantorowicz notes, "The play illustrated perhaps too overtly the latest events of England's revolutionary history, the 'Day of Martyrdom of the Blessed King Charles I' as commemorated in those years in the Book of Common Prayer. The Restoration avoided these and other recollections."[156]

The play had notoriously occasioned controversy in 1601, when Essex's supporters commissioned the Lord Chamberlain's Men to mount a special performance of the play to help rouse public support for Essex on the eve of his rebellion.[157] But Tate endeavored to make the play safe for royalty. He eliminated most of Richard's foibles and concentrated not on the King's shortcomings but on his relation with his second Queen, whose part he expanded. In words from his Dedicatory Epistle, every scene "was full of respect to Majesty and the dignity of courts." Nevertheless, on its third performance in December 1680, the play was banned. The following month the play resurfaced in a thinly disguised Italianate version, *The Sicilian Usurper*, only to meet an even more severe fate: the patent theater in which it had been played, the King's Theatre at Drury Lane, was shut down for a period of ten days. Although twelve years later he would be named England's poet laureate, in the wake of the controversy Tate "was labeled a radical."[158] As Odai Johnson writes in a perceptive essay on the episode, "The closing of the theatre became a regulation of the collective memory, physicalized as an illegitimate trespass on Royal property."[159] The play, by virtue of its being "banished from the theatre, became itself a sort of Bolingbroke figure, gathering charisma by its absence."[160] Tate did not passively accept these acts of theatrical censorship. In 1681, less than a year after its suppression on stage, he delivered his play from oblivion through the medium of print, representing its publication as an act of memorial rescue, not of Richard's political reign but of Shakespeare's theatrical one:

> 'Twas thought perhaps that this unfortunate Offspring having been stifled on the *Stage*, shou'd have been buried in Oblivion; and so it might have happened had it drawn its Being from me Alone, but it still retains the immortal spirit of its first-Father, and will survive in Print, though forbid to tread the *Stage*.[161]

The context for the controversy engendered by Tate's sanitized representation of Richard was the ongoing Exclusion Crisis. The Exclusion Bill, first proposed in 1678, would have excluded King Charles II's brother and presumptive heir James, a Roman Catholic, from the succession. The Whigs supported the bill whereas the Tories opposed it. Wars for the nation's historical memory were fought on both sides, in ways that implicated the larger crisis, the Civil Wars, that occasioned the parliamentary Act of Oblivion. Tories kept alive memories of what they perceived to be the tyrannical excesses of Cromwell's Commonwealth government. For their part, Whigs reminded the nation of the so-called Popish Plot of two years earlier. Although it was a fictitious conspiracy concocted by Titus Oates, who implicated, among others, James's personal secretary Edward Colman, exposure of the "plot" caused a wave of anti-Catholic sentiment from 1678–1681. Anti-Catholic fervor was kept alive by the memory of Elizabeth herself, as the anniversary of her accession was commemorated in London by huge processions in which the Pope was burnt in effigy. In this divisive atmosphere, Charles II's successful suppression of Tate's *Richard II* and the replacement of the offending play with Charles Saunders's *Tamerlane the Great* (1681) represented, according to Johnson, "a brilliant coup de théâtre," in which "Charles reappropriated the medium to unequivocally reassert his absolutism. That gesture marked the final defeat of the Exclusion Bill and the beginning of the rout of the Whig party."[162] On the issue of succession, Royal prerogative triumphed over the popular will.[163]

For his part, Tate denied any topicality to his play, any connection of his version of *Richard II* to contemporary events, including the Exclusion Crisis. In his Epistle Dedicatory, he insisted, "To form any Resemblance between the Times here written of, and the Present, had been unpardonable Presumption in Me . . . Why a History of those Times shou'd be suppresst as a Libel upon Ours, is past my Understanding."[164] In other words, he cast himself as a Richard, a character who, as I have indicated, showed no interest in or talent for connecting past and present, even though the play as a whole had a scandalous history in this regard. It was difficult indeed not to have connected Richard's past with the Elizabethan present of 1601, as Queen Elizabeth's famous comment to the Elizabethan antiquarian William Lambarde in the wake of the Essex rebellion suggests ("I am Richard II. Know ye not that?"). In other words, Tate met suppression with repression, namely, his own repression of the play's record of incendiary topicality and its all too obvious connections with the ongoing Exclusion Crisis, as hard to deny as the play's topicality in the waning years of Elizabeth's reign. The further irony of these twin acts of oblivion, as it were, is their fictional ancestry in Richard's own denial of history. It is as if Tate took his cue from Shakespeare's anti-historical protagonist. *Richard II*, I have argued, dramatizes a king's denial of history followed by a traumatic birth of historical consciousness. No wonder it spoke in so loud and unsettling a voice to a nation that had recently lived through the trauma of the Civil Wars, and no wonder that Tate in his Dedicatory Epistle had to speak in so Ricardian a voice to defend himself from charges of topicality. For a nation that sought to respond to its own historical rupture and the trauma it produced through various acts of oblivion, *Richard II* embarrassingly enacted the birth of a historical consciousness from traumatic loss, the very thing that the Restoration monarchy sought to efface.

Like the period of the Restoration, Elizabethan and Jacobean England looked back upon a prolonged traumatic event that would necessitate official attempts to legislate the memory of a nation. Studies like David Cressy's *Bonfires and Bells* and Ronald Hutton's *The Rise and Fall of Merry England* have demonstrated the extent to which Elizabethan and Jacobean England's sense of the past had changed and was continuing to change as a result of the Protestant reform of the old Catholic seasonal calendar.[165] Shakespeare's decision to subject to theatrical treatment figures such as King John and Sir John Oldcastle, each the subject of divided historiographical traditions, capitalized on those divisions. His dramatizations of these figures, although less overtly partisan than works like John Bale's *King Johan*, the anonymous *Troublesome Raigne of Iohn King of England,* or *The Life of Sir John Oldcastle* by Michael Drayton and others, do not exactly constitute imaginative acts of oblivion designed to make England forget its internal differences. Rather, they call attention to the social and political dynamics of remembering and forgetting, foregrounding the play of power implicit in such acts. As I will explore more directly in the next chapter, Shakespeare's second tetralogy comments on the act of oblivion—the suppression of the name of Oldcastle—that stands at its center.

The parliamentary Act of Oblivion demonstrated the importance of forgetting for the "restoration of national unity."[166] It was consistent with King James VI/I's argument for union before the English parliament more than half a century earlier, in which he uncannily perceived the role that forgetting would play in the development of an expanded national unit. James conceived of a Great Britain that needed to be founded upon acts of erasure. The old names of England and Scotland, which James implied could only signal difference and division, would be submerged in the old/new name of Britain. Adopting the title King of Great Britain without parliamentary consent, James traced his ancestry back to one Brutus, King of all Britons, rewarding antiquarians like Thomas Lyte who supported the historical myth. James projected a vision of "one king, one faith, one language; one law, one parliament, one people alike in manners and allegiance."[167] Furthermore, he spoke of the union of the kingdoms as a reunion: "the blessed Union, or rather reuniting, of these two mighty, famous, and ancient kingdoms of England and Scotland under one Imperial Crown."[168] That the Project for Union, James's personal Act of Oblivion, might wear the aura of legitimacy, James was careful to cloak it in the rhetoric of remembrance. In this respect he resembles Shakespeare's Henry V: a figure who, as I will show in a later chapter, demonstrates an increasing identification of political power with skill at orchestrating social memory and collective amnesia. Unlike James, however, Shakespeare does not simply promote the idea of an expanded national unit. Exploring the dynamics of how a national identity is formed, Shakespeare's second sequence of histories paradoxically reminds us that the imagined community that is a nation is produced by repeated acts of oblivion. They do not allow us to easily forget the sacrifices of memory at the stripped or purified altar of the Protestant nation

2 All Is Truancy
Rebellious Uses of the Past in *1 Henry IV*

Is it oblivion or absorption when things pass from our minds?
—Emily Dickinson to Thomas Wentworth Higginson[1]

In his speech "What Is a Nation?" delivered in 1882 at the Sorbonne, French philologist, philosopher, political theorist, and historian Ernest Renan asserted, "Forgetting, I would even go so far as to say historical error, is a crucial factor in the creation of a nation, which is why progress in historical studies often constitutes a danger for [the principle of] nationality."[2] Renan's statement accounts for many of the appealing eccentricities of *1 Henry IV*. It helps account for the convergence of two of the most prominent features of the play: an extravagantly fractured nation, the English contending against the Welsh and the Scots, and equally divided perceptions of the past within the play itself. More precisely, it helps to explain why a play with manifold dangers for the principle of nationality should devote so much attention to lapses of memory. Or why Shakespeare might be tempted to reflect such lapses among his characters with one of the most outrageous "historical error[s]" of his career: an "error" that one can only characterize as Falstaffian in its extravagance.

"Historical error" may well describe Shakespeare's underlying and in some ways rebellious method in this play in which forgetting performs so many important social and political roles. Certainly no one has ever accused *1 Henry IV*, with its grotesque portrayal of the Lollard knight and Protestant martyr Sir John Oldcastle, of constituting "progress in historical studies." Indeed, the play's underlying paradox is this: its most memorable character[3] seems a calculated affront to historical memory. Frequently accused of "abolishing the bonds of memory," the Protestant Reformation witnesses one of its own heroes and martyrs subjected to a similar process in *1 Henry IV*.[4] The history of a pre-Reformation martyr is itself reformed out of recognition.

On the other hand, what better way to meet a period of civil strife in English history than with a character whose remembrance would inevitably accentuate the deep divisions within Elizabethan religious life? The historiographical traditions regarding Oldcastle—traitor and heretic in some chronicles, zealous reformer and proto-Protestant martyr in revisionist accounts by William Tyndale, John Bale, and John Foxe[5]—were as sharply divided as those of King John. There was as much discord in the textual background of the play as there was to be in the play itself.[6] As if to confirm Renan's thesis, this play, like its successors *2 Henry IV* and *Henry V*, shows the path of forgetting to support the principle of nationality, and historical memory to constitute a persistent danger sniping at the borders of the early modern nation.

Furthermore, so as not only to divide two regions of English historical memory, Protestant and Catholic, from one another, but, more dramatically, to separate historical memory from itself, Shakespeare makes this trigger of divisive historical memory a virtual emblem of forgetfulness. Oldcastle (later renamed Falstaff) almost singlehandedly raises all the important questions about the virtues of remembering and forgetting in early modern England: pressing questions, certainly, for a country that had decisively transformed itself earlier in the century and that had jettisoned a good deal of its material, ritual, and doctrinal past over the course of the Reformation. A Lord of Misrule who produces disorder not only in the tavern and on the battlefield but also at the court of history itself, Oldcastle/Falstaff calls the fundamental premises of a memorializing culture into question. A paradoxical logic with regard to memory informs the character of Oldcastle/Falstaff as well as the play as a whole: capable of spreading contending historical memories, he is recreated by Shakespeare as a walking plague of forgetfulness. He is both cause of and cure for the history wars he is liable to unleash.

It seems no accident that the play in which Shakespeare arguably took the most liberties with the past contains a character who does likewise. Shakespeare's Oldcastle may represent history written by a playwright—quite possibly while quaffing pints of ale in the taverns of London's suburbs—playing the truant to his historical task, as it were, like Hal shirking the sobriety and gravity of his father's court.[7] One of the most fascinating aspects of Oldcastle/Falstaff is the way he embodies the very conditions—namely, a deeply flawed memory, or at least a willingness to unhinge narrative from known facts[8]—that seemed to produce him in the first place. A marred reconstruction of not one past but two, those of Sir John Oldcastle and the fifteenth-century military man Sir John Fastolfe, he either neglects the past or else wildly reinvents it, like his author. For Falstaff, the past tense is an invitation to play. It is as if, in creating Oldcastle/Falstaff, Shakespeare drew a figure for the considerable license he allowed his own historical imagination in *1 Henry IV*.

In the play as a whole, Shakespeare governs historical memory rather loosely, as England itself was ruled by Henry IV, and plants a rebellion against historical thinking in the character of Oldcastle/Falstaff.[9] Memory, the theme that Hal will—spectacularly, memorably—make his own in *Henry V*, is unavailable to his father as a means of military inspiration or method of social and political control. Henry dares bring it to light only in his private interview with the Prince (3.2). The King is effectively checked from controlling or directing his people's memory, preoccupied as he is with making his people forget the process by which he achieved the throne and the persistence of a powerful rival claim to the throne, that of Edmund Mortimer. For the King, the past is matter for either avoidance or suppression. Falstaff's fear that Hotspur's corpse will arise again to challenge him on the field of battle resembles a second impersonation of the King, like the one he undertakes in the tavern in 2.4: it serves to remind us how dangerous the dead can be to the living, particularly a dead king to a living one and his heir.

By default, the theme of remembrance comes to define rebels, not royalty in *1 Henry IV*. Into the play's historical vacuum move the Percies, who claim the theme of memory for the opposition,[10] and that historical chimera, Sir John Oldcastle/Falstaff, for whom the past, like a battlefield strewn with the defeated, is free for the plundering. Given the manifest dangers of historical memory to the stability of Henry's reign, the nation drifts without historical anchoring. At the same time, the play displays a heightened awareness that it is the highway of forgetting chosen by Falstaff and Hal, and not the rebels' well-trodden path of memory, that will lead to greater national unity. Shakespeare represents an England separating itself from the dynastic principle that plays such an important role in the first tetralogy, and distancing itself from its medieval past in ways that reflected the Protestant Reformation, while charting the tensions and contradictions within the early modern imagining of the nation.[11] He demonstrates throughout the second tetralogy that the very idea of a nation is undergirded by the same spirit of revisionism from which the character Oldcastle/Falstaff had been born and which he grandly embodies.

In what follows, I build two related arguments concerning Oldcastle/Falstaff. First, rather than representing a bizarre anomaly or aberration, Oldcastle/Falstaff is instead largely consistent with Shakespeare's treatment of history in the second tetralogy: specifically, with the ways in which the operations of various kinds of forgetting—rewriting, distraction, erasure—are inevitably implicated in historical memory. Second, the old Lollard's association with forgetfulness draws upon and resonates with contemporary associations of Protestantism, particularly its more radical manifestations, with a willful forgetting.

PADDING HISTORICAL MEMORY

A telling lapse in memory took place in the performance of a play at court before the Queen late in 1596, the probable date of the first performances of *1 Henry IV*. The performance was overseen by William Brooke, Lord Cobham, Elizabeth's fifth Lord Chamberlain. Not himself a descendant of Oldcastle, the fourth Lord Cobham and knight whom the English Reformation had virtually canonized,[12] Brooke held the title of Lord Cobham through his wife, Joan de la Pole. It is well known that Shakespeare originally named Prince Hal's companion Sir John Oldcastle, following his source, the anonymous *The Famous Victories of Henry the Fifth*. It was Brooke who most likely censured Shakespeare for his depiction of Oldcastle and caused him to change the name of the old rogue to Falstaff. [13] The old name of Oldcastle, it has often been pointed out, lives on in ghostly fashion in the revised play: for instance, in Hal's reference to Falstaff as "my old lad of the castle" (1.2.41).

It was Brooke's task to marshal the audiences that turned out for command performances like this one. A challenge to Brooke's authority issued from a recalcitrant member of the court audience named Edward Jones, described by Cobham's modern biographer David McKeen as a "hanger on at Court." Jones, who had risen from his place in order "to speak with his socially superior wife," was publicly confronted by Cobham. The Lord Chamberlain directed him in the sight of all to quit the area of the auditorium, chastising him for being, in McKeen's words, "impertinently forgetful of his place." Brooke, Jones complained in a letter he penned a few days later, "liften up [his] staff at me, called me sirrah, and bid me get me lower saucy fellow, besides other words of disgrace."[14] Jones was a Renaissance self-fashioner who, like Shakespeare, aspired to rewrite his identity by rising in rank. He hoped, albeit unsuccessfully, to raise himself at court by seeking Robert Cecil's support for an appointment as French secretary to the Queen. In spite of seating arrangements both at court and in the public theaters that were designed to remind audience members of their places, spectators might be suspected of privately indulging the fantasy of forgetting their "places" for the space of a couple of hours through identification with characters on stage. In such an environment of focused distraction, Jones seemed to catch the plague of self-forgetfulness. He was thereupon chastised by Cobham, who pointed toward him with his white staff and directed him to recall his place.[15]

Although the play in question may or may not have been *1 Henry IV*—both Gary Taylor and Robert Fehrenbach have argued that the play was performed at court during the Christmas season of 1596, and that Shakespeare changed the name of his character from Oldcastle to Falstaff before that performance[16]—this anecdote seems particularly illuminating for understanding the two-part *Henry IV*, where acts of forgetting figure prominently in both the textual background of the play and within the action of the play itself. In the same season, this Lord Cobham, who held the office of Lord Chamberlain from August 8, 1596 until his death on March 5, 1597, pointed an accusing finger (or perhaps white staff) at an impertinent Shakespeare for defaming the "honorable memorie" (Richard James, a generation later) of the Lollard martyr lampooned in the hugely appealing figure of Falstaff.[17] In a figurative sense Shakespeare, like Jones, was directed to recall his place.[18]

But the new name was not exactly innocuous. Thomas Fuller, a chaplain and moderate royalist during the English Civil Wars, expressed satisfaction that "Sir John Falstaff hath relieved the memory of Sir John Oldcastle, and of late is substituted buffoon in his place."[19] In his *The History of the Worthies of England* (1662), however, a county-by-county description of England with short biographies of the "worthies" of each, he complained that the new name of the character was as offensive as the old:

> Now as I am glad that Sir John Oldcastle is put out, so I am sorry that Sir John Fastolf is put in, to relieve his memory in this base service, to be the anvil for every dull wit to strike upon. Nor is our comedian excusable, by some alteration of his name, writing him Sir John Falstaff, and making him the property of pleasure of King Henry the Fifth to abuse, seeing the vicinity of sounds entrench on the memory of that worthy knight, and few do heed the inconsiderable difference in spelling of their name.[20]

The original "worthy," Sir John Oldcastle (c.1375–1417), was a friend of the Prince who served with him in the fight against Glendower's Welsh rebels in 1407. Like Sir John Fastolfe, he was a parliament man, representing Herefordshire as a knight of the shire in 1404. Owing to his sympathy for the proto-Protestant religious movement of Lollardy, he was convicted of heresy in 1413 and imprisoned. Following his escape, Oldcastle may have led a failed religious insurrection against King Henry V, the nobility, and the church hierarchy in the following year. As Annabel Patterson has shown, Reformation historiographers expressed doubts as to whether such a rebellion even took place, let alone whether Oldcastle was its leader.[21] After a period in which he went underground, he was eventually captured and executed in 1417. The popular sixteenth-century Protestant martyrology known as John Foxe's *Actes and Monumentes* memorializes the old outlaw as "this most constant servant of the Lord and worthy knight."[22]

Curiously, the censorship that covered up the name of Oldcastle moved the character in one respect even closer to the historical figure. Peter Corbin and Douglas Sedge write of Oldcastle's years of serving the crown, during which time he probably already held the heretical Lollard views that would eventually lead to his execution, "[I]t is certain that throughout his royal service he was leading a double life."[23] The phrase uncannily applies to not only the historical Oldcastle, but also the dramatic character and especially the relation between the two. On Shrewsbury field, the Prince responds to his friend's arisen condition, "Thou art not what thou seemest," to which Falstaff responds, "No, that's certain, I am not a double-man" (5.4.132–3). Falstaff's line, by which he claims that he is neither a specter (so that his line would mean roughly, "I am not a ghost") nor two men (referring to his heavy cargo, Hotspur's body slung across his shoulder) belies itself, for the line itself, like its speaker, is double, with its twinned meanings referring to body and soul respectively and expressing a familiar way in which we are all double. The first meaning, "I am no ghost," also recalls the historical Oldcastle's prediction at his execution that he would be resurrected within three days, as reported by his medieval chronicler Walsingham,[24] adding further to the line's duplicity, as it causes the original name and identity of the character, Oldcastle, to peek out from behind the massive girth of Falstaff, reminding us of the palimpsest-like quality of the character.

The line also bears a certain aptness in light of the actor who was most likely its original speaker, Will Kemp. Falstaff's claim may be linked to the comic actor's "self-resembled show" (the phrase is Joseph Hall's) about which Robert Weimann writes: the Elizabethan clown, "in distancing the role, even in extricating himself from it, can be his own laughing subject-matter, an agency that, unbound by representation, is more than anything concerned to present and disfigure (and to laugh with the audience at) 'his self-resembled show.'"[25] Emancipated from his role, the actor playing Falstaff might claim to be single, not double, unlike the other members of his troupe who were more distinct from their roles. More recently, James Shapiro has noted that "leading clowns" like Kemp "were always playing themselves," a circumstance reflected in Shakespeare's stage directions and speech prefixes, which occasionally identify the actor Kemp instead of the part he played: for instance, in *Romeo and Juliet*, "Enter Will Kemp" instead of "Enter Peter."[26] Falstaff's line might also refer to the common stage practice of doubling parts, doubly necessary in history plays with their relatively large casts of characters. To take him at his word, perhaps Kemp playing Falstaff did not double parts.

In spite of this, and in spite of Falstaff's disclaimer, the phrase "double man" seems perfectly suited to describe so many aspects of the character—his fantastic size, the duplicity that he continually expresses in his theatricality or love of mimicry (Falstaff is a "double-dealer" in the stage tradition of the Vice analyzed by Bernard Spivack[27]), and not the least, the duplicity that resulted when the Oldcastle identity went underground as a result of censorship. It might even be claimed that his status as a "double man" requires not one but two plays. The two-part structure of *Henry IV* accentuates the doubleness of Falstaff: as lovable rogue and selfish dissolute, as delightfully irresponsible and youthful old rascal and as aging and ailing cynic. His portrait in *2 Henry IV* darkens considerably, as if the play were designed to show the other side of this double man.

Falstaff doubles meaning even as he denies duplicity. Like King John and Henry VIII, Oldcastle was a "double man" insofar as he was a subject of opposed historiographic traditions. Reviled by Catholic apologists as a heretic and traitor, he was revered as a martyr by a Protestant hagiographic tradition that included John Foxe and John Bale. Foxe even proposed that Oldcastle and his fellow Lollard martyr Sir Roger Acton play an instrumental role in the ongoing Protestant revision of the Roman Catholic calendar by nominating the days of their executions as red-letter festival days.[28] The division over Oldcastle's memory spilled over onto Elizabethan stages. The anonymous farce *The Famous Victories of Henry the Fifth* and Shakespeare's two-part *Henry IV* both stress the elements of riot and misrule in their treatment of Oldcastle and the Prince (although Oldcastle is a very minor character in the former play). It is as if Shakespeare, in his outrageous treatment of Oldcastle, were leveraging the reformers' radical revisionism against one of their own. In response to Shakespeare's plays, the Admiral's Men performed a new play titled *The First Part of the True and Honorable Historie, of the Life of Sir John Old-Castle, the Good Lord Cobham* in 1599 at the Rose Theatre. It was co-authored by a team of four men—Michael Drayton, Richard Hathway, Antony Munday, and Robert Wilson—bent on rescuing the Protestant martyr from the indignities suffered at the hands of the Lord Chamberlain's Men. A popular success, that play was followed by a *Part 2*, now lost, in March of 1600. Shakespeare's revisionist history was itself quickly revised. The new play's prologue accused Shakespeare, in language reminiscent of the actions of zealous Reformers, of defacing the past: "Let fair truth be graced,/ Since forged invention former time defaced" (Prologue, 13–14).[29]

Editorial explanations of Shakespeare's choice of Oldcastle as the name of his dissolute knight generally fall into one of two categories. The name was either a blunder[30] or a calculated satire of the prominent Elizabethan family the Cobhams through a parodic portrayal of their famous ancestor.[31] Herbert and Judith Weil, editors of the New Cambridge edition of the play, provide an interesting twist on the latter theory: "Whether Shakespeare lighted by accident or intention upon Oldcastle as a figure to couple with his princely reformer, there is wonderful propriety in the choice."[32] They note the

> multiple ironies in the fact that the Cobham descendants of Oldcastle belonged not to a persecuted sectarian minority but to a ruling class which fervently supported the union of church and state . . . Because Lollard views frequently coincided with those of the later radical independents and sectarians, Oldcastle's theology could have been as embarrassing to his heirs as was his alleged rebellion against Henry V.[33]

David Scott Kastan makes a similar point when noting another kind of doubleness in the character of Oldcastle: as simultaneous Protestant martyr and defier of royal authority, Oldcastle is "an uncomfortable hero of the Protestant nation."[34] Kastan argues that, regardless of Shakespeare's own religious sympathies, audiences were "far more likely to see the lampooning of Oldcastle as the mark of a Protestant bias rather than a papist one, providing evidence of the very fracture in the Protestant community that made the accommodation of the Lollard past so problematic."[35] Oldcastle's memory was potentially troubling to his Elizabethan descendants even if he were to be represented fairly straightforwardly, let alone in the carnivalesque manner of Shakespeare. Placing at the center of his history of Henry IV's reign a character who could not be comfortably remembered in any register, including the extremes of veneration and burlesque, seems consistent with the uneasy status of historical memory within the play, which functions largely as an instrument of rebellion. The inclusion of Oldcastle foregrounds the divisive nature of historical memory, placing it at the center of this history of civil contention.

Editors and critics have long noted parodic echoes of Puritan sermonizing in Falstaff's speeches. Placing the satire in the mouth of one of the Puritans' revered forerunners and martyrs of reform might have made some members of Shakespeare's audience think they were seeing double. Kristen Poole has shown that, in addition to satirizing reformist rhetoric, Oldcastle/Falstaff actually embodied a satirical portrait of the Puritan. Specifically, she sees the character as a revival of satirical representations of Martin Marprelate that graced pamphlets and stages during the pamphlet wars a few years earlier. Audiences of *1 Henry IV* would have had little difficulty recalling the recent controversy, Poole asserts, which "was remembered long after the silencing of the tracts and sensational stage manifestations."[36] Early modern audiences "would have laughed not only *with* Falstaff but simultaneously *at* him: Falstaff does not simply satirize puritans but in many ways is himself a satiric representation of a famous Lollard martyr."[37] Poole places Falstaff in the tradition of grotesque representations of Puritans in anti-Martinist tracts and in stage caricatures, of which Shakespeare's character was hardly the first. Both inside and outside the tradition he grotesquely represents, both satirist and satirized, Falstaff is a double man in his very orientation toward the large and influential Puritan community of London.

Falstaff's dual relation to Puritanism is also apparent in his uneasy relationship with memory, one that in many ways reflects Puritan attitudes toward the past. In other words, it is not only how the character causes us to recall (or forget) the historical Oldcastle, but also how the character himself recalls (or forgets) that makes him a potentially loaded figure for early modern confessional conflict. Puritan controversialists frequently inveighed against blindly following the ways of one's forefathers. In *A Briefe Discourse of Certaine Points of the Religion, Which Is Among the Common Sort of Christians, Which May Be Termed the Countrie Divinitie* (1581), structured as a dialogue between the godly Zelotes and Atheos, George Gifford (c. 1548–1600), a Puritan preacher in Maldon, Essex, has the latter, like most of the erring figures in his dialogues, advocate respect for and imitation of the religious practices of one's forebears. Zelotes responds by saying, in effect, "that here is nothing good except what God sets forth in his word; if they follow that, they may, in effect, forget their forefathers."[38] The dialogue follows the lines of a common debate in Elizabethan England. For Puritans, undue reverence for the ways of one's forefathers perpetuated superstitious and idolatrous beliefs and practices; for those who clung, fiercely or otherwise, to the traditional faith, the new faith weakened attachments to the past. As Dewey Wallace, Jr. summarizes, "Protestantism was thus a radical force in its modernizing impact and, where Puritanism in particular was involved, quite revolutionary in its break with tradition and custom."[39] Oldcastle/Falstaff's forgetfulness, as well as his creation by an outrageous act of historical revision, mirrors an association of the more radical forms of Protestantism with negligence or outright hostility to the past. It was a common accusation among Elizabethan Catholics that the Reformation, in Eamon Duffy's words, served as a "solvent of human community, divorcing the present from the past, husband from wife, child from parent, and abolishing the bonds of memory, responsibility and trust."[40] As solvent of Hal's bonds with his father, Falstaff may be, among other things, a grotesque portrayal of the indifference to one's forefathers so often imputed to radical Puritans.

This character named for a radical reformer who claims not to be a double man also has the power to evoke both sides of the Reformation's confessional conflicts. To his companion Bardolph, Falstaff confesses in an Eastcheap tavern, "An I have not forgotten what the inside of a church is made of, I am a peppercorn, a brewer's horse: the inside of a church! Company, villainous company, hath been the spoil of me" (3.3.7–10). No church papist or statute Protestant, Falstaff may claim not to be a "double man" by avoiding the kind of duplicity often associated with the churchgoing of those who grudgingly accepted the Reformation in Elizabethan England. According to Alexandra Walsham, recusancy propagandists "reviled outward conformity as a disturbing exhibition of dissimulation or 'feigning.'"[41] Outward conformity in churchgoing resulted in a widespread feeling of duplicity in Elizabethan England, recent studies of the important category of the church papist in the English Reformation have demonstrated. Citing priest and Catholic polemicist Nicholas Sander (c. 1530–1581), who went to Rome on Elizabeth's accession, Walsham writes,

> The literal divorce between a Catholic's mental resistance and his deputy's physical submission mirrored the schizophrenic contradiction inherent in outward conformity itself. Temporizing, Sander argued, "divideth one man into twain, setting the hart in one cumpanie, and the bodie in an other."[42]

Even texts from the other side of the debate gave voice to this concern. The recusant Mother in the Protestant Francis Savage's "A Conference Betwixt a Mother a Devout Recusant and Her Sonne a Zealous Protestant," still troubled after listening to her son's expatiations on the counterfeit faith he is imploring her to reject, worries about dividing herself in two. As Joseph Puterbaugh comments, "If she attends Protestant services and yet secretly professes Catholicism, she has fears of splitting her identity in two, resulting in a counterfeit of both faiths and disloyalty to the queen."[43] Catholicism itself was a counterfeit to many reformers: in Alexandra Walsham's words, "a counterfeit, skin-deep concept of Christianity measured by mindless muttering of prescribed prayers, mechanical fulfilment of priestly imposed penances, and robotic performance of ritual."[44] But the most common type of religious counterfeit, went the common Puritan complaint, could be found among the masses of the outwardly reformed but inwardly indifferent: in George Gifford's words, "the most in number . . . having Poperie taken from them, and not taught throughly and sufficiently in the Gospell, doe stand as men indifferent; so that they may quietly enjoy the world, they care not what religion come: they are like naked men, fit and ready for any coate almost that may be put on them," that last phrase echoing the pervasive imagery of clothing that has long been recognized as a salient feature of *1 Henry IV*.[45] The radical reformers counted the masses of the confessionally neutral who broke the Sabbath and haunted alehouses the most numerous counterfeits of the realm.

Falstaff's claim on Shrewsbury Field that he is "not a double man," together with his insistence that he is "no counterfeit," above all registers the confessional conflict that gave new inflections to words like "counterfeit" and "double." On the one hand, Falstaff's claim is belied by his resemblance to the confessionally neutral excoriated by radical reformers. On the other hand, his claim is supported by his memorable claim to have forgotten the interiors of churches. Recusancy, like that of Shakespeare's father, was the path taken by those who resisted the pressures to become double by faithfully attending church services that did not reflect their faith. The double life that Corbin and Sedge attribute to the historical Oldcastle, hiding his radical reformist views beneath a veneer of conformity during his years of royal service, was almost the mirror image of that of Catholic recusants in Elizabethan England, who hid their adherence to the traditional faith behind outward allegiance to a (partly) reformed religion. It might seem outrageous to see the character who started life with the name of a Lollard knight through the filter of Catholic recusancy, but, as I will try to show in the next chapter, this is precisely the outrage that Shakespeare commits in the name(s) of Oldcastle/Falstaff over the course of the tetralogy as a whole: the knight becomes a symbol for a "merry England" that was widely associated with the nation's pre-Reformation past, a past whose disappearance was widely blamed on the excesses of reform.

Stephen Greenblatt has proposed, somewhat controversially, another memory that Falstaff may have embodied for his playwright and at least part of his audience by claiming that Shakespeare modeled the character largely on his fellow playwright and nemesis Robert Greene, the man who branded Shakespeare an "upstart Crow" in his deathbed pamphlet *A Groats-Worth of Witte*.[46] Greenblatt connects "Falstaff's supremely ambiguous social position, the knight who is intimate with both the prince of Wales and a pack of thieves," to "the central paradox of Greene's life—that this graduate of Oxford and Cambridge hung out in low taverns in the company of ruffians."[47] According to Greenblatt, Falstaff embodies many of Greene's salient characteristics: his "bingeing and whoring, his 'dropsical' belly, his prodigal wasting of his impressive talents, his cynical exploitation of friends, his brazenness, his seedy charm," as well as "the noisy, short-lived fits of repentance for which Greene was famous, along with the solemn moralizing that swerved effortlessly into irreverent laughter."[48]

It is not that Oldcastle is a name without a referent, a fictional name so completely severed from its historical moorings as to allow a riotous freeplay of the signifier detached from any responsibility to a signified. On the contrary, this name sporting a prefix ("Old-") that directs us to look backward and pay our respects to the historically remote holds together a body of referents as bloated as Falstaff himself and as improbable as his tavern bill. The power of Falstaff to recall so much—the Vice figure in an older drama, the Lord of Misrule in early modern festivity, the familiar stage types of the parasite and the braggart soldier, the recent culture wars between the Martinists and anti-Martinists, the play *The Famous Victories of Henry the Fifth*, and a recently deceased rival playwright who was a huge presence and notorious name in London during his brief literary career, not to mention the more distant historical material of the Lollard rising, the knight Oldcastle, and the soldier and parliamentarian Fastolfe—makes him the memorial equivalent of bombast or cotton padding for his original audiences. "My sweet creature of bombast," Hal calls Falstaff, referring at once to the cotton used to stuff garments as well as to his friend's inflated rhetoric (2.4.270–1). The broadest level, therefore, at which he functions as a "double man" lies in his double duty as both a counter-historical figure of forgetfulness and overdetermined historical sign. There is so much historical noise in Falstaff that he becomes, by virtue of that very excess, a figure of mnemonic distraction rather than focused remembrance.

Shakespeare's revisionist Oldcastle doesn't merely bring down to earth, in carnivalesque riot, the sober nationalist project of representing the English nation and its past. The forgetfulness embodied so richly and diversely in Oldcastle/Falstaff itself becomes central to the nationalist project, as the last play in the sequence, *Henry V*, especially makes evident. If the nation, as defined by Shakespeare's second tetralogy, is founded on the need to forget regions of its past as well as on a common fund of public memories, then it is no wonder that Hal spends so much time with this prince of neglect. When, at the end of *2 Henry IV*, Hal rejects his old friend, he does not reject the principle for which he stands. In fact, the rejection of Falstaff signals the beginning of Henry's dazzling incorporation of selective amnesia into his careful orchestration of the national memory in *Henry V*. Falstaff becomes superfluous as his function, the thing he represents, namely a gift for forgetting, becomes increasingly arrogated to the state. In the process, Oldcastle/Falstaff must disappear, become invisible. The pervasiveness of forgetting, in other words, must itself be forgotten in order for the Prince eventually to seize control of a recalcitrant and variable public memory and govern it with a firm hand.

Falstaff's enactment of forgetfulness doubles his author's. Indeed, historical truancy, *1 Henry IV* reminds us, is an essential element of stagecraft. A play based on a chronicle source, a truncated representation of the printed text on which it is based, must of necessity have an uneasy and troubled alliance with historical memory. Falstaff represents nothing less than the carnivalesque spirit of forgetfulness at the heart of theater, even a theater of remembrance like Shakespeare's history plays: a spirit that Henry V must not reject but rather clandestinely steal from his erstwhile friend so that, under the cloak of remembrance, he may manage the kingdom's unruly and rebellious memories in order to produce the forgery that was the early modern nation.

FORGETTING AS REBELLION WITHIN THE KINGDOM OF MEMORY

A penchant for forgetting helps define two seemingly opposite characters in *1 Henry IV*: Hotspur and Oldcastle/Falstaff. Both characters belong to the legion of the single-minded, whose very identities are founded on neglecting most of the world's concerns. Prince Hal meets Falstaff's opening line with the charge of self-forgetfulness: "Thou art so fat-witted with drinking of old sack, and unbuttoning thee after supper, and sleeping upon benches after noon, that thou hast forgotten to demand that truly which thou wouldst truly know. What a devil hast thou to do with the time of the day?" (1.2.2–5). The word "forgotten" in Hal's opening salvo against Falstaff proves significant. Like a mad chronicler, Oldcastle/Falstaff distorts everything he relates. It is not that he has no interest in recording events and lending them the durability they frequently achieve through narrative. He threatens the Prince and Poins, whom he accuses of cowardly desertion, that if he is caught, he will have "ballads made on you all, and sung to filthy tunes" (2.2.35–6). Any recording of the past, however, will be subject to maximum distortion to serve the ends of this prince of pleasure, who serves as a grotesque mirror of the degraded status memory appears to hold for the royal forces in general in the play. Falstaff's lies are "gross as a mountain, open, palpable" (2.4.189–90); those of the "subtle King" (as Hotspur calls him, 1.3.167), less so, and therefore considerably more dangerous.

In the next scene, Hotspur introduces himself with a contrasting phrase, "But I remember" (1.3.29). The apparent contrast between the two characters' memories, one active and alert and the other drowsy and neglectful, soon dissolves. Recalling in unusually vivid detail an incident on the battlefield when a foppish messenger from the king arrived to demand his prisoners, Hotspur forgets—or at least, pretends to have forgotten, in a gesture that strikingly anticipates similar royal acts—the critical part of the narrative, the answer he gave to the king's messenger, putting in its place the distracting details of the envoy's appearance:

> I then, all smarting with my wounds being cold,
> To be so pestered with a popinjay,
> Out of my grief and my impatience
> Answered neglectingly, I know not what,
> He should, or he should not, for he made me mad
> To see him shine so brisk, and smell so sweet,
> And talk so like a waiting-gentlewoman
> Of guns, and drums, and wounds, God save the mark! (1.3.48-55)

Hal has introduced Falstaff to us as one who "hast forgotten to demand that truly which thou wouldst truly know," and in nearly perfect symmetry, Hotspur in the following scene functions as one who cannot tell—either the audience or the king—that which we would truly know, for at the heart of his account there is a blank space in memory's ledger: Hotspur answered the King's messenger "neglectingly, I know not what." Hotspur recounts a soldier's distraction by the unexpected and incongruous appearance of a courtier on the battlefield, which anticipates the game that Shakespeare plays throughout, of shuffling characters from one world—court, tavern, or battlefield—to another in a way that distracts rather than focuses our attention. But Hotspur's narrative about being distracted is itself a highly distracting narrative by virtue of its length and colorfulness. It performs or recreates his own preoccupied mental state on the battlefield by diverting the King, the court, and the play's audience from the carefully staged lapse of memory. Hotspur's is a speech act that distracts with a tale of distraction. Hotspur answered (on the battlefield) *and* answers (in the court) "neglectingly." Hotspur's account of his own forgetfulness seeks to make King and nobles forget their questions, and incidentally might make us forget ours, as audience members. What exactly did he answer to the King's messenger? Did he deliberately withhold his prisoners from the King? If so, what are his motives? His lengthy and colorful account has the power to make us forget that which we would truly know. To Hotspur, words themselves represent a diversion, a detour from the straight path of action, so it is not surprising that his first speech be a distracting performance about the distracting power of the King's messenger's words.

But although this scene seems carefully stage managed, we soon learn that distraction is indeed the blustery Hotspur's characteristic mental state. The same scene features Hotspur's stammering and unsuccessful attempt to remember the name of Berkeley Castle:

> In Richard's time—what do you call the place?
> A plague upon it, it is in Gloucestershire.
> 'Twas where the madcap Duke his uncle kept—

His uncle York—where I first bowed my knee
Unto this king of smiles, this Bullingbrook—
'Sblood, when you and he came back from
Ravenspurgh—(1.3.239–44)

Later, at the convening of the rebel leaders, Hotspur will repeat the oath, "A plague upon it!" when he announces, "I have forgot the map" (3.1.4–5). At the same time, Hotspur, a prominent soldier in Shakespeare's corps of the single-minded, leads the rebels in sounding their refrain of the King's forgetfulness. Hotspur, in other words, bears as contradictory a relationship to memory as does his apparent foil, that slayer of honor if not of the warrior who zealously pursues it, Oldcastle/Falstaff.

The Percies repeatedly complain of their "good deserts forgot" (4.3.46). Worried about future memory of present times, and in particular the "shame" that may devolve upon his family, "fill[ing] up chronicles in time to come" (1.3.169), Hotspur chastises his elders Worcester and Northumberland who "set the crown/ Upon the head of this forgetful man" (1.3.158–9). With that last phrase, Hotspur symbolically dethrones Henry, turning his purported forgetfulness against him by obliterating his title.[49] Late in the play, Worcester adopts a Prospero-like role in parley with the King: "And yet I must remember you, my lord,/ We were the first and dearest of your friends" (5.1.32–3). The King, he charges, "Forgot your oath to us at Doncaster" (5.1.58). The trick of the King's response is to challenge the rebels' alleged possession of a settled and reliable version of history. He defuses their oft-recited grievances, which represent a potentially subversive reconstruction of the past or counter-memory, by linking them to fashion, newsmongering, and deceptive painting: in short, with the unsettled Rumour that holds sway over the stage at the beginning of *2 Henry IV*. They "please the eye/ Of fickle changelings and poor discontents,/ Which gape and rub the elbow at the news/ Of hurly-burly innovation" (5.1.75–8).

The issue of the selectiveness of the King's memory helps determine Worcester on his course of treachery toward his fellow rebels. He considers, "My nephew's trespass may be well forgot,/ It hath the excuse of youth and heat of blood" (5.2.16–7), a prediction borne out in Hal's eulogy for Hotspur. Remembrance is so persistently the theme of the rebel forces that it might appear that in the last play in the series, *Henry V*, Hal will enter France under the banner of his father's enemies—except that Hal takes the first steps toward recapturing the theme from the rebel forces before the end of the play. The reclamation of the national memory is as important a struggle as the reclamation of France. Before the Battle of Shrewsbury, Sir Richard Vernon relates to Hotspur that Hal "spoke your deservings like a chronicle" (5.2.57). Over the fallen body of Hotspur, Hal eulogizes, "Adieu, and take thy praise with thee to heaven!/ Thy ignominy sleep with thee in the grave,/ But not remembered in thy epitaph" (5.4.98–100). Honoring his defeated opponent in chivalric style, Hal at the same time reveals a desire to command historical memory that will become especially pronounced after he assumes the throne. Ironically, nothing of Hotspur, neither ignominy nor praise, will be long remembered, at least in subsequent plays. As Robert C. Jones comments, "No more than he had recalled or revived any past model will Hotspur himself continue to live as an inspiring memory."[50] Hotspur's death confirms the fear that dominates the earlier *Henry VI* plays, namely, that military defeat spells oblivion or erasure from the historical record.

Even though his pursuit of honor would seem to mark him as one committed to a memory that outlives mortality, Hotspur's distraction, which comes with the territory of an obsessive personality, makes him as forgetful a man as his enemy. He is neglectful of everything that does not pertain to his single consuming interest. Easily distracted, he claims that Glendower's magical cant causes him to forget or deny his religious belief: it "puts me from my faith" (3.1.149).[51] Of course, it requires no magus come from the North to effect this kind of forgetting: his own single-minded quest for honor on the battlefield proves sufficient for the task.

Similarly, Falstaff's equally relentless pursuit of pleasure in the tavern makes him Hotspur's squire, as it were, in the ranks of the single-minded. In the same scene in which he declares that he has forgotten "what the inside of a church is made of" (3.3.6), he tries to distract the Hostess from claiming the debt he owes her, while she fruitlessly assaults the memory of this figure of oblivion: "You owe me money, Sir John, and now you pick a quarrel to beguile me of it" (3.3.52–3). It is curious that this most outrageous object of historical revisionism, this character named for a Lollard martyr represented as a cowardly but convivial hedonist, should himself repeatedly revise the past before our very eyes. In the first tavern scene, for instance, Falstaff inflates the numbers of his assailants at Gadshill. Not a double man, he will later insist, he is most certainly a doubling man, as the number of purported assailants climbs precipitously from two to four, before the still odder claims of seven, nine, and eleven. The Prince lets patent numerical lies pass in gaudy procession, tripping his companion up on the more subtle inconsistency: his claim to have seen three "men in Kendal green when it was so dark thou couldst not see thy hand" (2.4.193–4). Falstaff's lies are not unlike the reports of the absurdly lopsided casualties at Agincourt in *Henry V*, numbers which even Holinshed regarded skeptically: six thousand French and twenty-five English. Holinshed noted that more plausible numbers for the English dead, as reported by both the French and English sides, ranged from one hundred to six hundred. Although his death is reported early in *Henry V*, his spirit of inflationary reporting appears to live on. By choosing to cite the more exaggerated and lopsided casualties, Shakespeare places at the heart of his nation's proudest victory Falstaff's spirit of "bombast" and historical revisionism.[52] Falstaff's self-reporting of his exploits as a would-be robber prepares us for Shakespeare's later reporting of the grander exploits (or theft on a very large scale) of the man who would be King of France.

On Shrewsbury field, Falstaff again rewrites events we have just witnessed by claiming to have fought Hotspur "a long hour by Shrewsbury clock" (5.4.140). Curiously enough, the Prince, who himself slew Hotspur moments before, agrees to support his friend's lies, which he hopes will make him "either earl or duke" (5.4.136). Falstaff rewrites history (what takes place on the battlefield), as he hopes to be rewritten himself, as earl or duke, with, no doubt, a newly concocted lineage to bolster the title, reflecting the plague of bogus genealogies in the period.[53] These primal scenes of historical revisionism, in the tavern and on the battlefield, reflect the countless similar acts that take place behind the scenes in the construction of the play. Of course, such acts are necessary in order to make chronicle history come alive, as it were. If they succeed in delivering "the true and perfect image of life indeed" (as Falstaff says of the life he has preserved by counterfeiting death on the battlefield), then perhaps they are no more "counterfeit" than the fallen Falstaff (5.4.113–6).[54] It is as if Shakespeare, in representing the resurrection of Oldcastle/Falstaff, were reflecting on the notion of chronicle history plays as a resurrection of the dead, a commonplace idea expressed, for example, in Thomas Nashe's defense of plays in *Pierce Penniless his Supplication to the Devil* (1592). Responding to attacks on the theater as an effeminate and feminizing pastime, Nashe asserted that the subject of plays is

> for the most part . . . borrowed out of our English Chronicles, wherein our forefathers' valiant acts, that have lain long buried in rusty brass and worm-eaten books, are revived, and they themselves raised from the grave of oblivion, and brought to plead their aged honours in open presence: than which, what can be a sharper reproof to these degenerate effeminate days of ours?[55]

Shakespeare's revisionist treatment of this idea on Shrewsbury field is dizzying in its implications for historical memory. Unlike one of Nashe's valiant dead, buried in our English chronicles and rescued from the grave of oblivion, Oldcastle/Falstaff spreads the plague of oblivion wherever he goes. He has a character named for a Lollard martyr and mimicking the speech and sermons of Elizabethan Puritans raise himself from a simulacrum of what Nashe called "the grave of oblivion." But that grotesque character is already not so much a living recollection as an effacement of his historical prototype. There is a certain aptness when Falstaff represents himself not as pulled from the devouring jaws of oblivion, like the cadre of characters so rescued by the period's acting troupes, but rather from what he regards as life-canceling honor. In short, Falstaff represents himself as *rescued from remembrance*—a dangerous, disembodying and disemboweling undertaking, as Falstaff represents it. It is the same "favour" that Shakespeare has performed for Oldcastle, whose historical identity lies forgotten or buried beneath the layers of padding that Shakespeare has added to the character.

Hal's eulogy over his friend's apparent corpse confirms this: it indicates a posthumous existence devoid of remembrance, quite unlike Hotspur's. In other words, Hal projects a posthumous condition quite like the one his author has fashioned for him. Oldcastle's Lollard legacy and martyrdom have become evacuated, hollowed out from the interior of the fat knight, even before censorship made of the character a palimpsest upon a palimpsest by nearly obliterating the name of Oldcastle. Oldcastle/Falstaff likes not grinning honor, and Shakespeare has obligingly provided Oldcastle with a legacy without honor, stripping him of the hagiographic dignities bestowed by Foxe and Bale.

Choosing life over the grave, Oldcastle/Falstaff does not "plead [his] aged honors in open presence," as Nashe would have it. Rather, he undertakes a sustained battle with the ideal of enduring memory that goes by the name of "honour," "peppering" it repeatedly on the battlefield. And far from offering a masculine reproof to "these dangerous effeminate days of ours," Oldcastle/Falstaff administers a thigh wound to that caricature of valiant masculinity, Hotspur, just as his author, his boon companion and partner in waylaying history, mutilates the values he represents.

In short, in Shakespeare's play it is difficult to sort historical remembrance from that which threatens it, "the grave of oblivion," because the latter is implicated in the former in Shakespeare's later histories in increasingly complex ways. Unlike the earlier *Henry VI* plays, the second tetralogy does not enact a battle waged for historical memory against an external enemy that threatens to efface it. Neither does it simply stage a rescue of the valiant dead from the grave of oblivion in the manner described by Nashe. In *1 Henry IV*, the monarch being recalled from the grave of oblivion is himself branded as a "forgetful man" by his enemies. Erasure, rewriting, and forgetting are so enfolded in the structure of this "history" that it fulfills both of the requirements for nationhood set forth by Renan in "What Is a Nation?": "Yet the essence of a nation is that all individuals have many things in common, and also that they have forgotten many things. No French citizen knows whether he is a Burgundian, an Alan, a Taifale, or a Visigoth."[56] *1 Henry IV* reminds us that a two-hour history play bears a paradoxical relation, at best, to the task of reviving "our forefathers' valiant acts . . . from the grave of oblivion": that such a representation inevitable makes us forget many things, as well as ensuring that we bear certain memories in common.

BACKWARD THINKING

Often characterized as a Machiavellian political schemer, Henry IV is unable to fulfill one of Machiavelli's fundamental principles, articulated in the *Discourses on Livy* (1513–7). In Book Three of the *Discourses*, Machiavelli describes the need for all communities, whether kingdoms, republics, or religious institutions, to counteract the shortness of human memory by a periodic "return to their starting point."[57] *The Discourses* as a whole aim to show the structure and advantages of a republic, unlike his better known work *The Prince*, which lays out the means of achieving and maintaining power in a principality. Nevertheless, Machiavelli is explicit that what he says about the need for periodic renewal applies to kingdoms as well as republics: "Kingdoms also need to be renovated and to have their laws brought back to their starting points."[58] Over time, fundamental beliefs get lost as "men begin to change their habits and to break the laws."[59] The inevitable process of lapsing from origins needs to be periodically reversed.

In *I Henry IV*, by contrast, power is achieved through the occlusion of and movement away from origins. Shakespeare's *Henry IV* plays, like the monarch after which they are named, have a troubled relation with the past. As David Riggs has written, "[T]he principal figures of *Henry VI* all can give their personal assent to the heroic traditions that secure their public identities," whereas

> Richard III, Henry Bolingbroke, and his son Hal inhabit a world that is considerably less assured about its relationship to the ideal past of epic and romance. They participate in the rituals of chivalry and courtly display, but they do not, and cannot, wholly identify themselves with what they have come to recognize as a political myth.[60]

In his two-part *Henry IV*, Shakespeare revives a past that is itself sealed off from the past it would revive. Because the King is unwilling and unable to rehearse the means by which he came to power, historical memory appears to be the rebels' trump card. Unlike his son, who will masterfully manipulate the memory of his soldiers and people in *Henry V* in order to tighten his grip on power, Henry IV rarely invokes his predecessors. An exception occurs when he chides Hal that his "affections . . . do hold a wing/ Quite from the flight of all thy ancestors" (3.2.30–1). But it is telling that this instance appears in a private interview rather than on the public stage. Privately the King cannot forget what publicly he cannot afford to remember.

Instead of invoking and manipulating memory as a means of social and political control as his son will do so brilliantly as Henry V, he relies on the theatricality of kingship, a manipulation not of the past but of the present tense. Rather than casting his presence in terms of noble ancestors, he has managed to keep it new "by being seldom seen": "Thus did I keep my person fresh and new, / My presence, like a robe pontifical,/ Ne'er seen but wondered at" (3.2.55–7). "Presence" has a temporal as well as spatial resonance. Because he cannot invoke remembrance to bolster the themes of power and national solidarity, Henry IV appears to occupy an historical abyss, to be trapped in a perpetual "present" from which he cannot be rescued by the troupe of actors who represent him, the Lord Chamberlain's Men. Engaged in the public, collective act of remembrance that is a chronicle history play, a troupe of players remembers a monarch who himself cannot afford to remember, at least publicly: a monarch who in Shakespeare's own time must have seemed particularly cut off both from the players who raised him "from the grave of oblivion" (Nashe) and from audiences witnessing his revival.

The past is dangerous territory in *1 Henry IV*, not the least because for nations like Wales and Ireland, Machiavelli's principle that periodic renovation of a state requires a return to founding principles could very well foment rebellion. A nation that by the end of Elizabeth's reign had been effectively absorbed into the fabric of English political and religious life, Wales is relegated to the role of an exotic and rebellious outpost, not unlike Ireland in the 1590s. As Christopher Highley has argued, in sixteenth-century England there was a "general identification of the two countries," especially in the context of a foreign policy of conquest and absorption. "The English conquest and settlement of Wales" was routinely invoked "as an example to guide and justify current colonial policy in Ireland."[61] Hotspur links the two when he responds to the prospect of Lady Mortimer singing in Welsh, "I had rather hear Lady my brach howl in Irish" (3.1.230).[62] Highley has connected the Glendower rebellion in *1 Henry IV* with the ongoing Irish uprisings—the Nine Years' War or Tyrone Rebellion—and noted specifically "the biographical affinities between Glendower and Tyrone."[63] He notes how the marriage of Edmund Mortimer "to Glendower's daughter brings to the surface a collection of cultural anxieties about the attraction of native society for English settlers in Ireland."[64]

For the political unconscious of sixteenth-century England, Wales and Ireland were linked by the common aim of eroding the "name and memorie" of the "little brookes" of the kingdom, as King James would say in his first speech to the English Parliament, although *1 Henry IV* represents anything but an England that has successfully displaced the cultures of its borderers.[65] The Welsh leader Owen Glendower has learned English at court, but he stands in no danger of being mistaken for an Englishman. He bears every mark—language, dress, superstition—of the exotic outsider, and his daughter speaks no English at all. This aspect of Glendower, although it stands in gaudy contrast to the practical, scheming English politicians of the play, is consistent with the larger pattern linking the rebel camp to memory and the royal camp with forgetfulness. Just as the Percies persistently hammer at the theme of remembering their kingmaking acts, so does the rebel Glendower represent a persistent, pronounced, and unruly cultural inheritance that resists assimilation or erasure. Although scorn for Glendower's cultural differences from English norms are expressed mainly within the rebel party, by Hotspur, the play may have reminded many Elizabethan spectators of the Tudor policy of displacing Welsh language, laws, and customs with English ones, a policy that was being practiced to an even greater extent on a resistant Irish population in the 1590s. For both Wales and Ireland, the insistent theme of memory was potentially as much an instrument of resistance as it is for the Percies.

There is yet another way in which Machiavelli's injunction to "return to their starting point" was fraught with danger to the Elizabethan state. Thinking backward to medieval England was frequently an oppositional gesture associated with recusancy. Henry's awkward relation to historical memory reflects a similar unease within Elizabethan England, which from the beginning waged a kind of war upon its Catholic past. As Eamon Duffy writes,

> The Elizabethan injunctions of 1559 recognized that the very stones of the parish churches remembered their Catholic past, and attempted to bulldoze away that material memory: the clergy were enjoined to "take away, utterly extinct and destroy all shrines, covering of shrines, all tables and candlesticks, trundles or rolls of ware, pictures, paintings and all other monuments of feigned miracles, pilgrimages, idolatry and superstition, *so that there remain no memory of the same* in walls, glasses, windows or elsewhere within their churches or houses. And they shall exhort all their parishioners to do the like within their several houses."[66]

As Duffy notes, "in many communities this purging of the memory just did not happen"; others, like Stratford, were "slow to implement the injunction."[67] Tangible remains of England's Catholic past persisted, frequently in hiding. During the Northern Rising of 1569, "concealed alterstones and holy water vats were resurrected from the dunghills and gardens where they had been buried and became the focus of the Elizabethan settlement."[68]

After the early chroniclers, who condemned Oldcastle as a traitor, and the historical revisionists Bale and Foxe, who recreated him as a martyr, Holinshed's *Chronicles,* as Annabel Patterson notes in her study of that massive source material for Shakespeare's histories, "passed on to his readers a set of doubts about what had actually happened" in the Lollard revolts of Lancastrian England.[69] Shakespeare responded to the doubts and the danger largely by mimicking Prince Hal's role, coming as close to truancy as a playwright-historian might. In his adopted (and, like Hal's, temporary) role as reluctant member of the court, he managed to offend the Cobham descendants, as Hal offended his father. Nonetheless, it was probably a safer form of rebellion than the other kind depicted—and secretly enacted—in the play, that of the disaffected nobles Worcester, Northumberland, and Hotspur.

An alternative approach to the practice of historical remembrance and revival is the drowsy forgetfulness of Falstaff himself, a forgetfulness that at some level informs the play as a whole, which manages to erase the context of Lollardy that was so central to the reigns of Henry IV and Henry V. Like the man who has forgotten what the inside of a church looks like, Shakespeare ostensibly evacuates religion and religious dissent from the inside of his play, even though John Donne, in a sermon preached at Lincoln's Inn, maintained that "The art of salvation, is but the art of memory . . . Plato placed all learning in the memory; we may place all religion in the memory too . . . All instruction, which we can give you today, is but the remembering you of the mercies of God, which have been new every morning."[70] According to Donne, to forget religion is therefore to forget the art and aim of memory itself. Shakespeare almost forgets religion and the religious divisiveness that linked his own time to that of Henry V, just as he almost cancels the name of Oldcastle. The gradual displacement of Oldcastle/Falstaff and the poignancy of his being forgotten by his old friend and companion the King need to be understood in terms of the dilemma that Oldcastle presented to "sixteenth-century Protestant apologists," who faced "the problem of legitimizing a figure who presented a direct challenge to the popular monarchy of Henry V."[71] One approach to the problem is simply to forget both Oldcastle, as Henry V will, and the movement in which he played such a prominent role, as Shakespeare does throughout the *1–2 Henry IV.* Shakespeare has been widely characterized as sidestepping religious issues and controversies throughout his plays, but in *1 Henry IV* he does not simply avoid the difficult inheritance of Lollardy. Instead, he reminds us of what power wishes us to forget, calling attention to the divisions within historical memory in both Lancastrian and Elizabethan England.

Prefiguring his later emergence as a figure of memory—a counter-theme, as it were, to his gross friend's habit of forgetting—Hal inadvertently masters men's names. In *King John*, the Bastard Falconbridge imagines his newfound privilege—obligation, even—to forget men's names after he is acknowledged a Plantagenet: "'Good den, Sir Richard.'—'Godamercy, fellow.'/ And if his name be George, I'll call him Peter;/ For new-made honour doth forget men's names" (1.1.185–7). And in the next play in the sequence, *2 Henry IV,* Hal will concur: "What a disgrace is it to me to remember thy name," he scoffs at his boon companion Poins (2.2.11–12). But in *1 Henry IV,* Prince Hal, dubbed "the king of courtesy" by tapsters, mockingly boasts to that same companion, "Sirrah, I am sworn brother to a leash of drawers, and can call them all by their Christian names, as Tom, Dick, and Francis"(2.4.5–7,9). Like the Prince, the play takes pains to call working men and servants—including several who do not even appear in the play—by name. "Is Gillams with the packet gone? . . . Hath Butler brought those horses from the sheriff?" Hotspur asks another servant (2.3.59,61). Editors Herbert and Judith Weil observe, "Why Shakespeare chooses to name these servants who never appear has not received clear explanation," and then go on to note the resemblance to an earlier scene where two carriers and an ostler name one another.[72] The First Carrier names the Ostler (Tom) and his own horse (Cut). The Second Carrier names the first ("neighbor Mugs") (2.1.5,36). And the brief scene is haunted by the comical-poignant reference to the previous ostler, similarly dignified with a proper name. The Second Carrier observes, "The house is turned upside down since Robin Ostler died," to which the First Carrier adds a lament: "Poor fellow never joyed since the price of oats rose, it was the death of him" (2.1.10–11). We are surely meant to laugh at the idea of a man's spirit being tethered to the price of oats. On the other hand, there is a kind of dignity gained by contrast with Falstaff's inflated language. Here is a type of inflation that produced real and widespread suffering.

In a more general way, the scene deflects our attention toward what may be termed the remainders of history: those not usually remembered by name in chronicles. Their pedestrian sufferings—for instance, at the hands of droughts and bad harvests, which, as the Weils point out, caused the price of oats to nearly triple in the three years before the play was written[73]—usually go unrecorded as well. Like Hal, Shakespeare plays "the king of courtesy" in *1 Henry IV* by taking pains to call servants by their Christian names. His next play, *2 Henry IV*, derives very little of its material from chronicles. It gives the impression that the materials they furnished for the reign of Henry IV have been nearly exhausted by the first play, and it will radically inflate the attention bestowed on the Robin Ostlers of history: the next way Shakespeare conceives of enacting a rebellious historiography. Hal begins to reclaim history for the monarchy at the end of *1 Henry IV*, repossessing it from the rebels. Like Hal, Shakespeare will eventually reclaim his place as national historian in *Henry V*, but not before committing further acts of historical truancy, by means of which he continues to explore the various borders of the nation's riven and dispersed memory in *2 Henry IV*.

I return to my book's epigraph, slightly paraphrased from Kundera: "[B]eyond the slender margins of the incontestable" (there is no doubt that the rebels led by Harry Percy lost the Battle of Shrewsbury) "stretches the realm of the approximate, the invented, the deformed, the simplistic, the exaggerated, the misconstrued, an infinite realm of nontruths that copulate, multiply like rats, and become immortal." I know of no better epitaph for Falstaff, Shakespeare's vice-regent in the territory of the invented, the deformed, and the exaggerated. Shakespeare ventures into this territory, I have tried to suggest, not simply to bring a holiday license to the genre of the history play, to confront Nashe's heroic view of the theater as rescuing England's past worthies from the night of oblivion with the spirit of the carnivalesque. Beyond this, Shakespeare stretched the genre of the history play to probe the very motivations informing historical memory and its attenuation or erasure in his own culture, one on which historical memory was a source of fractiousness and conflict. Shakespeare's histories do not merely recall the past: they also vigorously explore the politics of recalling and forgetting the past. At their center sits Falstaff, a compendium of the uses of forgetting in a post-Reformation culture of rising nationalism, mercantilism, and self-invention.

3 "Washed in Lethe"
Laundering the Past in *2 Henry IV*

The event of forgetting that dominates lives and societies, which, separated—or, as one still says, alienated—from what they are, move as though in their sleep seeking to recapture themselves.

—Maurice Blanchot, *The Infinite Conversation*[1]

Salomon saith, *there is no new thing upon the earth.* So that as Plato had an imagination, *that all knowledge was but remembrance*; so Salomon giveth his sentence, *that all novelty is but oblivion.* Whereby you may see that the river of Lethe runneth as well above ground as below.

—Francis Bacon, *The Advancement of Learning*[2]

In *1 Henry IV*, historical memory divides into opposed camps. England's civil wars are doubled by history wars, as the Percies' version of the past squares off against the King's. *2 Henry IV* poses a different challenge to a unified and homogeneous national memory consistent with royal self-interest. Rather than starkly opposed interpretations of historical events, *2 Henry IV* features multiple versions of the past marked by dispersion, heterogeneity, and fragmentation. Incongruous acts of recollection result in a patchy sense of national unity that is reflected in what may be judged a weakened artistic unity relative to the other three plays in the sequence. Shuffling attitudes toward the past expressed by king, nobles, and commons, *2 Henry IV* enacts a heterogeneous set of memories that resist digestion to a unified historical narrative of the kind that Henry V will attempt to command in the next and last play in the sequence. The diverse and largely popular means of regarding the past in *2 Henry IV* confirms the historian Adam Fox's conclusion that "popular traditions might bear little relationship to the significant historical events as recorded by antiquarian scholarship in this period."[3]

Memory is largely a form of distraction in this metatheatrical play that directs audiences' attention not so much to the historical reign of Henry IV as to the recent theatrical reign of *1 Henry IV*. The very idea of a distracting memory, the form of memory that dominates *2 Henry IV*, might seem a contradiction. It defies the elements of retrieval, of gathering in, concentrating, and assembling into a coherent picture, implicit in the idea of memory as re-collection. Heidegger defined memory as "the gathering and convergence of thought upon what everywhere demands to be thought about first of all."[4] But in *2 Henry IV* memory disperses rather than re-collects. The many specific evocations of the earlier play compete with the scant and theatrically unprepossessing historical materials in the later one. In fact, it may be said of the entire tetralogy that it develops in a state of mnemonic distraction. Harry Berger, Jr. writes, "What makes the *Henriad* a single text is that it unfolds a process of continuous revision in which earlier textual moments persist like ghosts that haunt and complicate later moments, and thus take on new meaning."[5]

Constructions of the past in *2 Henry IV* tend to be more private than public, but the numerous personal reminiscences do not exactly serve as a counter-memory to a national, public version of the past, because such a history has yet to emerge in both *Henry IV* plays. Or if something like a national narrative does indeed exist in the *Henry IV* plays, its condition is as feeble as the King's. Private reminiscences move into the historical breach, the mnemonic gap left by the nation's lack of a dominant, unified narrative. Unlike its predecessor *1 Henry IV* and its successor *Henry V*, *2 Henry IV* takes place in a hollow of history, a time predominantly of recollection and anticipation. Falstaff and his friends hope for advancement, the Lord Chief Justice for punishment or execution, and Hal for his long-awaited and closely calculated entry onto the political stage. It is largely because the play is a patchwork of memories and preparations that it seems so easily forgotten itself. Because a spectator's memory has so little present action to latch onto, it is a challenging play to remember: consequently, one that foregrounds the activity of memory like no other in the Shakespearean canon. Set in the interstices of history, with sparse historical materials to command and a small fund of public memories on which to draw, *2 Henry IV* is punctuated by acts of oblivion, the most memorable of which is the Prince's rejection of Falstaff. It is no surprise, therefore, that the play itself is sometimes passed over or forgotten by critics,[6] as if it were destined to play Falstaff to the critic's Prince Hal. Bearing more than its share of lethargy—a physiological condition linked to an excess of phlegm according to humor theory, and ultimately deriving its name from the Greek *lethe*, forgetfulness[7]—*2 Henry IV* is notable for exploring the varieties of forgetfulness, including the forgetful memory of which the theater is capable. More than any other history play by Shakespeare, *2 Henry IV* explores the element of forgetting in plays ostensibly designed to help their audiences remember their common past: their historical abbreviations and omissions, their impersonations leading to self-forgetfulness, and the powerful nostalgias they are capable of generating.[8] By doing so, *2 Henry IV* advertises its suitability, and the suitability of history plays in general, to represent and even help produce the forgetful political construct known as a nation.

IN THE SHALLOWS OF HISTORY

In the entry "*De vita humana*" from *Timber: or, Discoveries* (1640) Ben Jonson suggests that theaters are powerful sites of forgetfulness and vehicles for the loss of self: "I have considered our whole life is like a play; wherein every man, forgetful of himself, is in travail with expression of another. Nay, we so insist in imitating others, as we cannot, when it is necessary, return to ourselves."[9] Our lives are like plays not in a positive sense that entails experimentation leading to recognition and self-discovery. All the world's a wide theater of self-forgetfulness, in Jonson's version of the conceit, insofar as the compulsion to imitate and the self-forgetting it produces are universal. In Adrian Poole's memorable formulation, "The theater is a place in which people partly forget themselves together, on stage and in the audience."[10] As Garrett Sullivan, Jr. and Zackariah Long have shown, antitheatrical literature of the period is filled with expressions of anxiety about "self-loss and transformation" effected by playgoing.[11]

As Marcel Proust famously distinguished voluntary memory, or conscious efforts to recall the past, from involuntary memory, in which everyday events or objects trigger recollection without effort, so does Jonson's figure suggest a distinction between two types of forgetting, voluntary and involuntary: the former, a willed effort by the professional actor, and the latter, a consequence of the familiar but often unconscious impulse to imitate others. In a theater, of course, actors return to themselves.[12] In life, Jonson's figure suggests, the risk is greater: identities may be permanently impaired or even lost by the involuntary form of forgetting that results from the pervasive compulsion to mimic, a contagious theatricality that spills beyond the edges of the stage and the confines of the theater. In *2 Henry IV*, the forms of forgetting run the gamut from the involuntary forgetting of Justice Shallow and his men to the willed obliteration of Hal's "I know thee not, old man" (5.5.43).

In *2 Henry IV* it is Falstaff who, like Jonson the satirist, spells out the mnemonic risks of impersonation. The man who in a few brief moments is about to be publicly erased from the new king's personal history muses on the contagious and forgetful imitation infecting Master Shallow and his men in terms that suggest that the impulse to imitate is a largely unconscious one. Furthermore, it seems to afflict persons of all degrees. But whether a servant imitates a master, or a master a servant, the compulsion to imitate in Falstaff's account leads invariably to a single destination: self-forgetting.

> It is a wonderful thing to see the semblable coherence of his men's spirits and his: they by observing him do bear themselves like foolish justices; he by conversing with them is turned into a justice-like servingman. Their spirits are so married in conjunction, with the participation of society, that they flock together in consent like so many wild

> geese. If I had a suit to Master Shallow, I would humour his men with the imputation of being near their master; if to his men, I would curry with Master Shallow, that no man could better command his servants. It is certain that either wise bearing or ignorant carriage is caught, as men take diseases, one of another. Therefore let men take heed of their company. (5.1.51–62)[13]

Falstaff's description of a reversible or reciprocal mimicry—the servingman aping the justice, and the justice, the servingman—recalls a memorable moment in *1 Henry IV*, but not in a way that signals a return to the festive world of that play. Instead, the echo registers a distance between the nostalgic *2 Henry IV* and its festive predecessor. In the earlier play, Hal and Falstaff engage in a rehearsal for Hal's upcoming meeting with his father by impersonating, in turn, King and Prince in the Boar's-Head Tavern in Eastcheap. The subject of these imitations, like that of Falstaff's soliloquy in *2 Henry IV*, is the contagion unleashed by "the participation of society": "Let men take heed of their company," although in *1 Henry IV* the mock-king's message has a far more limited application: let Harry take heed of his company. Falstaff's impersonations of Prince and King, together with Hal and Falstaff's reversible portrayals, recall the upside-down worlds associated with festivals and reinforce our impression of Falstaff as a holiday Lord of Misrule.[14] In *1 Henry IV*, the inversions are temporary, whether the play-like scene within the tavern just alluded to or Hal's carefully orchestrated play of contagious imitation. As in festivals that sanctioned a temporary inversion of the roles of master and servant, Hal, we know from early in the play, will return to playing a prince once the holiday mood of the play's middle, as distended as Falstaff's belly, yields to the stern demands of policy and warfare. By contrast, the inversions that Falstaff describes in *2 Henry IV* conspicuously lack mirthful overtones. There is no festival release implied by Shallow's aping of his servingmen, or vice versa. Furthermore, the inversions of *1 Henry IV*, like the festival occasions they resembled, reinforce the traditional order through carefully controlled subversions of it. Their humor and release depend on memory—on one's remembering who one is, while impersonating someone else. By contrast, the mutual mimicry that Falstaff mocks in *2 Henry IV* confounds social difference. Justice and servingmen become as indistinguishable as wild geese: "[T]hey flock together in consent." Rather than reinforcing memory of who or what one is, the largely unconscious form of mimicry in *2 Henry IV* threatens to produce a contagion of self-forgetfulness.

Earlier in the play Falstaff identifies a more colorful side of this gray world of social in-difference, in which mimicry across class lines is thoroughly drained of festive associations. These are "costermongers' times," as Falstaff pretends to complain, although he is the first to try to turn a profit: "A good wit will make use of anything: I will turn diseases to commodity" (1.2.134, 194–5). "Costermonger" is a name for a petty tradesman, originally a street vendor of costards or apples. Like the many other references to apples in the play, this one may speak of a fallen world and innocence lost. Part of the play's rampant nostalgia is directed at a world before these costermongers' times, a time, presumably, before names, identities, and histories became commodified and pasts themselves became subject to change. Because the Elizabethan theaters' entertainments were driven by the marketplace and owed their very life to a costermongers' world dominated by the values of trade and exchange, the theaters in turn reflected the values of the marketplace in many respects, trafficking and profiting as they did in the exchange of identities.[15] Mercantilism produced not only new wealth, but also, as in a theater, new identities. New titles were created and, not infrequently, new histories to help authorize them, a circumstance reflected by *2 Henry IV*'s Falstaff, who is accused of misappropriating the title of knight. As Adam Fox writes,

> New and spurious versions of the past were being written in the early modern period . . . It was the arriviste gentry of Tudor England, with the aid of the heralds, who were as responsible as anyone for the creation of bogus versions of history in the fantastic genealogies which they fabricated in an attempt to dignify family lines with spurious longevity.[16]

In other words, the mimicry of the stage, essential to the production of a play, was already widespread in the social world that visited public theaters in early modern England.

Besides harboring a vagrant nostalgia for a lost festive world, Falstaff's mockery of Shallow and his men also augurs the sudden and somber dislocation of identities that takes place four scenes later. Falstaff is forgotten by the future King at the very moment that the Prince puts his own past under erasure ("Presume not that I am the thing I was," 5.5.52). Doing his best imitation of his father, Hal mimics Henry's rebuff of the Percies with his rejection of Falstaff. After submitting articles of grievance to the King, the Archbishop confidently expects an act of oblivion of sorts from Henry IV, whom he describes as "weary/ Of dainty and such picking grievances" and who therefore will "wipe his tables clean/ And keep no telltale to his memory/ That may repeat and history his loss/ To new remembrance" (4.1.197–8, 201–4). The King covets such an act, both for himself and for his son. In soliloquy he implores sleep to "steep my senses in forgetfulness" (3.1.8). Later he advises Hal to "busy giddy minds/ With foreign quarrels," and thereby "waste" or rub out "the memory of the former days" (4.2.341–3). The King's craving for forgetfulness, as if for a drug, will eventually stand in stark contrast to the Prince's determination to guide and control the national memory in *Henry V*. Henry IV desperately wishes to be visited by the devil of oblivion; Henry V will make a private pact with the same devil, but while publicly donning the robes of a prince of remembrance. Hal's ambition to control public memory is forecast by his private act of oblivion, his rejection of his old friend curiously repeating the erasure of Falstaff's old identity, Sir John Oldcastle, as if the Prince were his own Lord Chamberlain and a historical censor determining who will be remembered and by what means. Ironically, his control of the public memory will be achieved with the same spirit of revisionism that his rejected friend Falstaff embodied, and that he has now appropriated as his own. Hal will reject Falstaff but not the spirit of revisionism for which he stands, as his behavior at his father's deathbed makes clear. To his sleeping father he says as he lays hold of the crown, "My due from thee is this imperial crown/ Which, as immediate from thy place and blood,/ Derives itself to me" (4.2.171–3). His father subsequently awakes and rebukes him, in response to which Hal weeps and no doubt deliberately distorts his remembered apostrophe to the ring of gold: "I spake unto this crown as having sense,/ And thus upbraided it: 'The care on thee depending/ Hath fed upon the body of my father;/ Therefore thou best of gold art worse than gold'" (4.2.286–9). As James Bulman perceptively comments, "Hal's memory of what he said . . . amounts to a theatrical fiction intended to exculpate him—the sort of revisionism at which Hal repeatedly proves himself skilled."[17]

Before the climactic repudiation of Falstaff takes place, the future king and Lord Chief Justice exchange charges of forgetfulness. The scene refers to one of the more notorious legends about the wild youth of Henry V, Hal's striking of his father's Lord Chief Justice, which resulted in the Prince's being committed to jail for a brief time.

> How might a prince of my great hopes forget
> So great indignities you laid upon me?
> What! Rate, rebuke, and roughly send to prison
> Th'immediate heir of England? Was this easy?
> May this be washed in Lethe and forgotten? (5.2.67–71)

Invoking liquid imagery that, as Adrian Poole has shown, has been associated with forgetting since antiquity, [18] the Lord Chief Justice retorts, in effect, that it was Henry who had already bathed in Lethe's waters when he struck the Justice, for the Prince had forgotten whom the Lord Chief Justice represented. Indeed, the Chief Justice's account suggests that the risk of forgetfulness inheres in the very process of representation, a process ostensibly guided by memory, as the representative recalls or makes present a figure who is absent. Reminding the Prince of the particular circumstances leading up to his imprisonment, the Lord Chief Justice also delivers a general lesson on the relationship between representation and remembrance:

> I then did use the person of your father:
> The image of his power lay then in me;
> And in th'administration of his law,
> Whiles I was busy for the commonwealth,

> Your highness pleasèd to forget my place,
> The majesty and power of law and justice,
> The image of the king whom I presented,
> And struck me in the very seat of judgment. (5.2.72–9)

What the Lord Chief Justice describes seems distant from the ungoverned mimicry let loose by Shallow and his men. A sturdy government apparatus supports his sanctioned representation of the King. In fact, the Lord Chief Justice comes to represent a kind of Falstaff in reverse. Both men impersonate the King, and in a way that ultimately supports the social order: the Lord Chief Justice, directly, and Falstaff, indirectly, by providing the means for holiday release. The focus of their kinship becomes sharper as the scene develops. In a turn reminiscent of Hal and Falstaff's memorable impersonations of father and son in the tavern scene of *1 Henry IV*, the Lord Chief Justice proposes, "Be now the father and propose a son" (5.2.91) and casts himself as Hal ("And then imagine me taking your part," 5.2.95). The Lord Chief Justice effectively returns imitation to something like the status it held in *1 Henry IV*: no longer a leveling force that spreads a plague of self-forgetting, as it does in the homely world of Justice Shallow and his men and in London's theaters, according to anti-theatricalists of Shakespeare's time, imitation (and specifically, imitation of a king) ultimately reinforces rather than erodes memory of place, of who one is and where one stands.

In a move reminiscent of the ending of *1 Henry IV* and foreshadowing the fate of memory in *Henry V*, where it appears to have been reappropriated by the King following its long association with the rebel forces in the *Henry IV* plays, the Prince deemed forgetful by the Lord Chief Justice ("Your highness pleasèd to forget my place," 5.2.76) lays hold of the theme of remembrance, confiscating it for the crown. Confirming the Justice in his office, Henry applies the word "remembrance" in a legal sense, as a "note entered in the records."[19] He proffers the Sword of Spiritual Justice "With this remembrance: that you use the same/ With the like bold, just, and impartial spirit/ As you have done 'gainst me" (5.2.114–6). Closing the speech with a repetition calculated to aid or reinforce the memory, "As I before remembered," the prince transforms himself from Prince of Oblivion, forgetful of father, place, and duties, to King of Remembrance, fulfilling a prediction made by Warwick: "The prince will in the perfectness of time/ Cast off his followers, and their memory/ Shall as a pattern or a measure live/ By which his grace must mete the lives of other" (4.2.74–7). What the father regards as his son's careless neglect turns out to have been a conditioning of his memory for his future reign. Seeming to make a career of forgetfulness, Hal has in fact been laying up a store of memories by which to measure and "mete the lives of other" men and women. Of course, Warwick will prove to be only partly right. Rather than accumulating memories as a pupil would learn his tables, Hal has been studying how he may develop a firm grip on the public memory. Neither mnemonist, as

Warwick sees him, nor oblivionist, as his father regards him, Hal understands better than either of these figures how the alliance or partnership of memory and forgetting can make for a pliant body politic.

THERE'S SOMETHING ABOUT "MERRY," OR WHAT "MERRY" MEANT TO EARLY MODERN ENGLAND

For the rebels in *2 Henry IV* what has recently transpired requires tempering by time and oblivion. The past is still a thorn in the present, claims the Archbishop of York, who, speaking on behalf of the rebels, names memory as a cause of the present insurrection:

> The dangers of the days but newly gone,
> Whose memory is written on the earth
> With yet-appearing blood, and the examples
> Of every minute's instance, present now,
> Hath put us in these ill-beseeming arms. (4.1.80–4)

York's position seems incongruous with most accounts of memory in the play. It indicates the extent to which the rebels are out of step not only with the rest of the nation but also with the play's audiences as well. For the rebels, memories are all too vivid, like fresh wounds that have not yet healed. But the play repeatedly belies York's claims. Whether or not in punning reference to the old name of the old knight, Sir John Oldcastle, in *2 Henry IV* virtually everything seems old: the quarreling ("By my troth, this is the old fashion: you two never meet but you fall to some discord," the Hostess chides Doll and Falstaff, 2.4.45–6), the pranks, the rebellion, the jokes, even the apples—either last year's pippins or shriveled apple-johns, which Falstaff cannot endure presumably because they remind him of his own age.[20] As James Bulman notes, Falstaff himself seems "an older, more diseased, and more corrupt figure than he was in *Part 1*."[21] The play-world of *2 Henry IV* is a superannuated one, and the play as a whole a sequel about the belatedness of sequels: not only *Part 2* as a sequel to *Part 1*, but also the diminished present as sequel to a merrier world, Reformation England as disappointing sequel to its late medieval past.

The play's structure, with its echoes of speeches, situations, and events in *1 Henry IV*, replicates its characters' frequent acts of recollection. It causes us unwittingly to imitate, in Shallow fashion, characters' acts of remembrance as we inevitably recall the earlier play. Hal and Poins' brief barb at Francis' expense, "Anon, anon, sir" (2.4.230), recalls their more elaborate but similarly placed jest at the drawer's expense in the earlier play. Gad's Hill is both briefly reenacted and recollected in the same scene. Hal and Poins enter the tavern disguised, and after the abbreviated jest unravels Hal says, "Yea, and you knew me as you did when you ran away by Gad's Hill" (2.4.248–9). Henry's announcement of an expedition to the Holy Land recalls the opening of *1 Henry IV*. Feeble's proverbial "we owe God a death" (3.2.192–3) is a feeble recollection of the far more memorable exchange between Falstaff and Hal on Shrewsbury field. And so forth. It appears that there is no alternative to recollection in this play, because all action releases echoes of the past, particularly of the past play *1 Henry IV*.

In the tavern, an anonymous drawer who has just brought in a plate of apple-johns—named for St. John's Day, December 27, around which date the apples are mature—initiates a chain of reminiscences. He relates an incident from an indeterminate time in the past that illustrates Falstaff's dislike for these apples, which are ordinarily eaten when shriveled. The Prince had set down before Falstaff a plate of five apple-johns, telling him "there were five more Sir Johns . . . 'I will now take my leave of these six dry, round, old, withered knights.' It angered him to the heart, but he hath forgot that" (2.4.4–6). The lazy indefiniteness of the pronoun "that" allows it to serve as a vehicle of the drawer's remembrance as well as of Falstaff's forgetting. Does it refer to Hal's jest or to Falstaff's response, his anger? "That" also allows for a certain ambiguity in the quality as well as the object of Falstaff's forgetting. His might be either a willful act—he has forgotten his anger toward his old friend through an act of forgiving[22]—or an involuntary process, the result of a moral lethargy that has caused his anger to sink into oblivion and canceled Hal's act of turning the apple-john into an edible *memento mori*.

Triggered by the sight of the apple-johns, the drawer's act of reminiscing reflects the subject matter being recalled: that is, the very time seems as shriveled as those apple-johns because of the ubiquity of recollection in the play. Another drawer, Will, enters. True to his name, he shifts the discourse to the future tense. Twice he utters the future auxiliary ("will") in his first and only sentence (2.4.12–14), promising to temporarily lift the burden of remembrance. But as happens throughout the play—in fact, as Warwick's speech to the King on "a history in all men's lives" (3.1.79) predicts—the future turns out to be another image of the past, as Francis's next remark suggests. "By the Mass, here will be old utis" (2.4.14), Francis says with relish of the Prince and Poins' strategem against Falstaff, employing a word that was ostentatiously archaic ("utis," meaning "festivity," "clamor," "din," or "outcry," "old utis" meaning roughly "a fine to-do"[23]). He thereby causes even this moment of eagerly anticipated fun to point backward.

In addition, Francis' oath "By the Mass" links Roman Catholic ritual, by now long outlawed in England, to the nearly ritualistic pranks at the expense of Falstaff. In the first *Book of Common Prayer* (1548–1549) issued under Edward VI, the heading for the communion service read "The Holy Communion, commonly called the Masse," but the word was dropped from the second and third editions under Edward (1552) and Elizabeth

(1559). Because Falstaff was originally named after the Protestant martyr Sir John Oldcastle, the oath's rhetorical linking of the Mass and the tricking of Falstaff may cover a pointed Shakespearean jest beneath the surface jests of the tavern world. The pairing might very well have reminded many in Shakespeare's audience of "the collapse . . . of festivity"—"old utis" on a larger, national scale—that issued from the Protestant Reformation in early modern England.[24] Ronald Hutton writes in his study *The Rise and Fall of Merry England: The Ritual Year 1400–1700*, "Indeed the impact of the Elizabethan Reformation upon ritual was very swift, apparently sweeping away that of the former Church even faster than Edward's measures."[25] The attack on ceremony was often joined with an attempt to curb festivity and the social disorder it could sometimes breed, so that "it becomes easy to understand why grumbles were heard that the Protestant Reformation had destroyed a happy society. In 1552 Dr John Caius either coined or appropriated what was to become an enduring expression, when he wrote of 'the old world, when this country was called merry England.'"[26] Many of the reforms dated from the Elizabethan period. As noted in my first chapter, it is no longer tenable to maintain the old idea that the process of Reformation came to an end in 1559 with the Elizabethan Settlement.

In a study that balances skepticism toward early modern expressions of nostalgia with hard evidence for comprehensive cultural change, Patrick Collinson notes that nostalgia for "Merry England" has enjoyed a remarkable longevity and has not been limited to a single historical period. By the time of Charles II, "Merry England was synonymous with the Elizabethan age; for Dryden it lay in the early seventeenth century. By the time of Walpole, it was located in the reign of Queen Anne . . . Always the day before yesterday."[27] Whether or not nostalgia for a festive world, "merry England," was warranted in Elizabethan England, such nostalgia appears to have been widespread. Furthermore, it was charged with political and religious meaning, the full implications of which have yet to be brought to bear on an understanding of the outrages Shakespeare committed upon the memory of Oldcastle: outrages directed simultaneously at Protestant pieties and Catholic nostalgia for England's "merry" past.

The more sober and less festive of the two plays Shakespeare wrote on the reign of Henry IV, *2 Henry IV* marks the passing of "merry England," although in a way that challenges all the manifold nostalgias it evokes. The play as a whole is no less outrageously revisionist than the figure of Oldcastle himself, the Lollard martyr rewritten as liar, rogue, and hedonist, a dedicated pursuer of pleasure as well as one of its principle purveyors on the Elizabethan stage. As Collinson writes, "Merry England is almost the same thing as Catholic England," and in Elizabethan England, by "legislated means, Catholic England did die, and not of natural causes."[28] What Shakespeare does in the *Henry IV* plays is to enact the passing of "Merry England," although, improbably, with a character bearing the name of a militant reformer as its symbol. In other words, Shakespeare installs a representative of the forces that many Elizabethans held responsible for the demise of England's merry past as a synecdoche for that very past. And if Oldcastle/Falstaff was in fact originally acted by Will Kemp, the historical irony would have been one layer deeper, at least when Kemp decided eventually to quit the Lord Chamberlain's Men in 1599: as Collinson writes, Merry England, or Catholic England, and "Will Kemp had long since parted company. When did Kemp begin his morris dance to Norwich? On the first Monday in Lent. Either the old Catholic calendar had been forgotten, or it was being deliberately flouted."[29] A reformer of Merry England becomes its symbol, owing to Shakespeare's Falstaffian reformation of history itself. By fusing, or confusing, the wildly distorted figure of a Reformation martyr with the merry world the Reformation was thought to have swept aside, Shakespeare outrageously constructs a figure of forgetfulness and historical revisionism as the object of a powerful, irresistible nostalgia.

Is Shakespeare merely playing a prank on his audiences, a rarefied version of the one Hal plays upon the tavern drawer Francis in *1 Henry IV*? Hal and Poins play a tasteless joke by stationing themselves in adjacent rooms, Poins calling Francis while the Prince holds him in conversation. Does Shakespeare similarly call our historical memories in two directions at once? Might he be exposing the distortions of nostalgia as equal to the distortions that produced his character Oldcastle/Falstaff in the first place, by making an outrageous revisionist *and* product of revisionism an object of nostalgia? Perhaps, but a fuller answer demands more patience. *2 Henry IV* shows nostalgia, which to some degree must have been shared by every viewer of the play who had previously seen *1 Henry IV* and which seems largely held by commoners in the later play, as being difficult to dismiss with a series of jests. On the one hand, Collinson (following Keith Thomas) notes, Merry England always was "the day before yesterday." On the other hand, it is undeniable that sixteenth-century England witnessed "a drastic renunciation of what had gone before."[30] If a nostalgia like that of John Stow in his *A Survey of London* (1598), roughly contemporaneous with *2 Henry IV*, for the "merrie and sportful" pastimes of old, might seem "Shallow," it also showed another, more vigorous side: it served as a potentially subversive counter-memory to the narrative being fashioned, controlled, and manipulated by the state.[31]

The word "merry" and its related forms ("merrily," "merriment") occur more frequently in *2 Henry IV* than in any other play of Shakespeare's, even the play that sports the word in its title, *The Merry Wives of Windsor.*[32] In this somber sequel to its more festive and playful partner, the word substitutes for the thing itself. Merriment has largely vanished; only the word remains. In the less than merry world of *2 Henry IV*, "merry" signals the absence of the very thing to which it refers. As the merry world of *1Henry IV* recedes into audiences' memories, the word becomes more insistent, occurring no fewer than fifteen times in the play's final act, serving as the refrain of the play as a whole as well as a refrain, of sorts, of the ballad sung by Justice Silence. The fifth act is filled with anticipation for the return of an idyllic world evoked by the country justice Silence's song in Act V, scene 3, as Falstaff and friends seem convinced that Hal's imminent coronation spells the return of merriment:

> Be merry, be merry, my wife has all
> For women are shrews, both short and tall.
> 'Tis merry in hall when beards wags all
> And welcome merry Shrovetide, be merry, be merry. (5.3.27–30)

Shrovetide was mostly known as a time of festivity preceding Lent, "an occasion for eating up the remaining stocks of meat, eggs, cheese, and other commodities which could not be consumed during the long season of fasting now at hand."[33] It frequently produced riot and disorder, especially in London.[34] Although Shrovetide was associated with a period of intense indulgence, feasting, and festivity before the fasting of Lent, it also included, as its third day, Shrove Tuesday, a day of "shriving" or confessing one's sins and seeking absolution, although as Hutton observes, even this day of shriving "was more celebrated . . . for eating and merry-making, with the prospect of austerity to come lending a peculiar fervour to both."[35] Followed by what Cressy characterizes as the "anti-climax" of Lent,[36] Shrovetide and its successor, the long period of fasting and denial, were prominent features of the ritual year in England. Anyone watching *The Second Part of Henry IV* while carrying the memory of *Part 1* might well have recognized the theatrical equivalent of the transition from Shrovetide to Lent, "the time when *2 Henry IV* is set . . . and the season that governs *1 Henry IV*,"[37] in the sequence of the two plays. Silence, of course, has the year backwards. Although his song looks forward to Shrovetide, it is clear that merriment lies in the past. Shrovetide corresponds roughly to *1 Henry IV* and the reign of its Lord of Misrule, Oldcastle/Falstaff. As a sequel, Shakespeare gives us the familiar continuation of Shrovetide, the "lenten entertainment" (*Hamlet*, 2.2.282) of *2 Henry IV*. Theaters were closed during Lent in Elizabethan England, but in *2 Henry IV* Shakespeare manages to convey something like a theatrical equivalent to the abrupt cessation of festivity that the people of early modern England experienced annually at Shrovetide's end. For at least some parishioners who harbored a nostalgia for Catholic England, the Elizabethan era itself must have felt like a Lenten sequel to the Shrovetide of merry England.

Puritan polemicists and preachers in the Elizabethan period regularly complained about a persistent nostalgia that signaled a dangerous or unthinking residual Catholicism. In both the play and in Puritan propaganda, the heart of such nostalgia is to be found in the countryside, among the "common sort," the rural laity. In *2 Henry IV*, rural Gloucestershire is the stronghold of nostalgia for England's "merry" past. Shakespeare set three scenes in Gloucestershire: 3.2, the recruitment scene, and

5.1 and 5.3, both of which take place in Justice Shallow's home, featuring the planning and execution of a festive dinner in honor of Falstaff. Until this point, the play rings with the occasional references to "a merry song" (Falstaff, 2.4.225), Shallow's nostalgically recalled "merry night" spent in the Windmill in St. George's Field (3.2.163), and Henry's bitter excoriation of his son, who has tried on the crown upon thinking his father dead: "[B]id the merry bells ring to thine ear/ That thou art crownèd, not that I am dead" (4.2.240–1). As if in reference to the oscillating moods of the play itself, the Archbishop Scroop cheers the ill-feeling Mowbray, "Against ill chances men are ever merry,/ But heaviness foreruns the good event" (4.1.309–10), which the Earl of Westmoreland quickly reaffirms, "Therefore be merry, coz, since sudden sorrow/ Serves to say thus: some good thing comes tomorrow" (4.1.311–2). But it is at the festive Gloucestershire scene, Act 5, scene 3, a brief reprise of the festive world of *1 Henry IV*, that the word "merry" proliferates, occurring no fewer than fourteen times: for example, this line sung by Silence, "And praise God for the merry year" (5.3.14). Silence's phrase would have reminded many in Shakespeare's audience of the festive ritual year that had been severely reduced—silenced, one might say—in the course of the Reformation. His repeated injunction "Be merry," both sung and spoken, bespeaks the general hope in this rural community for the return of the merry world once the Prince is crowned. I do not want to claim that the heavy use of "merry" at the end of the play necessarily marks its country justices, Shallow and Silence, as church papists,[38] those who outwardly conformed but remained inwardly bound to the old faith, but I do not hesitate to assert that the word would have elicited for Shakespeare's contemporaries controversies over the persistent attachment to the past that recent scholarship has shown to be a widespread feature of Elizabethan England's religious landscape, not limited to recusant Catholics.[39]

The proliferation of nostalgia in *2 Henry IV*'s rural scenes reflects complaints by Puritan controversialists, who expressed particular frustration at the countryside and the "residual rural Catholicism persisting within the Church of England."[40] According to Alexandra Walsham, Puritans singled out the rural sort for their "shallow knowledge" of the religion they professed.[41] It is precisely the rural sort that George Gifford, a Puritan preacher from Maldon, Essex, excoriated for their proneness to nostalgia for England's "merry" past. In a series of dialogues and sermons, he numbered among the persistent errors of what he termed "countrie divinitie" a nostalgia for the old days and an attachment to the customs of one's forefathers.[42] In *A Dialogue betweene a Papist and Protestant, Applied to the Capacity of the Unlearned* (1582), Gifford's Professor of the Gospel scorns those who know little doctrine and "speake of the merry world when there was lesse preaching, and when all things were so cheape, that they might have xx eggs for a penny."[43] The complaint was common in Protestant polemics. In *Antiquitie Triumphing Over Noveltie* (1619), John Favour writes,

> Are not these the words . . . in the mouthes of all the old superstitious people of this land? And do not the yong learne of the old? *When we prayed to our Lady, and offred tapers on Candlemasse day, and heard Masse as we have done . . . then we had plentie of all things, and were well, we felt no evill. But since we have left the religion of our fathers . . . we have scarsnesse of all things.* The old superstitious people of Christ-Church in Hampshire, would say, that there came fewer Salmons up their River, since the masse went downe: for they were wont to come up when they heard the sacring Bell ring . . . the pretence is still, that the former way was the Old way, and that Old way was the best way.[44]

The interlocutors who challenge the pious and zealous in Gifford's dialogues inevitably fall back on an appeal to precedent and the ways of their forefathers. In *A Briefe Discourse of Certaine Points of the Religion, Which Is Among the Common Sort of Christians, Which May Be Termed the Countrie Divinitie* (1581), Atheos, the antagonist of the zealous Zelotes, expresses a stubborn commitment to the ways of his forefathers. He vows,

> I praye God I may follow our fore fathers, and doe no worse then they did: what should wee seeks for too be wiser or better then they: I would wee could doe but as well as they did . . . then they lived in friendshippe, and made merrie together, nowe there is no good neighborhoode: nowe every man for himselfe, and are readie to pull one another by the throate.

Their forefathers pleased God "better than we doe nowe."[45] Complaining about excessive citing of the scriptures in sermons, Atheos maintains, "It was never merry since men unlearned have meddled with the Scriptures."[46] His portions of the dialogue are suffused with "nostalgia for the past and the 'forefathers' when things were both more virtuous and 'merrier.'"[47] Gifford's dialogue implies that the nostalgia of rural folk stems from their shallow understanding of the faith and their persistent attachment to the outward forms of worship. "Is it not enough for plaine countrie men, plow men, taylours, and such other, for to have their ten commaundments, the Lords prayer, and the beliefe?" protests Atheos.[48] The attachment to outward forms, to which reformers frequently attributed nostalgia for the old faith, was a common object of Puritan complaint. In one of the most influential Puritan polemics of the day, *The Plaine Mans Path-Way to Heaven* (1601), Arthur Dent complains, "The common sort of people thinke indeed, that all Religion consisteth in the outward service of God, though their hearts bee farre from him."[49] As Gifford's mouthpiece, the pious and zealous Zelotes, responds to Atheos' appeal to the ways of their forefathers by asserting "that there is nothing good except what God sets forth in his word; if they follow that, they may, in effect, forget their forefathers."[50] Historian Dewey Wallace, Jr.

concludes that for a large body of Elizabethans, nostalgia was at least as important a motive of Roman Catholic resistance to Protestant reforms as adherence to any particular doctrines rejected by the reformers. Resistance, he argues, needs to be understood "as a compound of nostalgia for the time when things were 'merrier,' loyalty to customary usage, and the greater ease with which the old faith was accommodated to the everyday 'magical' and 'folk-religious' practices which provided so much comfort to ordinary individuals."[51]

I do not want to suggest that Puritan preachers expressed a uniform hostility to the past or regarded it solely as a repository of error and superstition. But the Puritan use of history tended to be unusually narrow and selective. When Puritan preachers looked backward, it was frequently to draw a parallel between either the deliverance or the punishment of the Hebrew nation and that of Protestant England. Michael McGiffert shows how such preachers constructed a moral nationalism by articulating parallels between England and Israel. Looking back upon a "dazzling run of deliverances," which included the accession of Elizabeth, the defeat of the Spanish Armada, and, in the Jacobean period, deliverance from the Gunpowder Plot, Puritans used the historical record to prove "that God was especially English. The past thus served the preachers, and they in turn . . . bestowed on England a national character."[52] Nostalgia, on the other hand, did not figure among the attitudes toward the past sanctioned by radical reformers. It was not to be found in the Puritan preaching of Shakespeare's day, except as an object of either ridicule or excoriation.

The pseudonymous Marprelate pamphlets, launched by extreme Puritans against the bishops whom they accused of abusing their temporal power, also targeted nostalgia, linking it to a debilitating self-forgetfulness. As in the Jones anecdote about a court performance examined in the preceding chapter, self-forgetfulness issues from witnessing an act of impersonation. In the pamphlet *Hay Any Worke for Cooper* (1589), a reply to Thomas Cooper, Bishop of Winchester's *An Admonition to the People of England*, Martin tells the tale of a vicar in Halstead, Essex known for his antics in the pulpit. Good Gliberie, he informs us, "was sometimes . . . a vice in a playe." One day Gliberie ascended his pulpit with the resolve "[t]o do his businesse with great commendations." During his sermon a distraction presents itself: "A boy in the Church hearing either the sommer Lord with his Maie game or Robin Hood with his Morrice daunce going by" rushes from the church. Seeing the boy sneak out the door to follow provokes in Gliberie a nostalgia for his own past: he "had a minde to his olde companions abroad (a company of as merrie grigs you must think them to be as merie as a vice on a stage)." Overcome with recollection, he shouts, "[H]a, ye faith boie, are they, there, then ha wt thee," as he follows the boy out the church and entirely forgets his pastoral responsibilities.[53]

Gliberie's forgetful nostalgia does not feed directly off of the revelers' actions but rather off of a boy's response to those revelers. The intermediary of an absorbed spectator is necessary in order for the pastor to forget his present duties to his flock and attempt to recapture the past: not only his private past but that of his nation as well. For Martin's anecdote dovetails the private nostalgia of his erratic and susceptible parson with a collective one. In sixteenth-century England, the Robin Hood legends became a locus of fond recollection for early Tudor festivity that went by the name of "merry England," now in demise.[54] Gliberie's actions imply that for some in Elizabethan England, such festivity had not waned sufficiently: that English parishioners needed to be administered further doses of forgetfulness in order to resist its nostalgias, which distracted them from the true object of memory, religious devotion.

Orson Welles saw a nostalgia for a faded world feeding all of the Prince Hal plays. He used "the death of Merrie England . . . the age of chivalry, of simplicity, of Maytime and all that" as the guiding idea for his film adaptation *Chimes at Midnight* (1966).[55] More than Welles' adaptation, however, Shakespeare's play allows us considerable latitude in our response to its expressions of nostalgia: a reflection of the wide range of responses to nostalgia for "merry England" in the early modern period. Furthermore, the play periodically reminds us that, as Svetlana Boym writes, "Nostalgia (from *nostos*—return home, and *algia*—longing) is a longing for a home that no longer exists or has never existed."[56] From one perspective, nostalgia is the diachronic version of the mutual imitation of Shallow and his men. It represents another way to lose oneself in a play that is a virtual compendium of the ways and means of self-forgetting. Nostalgia, the willful habitation of a time that never was, is the historical equivalent of the widespread theatricality that Ben Jonson and Falstaff describe and deplore. *2 Henry IV* is extraordinary for its demonstration that theater and history are indeed a potentially "lethel" combination.[57]

On the other hand, Shakespeare makes it hard for audiences to merely dismiss the commoners' expressions of nostalgia, because we are prone to share a longing for, or at least a fond remembrance of, the more festive world of *1 Henry IV*, a theatrical embodiment of "merry England" and its spirit of companionship, conviviality, and good humor.[58] Given the many specific parallels of scenes and incidents in the two plays, it would be nearly impossible for an audience that had seen the earlier play to watch *2 Henry IV* without recalling *1 Henry IV*. Many in the later play's first audiences might have shared Francis' relish for the same old—either for the theatrically tested and proven devices of its predecessor or for the pre-Reformation historical period it represented, with its ritual year intact: the "English calendar of celebrations" that was transformed "almost out of recognition" by the Reformation.[59] Others, however, are likely to have taken the pervasive quality "old" in *2 Henry IV* in a different spirit, as evidence that the dilated play about *Henry IV*, like the monarch it represents and like the "merry England" that Welles saw embodied in Falstaff, had outlived its allotted time, and now filled out its career as a bedridden thing. Monarch, play, and nation all stand in need of "reformation," a constant theme of the Prince Hal material.[60] In either case, the frequent attributions of age in *2 Henry IV* seem calculated, as if the play were musing on its own belatedness, its status as sequel and resemblance to "a last year's pippin" (5.3.2).

The most curious aspect of nostalgia for "merry England" in *2 Henry IV* is this: frequently associated with church papistry, it is here embodied by a grotesque version of an arch reformer, a Lollard, a spiritual ancestor of those very preachers who decried nostalgia for merry England as a misguided attachment to the nation's Catholic and error-ridden past. The second tetralogy makes Falstaff a virtual synecdoche for a merry England that has become permanently lost.[61] Although he fuels nostalgia for a merrier past and although his very character is constructed from false historical memories, he also, like a good Puritan, mocks the errors and false memories that nostalgia inevitably disseminates. In this respect Falstaff in *2 Henry IV* develops well beyond the figure of oblivion that he embodies in *1 Henry IV*. Shallow's false memory syndrome is a widespread affliction, one that in many ways infects the entire tetralogy as well as many characters within it, and Falstaff challenges it on many levels, even after his death is reported in *Henry V*.

Following Falstaff's death, his erstwhile friend and king can now replace him as a favorite object of Elizabethan nostalgia. The telos of Shakespeare's second extended foray into English history, Henry V embodied a code of chivalry for which many Elizabethans felt nostalgic.[62] Falstaff's skeptical voice has been silenced, although memories of his grotesque inversion of the code of chivalric conduct still hold the power to unmask that nostalgia, which Shakespeare's warrior king both satisfies and feeds. At the same time, Falstaff embodies a nostalgia for a "merry England" perceived to be lost. The youthful adventures of Hal with Falstaff become a kind of theatrical shorthand for a more youthful England for which nearly everyone in *2 Henry IV* waxes nostalgic. *2 Henry IV* and even, in reduced measure, *Henry V* are suffused with a nostalgia for Falstaff and the festive world he represents, but as a skeptical voice corrosive to nostalgia, Falstaff permanently damages the very attitude he elicits from audiences. If, as Melchiori conjectures, Will Kemp delivered the original epilogue in which he affirms that "Oldcastle died martyr, and this is not the man" (Epi. 24–25),[63] and if Kemp also played Oldcastle/Falstaff, as is likely,[64] then his dual role of memorably embodying a past and denying its very existence is carried through to the very historical basis of the drama itself. Falstaff plays these doubled parts throughout the play, as Welles failed to grasp. The only compelling pasts in the play are invented ones, and they are exposed as such. Coming after a play in which memory is rarely invoked at all, a play in which the monarch himself wishes to sever ties to the past, *2 Henry IV* is the natural legacy of that severance. It shows history to be a process of continual reinvention, no more authorized than Rumour itself.

I do not want to suggest that all of Shakespeare's merry worlds lie in the past. In fact, *The Merry Wives of Windsor* anachronistically takes the contemporary of a late medieval monarch and object of considerable nostalgia and revives him in the town of Windsor in the Elizabethan present. In the course of the play, the word "merry" attaches itself not only to the wives of the title, Mistress Page and Mistress Ford, but also to the Host (by Justice Shallow) and to Falstaff himself (by the Host). As Marjorie Garber writes, the word "merry" in *The Merry Wives of Windsor* "has a distinct holiday cast, meaning the opposite of workaday or ordinary. Although this is not, strictly speaking, a play about a seasonal festival, it has many of the earmarks of 'carnival,' a world turned upside down."[65] If nostalgia is the illness from which so much of England suffers in *2 Henry IV*, then *The Merry Wives of Windsor* may be its antidote: a demonstration that the merry world for which Falstaff's companions pine in the earlier play may yet survive, if only in the circumscribed space of the stage.[66]

NOSTALGIC COMMONERS, REVOLUTIONARY ROYALS: SOCIAL CLASS AND PERCEPTIONS OF THE PAST

Although Welles was certainly right in seeing a rich vein of nostalgia running throughout the play, his film misses the larger contexts to which that nostalgia belongs: first, the monarchy's interest in seizing control of historical memory—because, to recall Foucault's assertion about popular memory, "if one controls a people's memory, one controls their dynamism"[67]—coupled with the welter of forms of memory in the play that resist homogenization and control; and second, religious divisions that caused nostalgia to pose an obstacle and even a danger to the cause of reform. Although nostalgia detaches a people from any actual past that may serve as a guide to the present, it also produces a disorderly body of memories that resist incorporation into a unified national consciousness of England's past. Depending on the political moment, nostalgia can fuel political unrest as well as subdue it. As Alison Shell writes, "England's post-Reformation Catholics knew all about the . . . rallying powers of nostalgia."[68] Nostalgia, as Adam Fox maintains in his study *Oral and Literate Culture in England 1500–1700*, could be dangerous to the reigning powers:

> In many of the reminiscences of eldest inhabitants is a nostalgia for the old days which can be characteristic of any age. It had been, after all, a much "merrier world" in the past: hospitality was greater and life was simpler, there were fewer lawyers and all things were cheap. To this extent there could be something inherently subversive about popular perceptions of the past. What ordinary men and women remembered was not usually the stuff of learned or officially approved versions of the past but instead interpretations of events which attempted to make

> sense of and justify the world as they saw it. As such their memories could be irreverent and even seditious in the details which they chose to retain or forget, and the way in which they chose to construe them.[69]

Social class has an enormous effect on the historical imagination in *2 Henry IV*. The play draws a stark division between learned and popular perceptions of the past, and popular perceptions in the play hold largely to a nostalgic course. The alternatives to nostalgia are voiced largely by the upper classes.

The tavern scene, punctuated by the words "old" and "ancient" (the latter in reference to Falstaff's ensign or ancient-bearer Pistol, most of whose reminiscences are literally "ancient," or classical), sets the stage for Henry and Warwick's discourse on history in the ensuing scene. But it does far more than merely prepare the stage for the great. It opens up the play to popular means of recalling the past. It introduces the remainder of England's private and collective memories after (or before) the official histories get told. Because there is little historical material of a prominence comparable to that of Shakespeare's other history plays, the door is opened to a disorderly array of "histories," alternative ways of preserving and conferring meaning on the past. Most of these are drenched in affection for that which is departed, and stand opposed to the king's desire to have his senses steeped "in forgetfulness" (3.1.8).

Whereas commoners in the play tend to wax nostalgic, viewing the past as remote and irretrievable, time moves in cycles for the nobility. This cyclicism takes many forms: the demoralizing vision of endless cycles of revolt; the bracing form of valiant deeds brought back to life as Henry V reenacts the earlier victories of Edward III and the Black Prince at Crécy and Poitiers; and the more neutral vision of Warwick, which makes the study of historical cycles a useful predictive tool. These alignments contravene our expectations and contribute to the sense of a world turned upside down. Ordinarily one would expect to associate the nobility with nostalgia and a persistent orientation toward the past, and commoners, most of whose lives were governed by an agricultural calendar, with a cyclical experience of time. But in the two-part *Henry IV* the monarch, who has inherited a burdensome past to match his burdensome crown, has been barred by his actions against Richard from making public visitations to the past, leaving the rights to its vast territories to be claimed by the likes of Justice Shallow.

The two conceptions of the past given expression by Shallow and Warwick are opposites in at least one important respect. Nostalgia is predicated on a belief that what happened in the past is unrepeatable. As Svetlana Boym writes in her study of *The Future of Nostalgia*, "Nostalgia, like progress, is dependent on the modern conception of unrepeatable and irreversible time. The romantic nostalgic insisted on the otherness of his object of nostalgia from his present life and kept it at a safe distance."[70] The nostalgic commoner in *2 Henry IV*, who wants nothing more than to inhabit the past, feels permanently exiled from it; King Henry, by contrast, would distance himself from the past, which, Warwick teaches, is nevertheless connected to the present by inevitable patterns of recurrence.

The nostalgic's belief in the otherness of the past is everywhere belied by the ubiquitous sense that so much of what transpires in the play echoes a prior speech or scene from *1 Henry IV*. Even as Shallow regards with bittersweet pleasure a past beyond recuperation, we witness the past everywhere returning before our eyes and ears, much like a play with its rounds of rehearsals and performances. On the other hand, although the nostalgia of Shakespeare's commoners is unmasked as self-indulgent and delusional, the play as a whole unquestionably "speak[s] of something that is gone," to cite Wordsworth's "Immortality Ode": events, speeches, and sentiments from *1 Henry IV* return relentlessly in *2 Henry IV*, but in a different, decidedly less festive, key.[71] The play also establishes the commoners' independence from "the revolution of the times," a view of history that the King himself associates with fatalism: an independence that translates into a comparative freedom to invent their own pasts and thereby reinvent themselves.

King Henry broaches the subject of historical memory by lamenting a certain kind of historical literacy that allows one to predict the future by reading the past. Comparing the former division between Richard II and Northumberland to his present breach with the Percies, Henry observes that Richard himself foretold "this same time's condition" (3.1.77). To have the dubious privilege to "read the book of fate/ And see the revolution of the times/ Make mountains level" would cause even "the happiest youth" to "shut the book and sit him down to die" (3.1.44–6,53,55). Warwick then delivers a more neutral account of the historical cycles that the King finds so demoralizing. Unlike Henry, he holds out the possibility that one might use the past as a means to predict the future and thereby gain some measure of control over it.

> There is a history in all men's lives
> Figuring the natures of the times deceased,
> The which observed, a man may prophesy,
> With a near aim, of the main chance of things
> As yet not come to life, who in their seeds
> And weak beginning lie intreasurèd.
> Such things become the hatch and brood of time,
> And by the necessary form of this
> King Richard might create a perfect guess
> That great Northumberland, then false to him,
> Would of that seed grow to a greater falseness,
> Which should not find a ground to root upon
> Unless on you. (3.1.79–91)

Voicing a classical argument for history as life's teacher, *Historia magistra vitae*, Warwick appears to provide an authoritative commentary and key to the structure of Shakespeare's histories. Yet his speech also seems far removed from the ordinary motivations of audiences, who come to the theater more for pleasure than for instruction, and who would therefore likely see their motives more nearly reflected in the nostalgia of the commoners than in Warwick's studied response to the past. Temporarily practicing collective acts of pleasurable and even nostalgic remembrance, whether for the merry world of *1 Henry IV* or for national rejuvenation in the reign of Henry V, which itself would have seemed at once an urgent need and remote possibility in the waning years of Elizabeth's reign, audience members most likely would have had immediate grounds for feeling an affinity with the Shallows of this stage-play world.[72]

Although Warwick appears to supply a commanding, metatextual description of Shakespearean history, it falls short of a public and collective vision of the past. It is essentially private, requiring special discernment to unlock what lies "intreasurèd." Its idiosyncrasy and privacy are confirmed by Henry's response, an apparent misconstruing of Warwick's intent, which was to reassure the King that studying the past might help him master the present. Henry instead stresses the deterministic side of Warwick's cyclical view of history: "Are these things then necessities?/ Then let us meet them like necessities" (3.1.91–2), the four-square nature of rhetorical question and response and the rhyming of "necessities" with itself finely underscoring the king's fatalistic sense of recurrence as well as the need to meet such "necessities" on their own terms. That Warwick and his King are unable to share a common interpretation of the former's remarks on the meaning of history reinforces the play's dominant sense that no public, collective idea of the past is likely to emerge under Henry IV, a monarch who, as we saw in the last chapter, can afford to do little with the past besides wish to cover it up.

In Warwick's next speech, the grand, intelligible, and instructive pattern of historical cycles he has just evoked brushes up against Rumour. The latter suggests not only unauthorized report—a masterless discourse, as it were—but also disorder and impermanence. Warwick counters the king's pessimistic estimate of the number of rebel troops, "It cannot be, my lord:/ Rumour doth double, like the voice and echo,/ The numbers of the feared" (3.1.95–7). Warwick curiously means to quiet such echoing rumors, captured in the assonance and alliteration of the phrase "Rumour doth double" (the trochaic "double" a dilated and dying echo of "doth" that repeats or doubles its first two sounds), with the false report "that Glendower is dead" (3.1.102). In the middle of *2 Henry IV*, history meets its double, rumor, and they prove as hard to distinguish from one another as the discourse of Shallow and his servingmen. At first, it is true, they seem poles apart. The history in men's lives remains obscured from most eyes. It lies "intreasurèd" in "weak beginning[s]" that require keen powers of observation.

Rumor, available to all, seems the multitude's poor, disordered equivalent to Warwick's intricately patterned history, available only to a historically literate elite capable of reading the "book" of the past and harvesting its predictions for the future. Requiring no discernment, rumor is the jester at the court of history. But jester and *magister*, rumor and history, may not be so easy to distinguish after all—may instead be the ideological equivalent of doubled parts. Searching the past for forecasts of "the main chance of things/ As yet not come to life" (3.1.82–3), as Warwick advises, is likely to turn history into an echo-chamber, a long corridor of guesswork, hear-say, and imagined resemblances. The example of *Henry V*'s Welsh Captain Fluellen, with his absurd invocations of precedents and archetypes, shows how close these two may become. Taking the idea of history as *magistra vitae*, life's tutor, to extremes, Fluellen thoroughly disrupts the distinction made in *2 Henry IV* between the keen discernment of historical patterns and unfounded speculation.

Warwick's reference to Rumour's doublings ("Rumour doth double") is doubled or echoed in the next scene by Shallow's repeated question about old Dooble: "Is old Dooble of your town living yet? . . . And is old Dooble dead?" (3.2.33,43): a line that also doubles the (false) report that "Glendower is dead" in the previous scene. The doubled name of Dooble, as Melchiori notes, suggests "by its cavernous sound a person doubled up by old age."[73] The whole play, I have been arguing, has this doubled up quality, because nearly everything in *2 Henry IV* echoes a speech, a line, or an incident in *1 Henry IV*. In addition to a figure for the superannuated play as a whole, Old Dooble seems potentially an allegorical figure for memory itself, which, as Shankar Raman writes in the course of an essay on *The Comedy of Errors*, "emerges as a form of doubling, a *re*-presentation of what had gone before: not in its living presence but in its name."[74] The report of Old Dooble's death seems consistent with what may be called the demise of memory in this play, relegated as it is to the very corners of the kingdom—to the Gloucestershire countryside, for example—following its appropriation by the rebel forces in *1 Henry IV*.

Shakespeare sandwiches Henry and Warwick's conversation about the cycles of history between two scenes—the tavern scene and the recruitment scene—featuring commoners' nostalgic reminiscence. Nostalgia, to be sure, is frequently transparent and predictable in its operations and inauthentic as a form of historical knowledge. As Michael Kammen writes in his study of the transformations in America's sense of tradition, "nostalgia and amnesia are natural antagonists of meaningful historical knowledge. . . . Nostalgia, with its wistful memories, is essentially history without guilt."[75] Nevertheless, in this play nostalgia faces very little competition from alternative ways of regarding the past. Aesthetically, nostalgia proves to be a surprisingly supple form of recollection. It modulates from Pistol's pseudo-classical "What, we have seen the seven stars" (2.4.150) and Shallow's inch-deep "Ha, cousin Silence, that thou hadst seen that this knight and I have seen!" (3.2.175–6) to Falstaff's resonant "We have heard the chimes at midnight, Master Shallow" (3.2.177). Falstaff's line reiterates his fellows' tender feeling for youthful carousing, but in a way that darkens and deepens the palette of Shallow's nostalgia, as Pistol's and Shallow's "seeing" yields to the more internal sense of hearing and to the ominous suggestion of a limen or threshold, midnight. The line may invoke, in addition to the festivity that Falstaff's aged fellows associate with their youth, the collapse of festivity as a historical development associated with the Reformation: two forms of threshold (historical rupture as well as the passing of youth) echoing the diurnal one, midnight. Unlike Shallow's reminiscences, Falstaff's may also suggest iterability. His midnight chimes, reinforced by the line's rhythmical uniformity (rather striking after Shallow's rhythmically shaggy line), help evoke the cyclicism of diurnal time, which is at odds with the nostalgic Shallow's sense of a past beyond recuperation. While giving the nostalgia of the commoners its most memorable expression, Falstaff also skeptically brings Pistol's and Shallow's nostalgia to the threshold of its dramatic alternative, the cyclical views of history articulated by Warwick and Henry in the preceding scene.

Nostalgia does not escape without receiving its well-deserved share of ridicule in *2 Henry IV*. After Shallow, with the very modest help of Silence, chronicles his own past, Falstaff easily plumbs what appears to be the shallowest of all orientations toward the past. If "the nostalgic desires to obliterate history and turn it into private or collective mythology, to revisit time like space," then Falstaff, like some warden of historical knowledge, would seem to deny Shallow his visitation rights.[76] It is not clear, however, that Falstaff himself is entirely immune to this disease of memory. In soliloquy, he mocks,

> This same starved justice hath done nothing but prate to me of the wildness of his youth and the feats he hath done about Turnbull Street, and every third word a lie, duer paid to the hearer than the Turk's tribute. I do remember him at Clement's Inn, like a man made after supper of a cheese-paring. . . . And now is this Vice's dagger become a squire, and talks as familiarly of John a'Gaunt as if he had been sworn brother to him, and I'll be sworn a ne'er saw him but once in the tiltyard, and then he burst his head for crowding among the marshal's men. I saw it and told John a'Gaunt he beat his own name, for you might have thrust him and all his apparel into an eel's skin (3.2.247–51, 258–63).

Like Shallow, Falstaff shamelessly reinvents his own past, as he transparently repeats Shallow's transparent practice of talking familiarly of John of Gaunt. Poins comments when reading "Sir John Falstaff, knight," a false title of which Falstaff continually reminds others, "Every man must know that as oft as he has occasion to name himself: even like those that are kin to the king": that is, those who claim kinship to the king, even if, as the Prince says, they have to "fetch it from Japhet" (2.2.85–7,91).

Framing as they do a scene in which a king earnestly wishes to forget, the pleasurable acts of inventing and recollecting private but shared pasts that take place in the tavern scene (2.4) and enrollment scene (3.2) gain unexpected force. The fond nostalgia of the poor, with their refrain of "that we have seen"—"Jesus, the days that we have seen!" (Shallow, 3.2.180)—serves as counterpoint to the nobility's "that which I would to God I had not seen" (Morton's report to Northumberland, 1.1.106). What most of us would probably characterize as the shallowest of all attitudes toward the past, nostalgia, bears a surprisingly skeptical force in this play, exposing as it does the hollowness of the King's declaration about the hollowness of history. Furthermore, because the commoners take pleasure in recollection, in spite of the "questionable shape" (*Hamlet*, 1.4.43) of what they recall, they seem far closer to the spirit of popular history, the collective enterprise of the Lord Chamberlain's Men and their audiences in fondly (affectionately and perhaps foolishly) resurrecting England's late medieval past, than do Shakespeare's kings and nobles.

The most important feature of nostalgia in *2 Henry IV*, whether the personal indulgences of Pistol, Silence, and Shallow, or the larger, collective nostalgia for "merry England" of which they are a part, is that it remains unaccommodated. It is neither joined to a larger narrative nor expunged. In this respect it differs from the nostalgia that fuels the Cade rebellion in *2 Henry VI*. In the earlier play, the subversive historiography of Holland's line, "Well, I say, it was never merry world in England since gentlemen came up" (4.2.6–7), is not left hanging.[77] Rather, it is silenced when Cade is revealed as a mask for the anti-historical forces that the English have been fighting in France, especially when he rants against literacy and the use of documents. Claiming to be a Plantagenet in a Falstaffian gesture of self-aggrandizement and intoxicating moment of self-forgetfulness and self-reinvention, Cade implicitly endorses and seeks to profit from the dominant, dynastic understanding of power in the first tetralogy. Cade thereby defuses the more subversive, alternative historiography voiced by Holland.

In *2 Henry IV*, nostalgia for the "merry world" never seems overtly politicized as it does in *2 Henry VI*'s Cade Rebellion, because such nostalgia for the most part wears the kindly and nonthreatening visage of aging rural folk, but politically subversive it is nonetheless. In an atmosphere in which the King urges his son to cancel the past—to "busy giddy minds/ With foreign quarrels" and thereby "waste the memory of the former days" (4.2.341–3)—and the responsibilities of tending to it seem to belong almost exclusively to the poor. It is the tavern, a place of oblivion purchased through drink, that paradoxically serves as the refuge of the historical sense in this play. Not only does it allow Shakespeare to remember the forgotten of history by directing attention to commoners and to the everyday, but it also helps preserve the diverse ways in which people remember, the heterogeneity of cultural memory beneath the apparent solidarity of national memory achieved in *Henry V*. The *Henry IV* plays do not simply register a fondness, a nostalgic affection, for an England that is passing or is past: rather, they dramatize what it is like for a people to be without a collective myth, guided by a monarch whose burden it is to perpetually try to make his people forget the circumstances of his having become king.

FROM TELLING TO TOLLING: THE KNELL OF HISTORY

2 Henry IV opens with what is for Shakespeare an unusual theatrical device, an Induction. It is delivered by Rumour, whose costume is "painted full of tongues," according to the stage direction for the quarto. The identity of Rumour, this figure of uncertainty, error, and false report, is paradoxically beyond question. Appareled in a costume decorated with tongues, his is the most legible body on stage: "But what need I thus/ My well-known body to anatomise/ Among my household?" (Ind. 20–22). In keeping with his legibility, he inadvertently betrays his office by speaking the truth—that the King and his troops have defeated the rebels at Shrewsbury—before speaking falsehood. Rumor, as Adam Fox writes, was a necessary feature of the conveyance of news in early modern England:

> In a society which had few means of confirming or denying news, in which political insecurity was often of the highest order, and in which the authorities tried to restrict and censor the circulation of intelligence, it is hardly surprising that fervent speculation and wild rumours were rife . . . In such an environment the scope for wild and unfounded stories was immense.[78]

The decade that witnessed Shakespeare's chronicle histories, the 1590s, "when economic crisis, coupled with the perceived threat of plotters from within the realm and invasion from without, created a climate ripe for such scaremongering," were especially susceptible to speculation in the form of prophecies and rumors.[79]

Rumour prefigures two characters, opposite in function, from the opening scene of the play: Lord Bardolph, who might very well have been played by the actor impersonating Rumour,[80] and Morton, who arrives with a reliable account of the rebels' defeat and Hotspur's death. Whereas Lord Bardolph is "cast from the beginning as Rumour or Bad Counsel,"[81] Morton represents something like faithful historical memory. Bearing the news to Hotspur's father Northumberland of his son's death, Morton comes close to being allegorized as Remembrance in Northumberland's lines,

> Yet the first bringer of unwelcome news
> Hath but a losing office, and his tongue
> Sounds ever after as a sullen bell
> Remembered, tolling a departed friend. (1.1.100–3)

The tongue of the bearer of bad news becomes a bell (captured in the assonance and consonance of ll. 102–3), ever after heard by the recipient as dolefully repeating its message of loss, no matter what else it tries to communicate. The infinite variations in a human voice are reduced to the repetitiveness of a clamoring bell and the monotony of a single discourse. The word "remembered" in l.103, with its repeated phoneme /em/, itself has a knelling quality, as if to imply that to remember is to mourn and that all telling is a tolling of what has inexorably and permanently departed. It is no accident, I presume, that the character who gives voice to the most powerful and affecting memory in any of the histories—the recollection of Falstaff on his deathbed (*Henry V*, 2.3)—should be named "Nell," and that her account of her friend's demise should rely heavily on a tolling repetition, resembling a death knell.[82]

Northumberland's image of the tongue as tolling bell is not an altogether doleful one. It implies that memory is constant and reliable, bearing a stability that seems in many ways preferable to the flights of Rumour and "the blunt monster with uncounted heads,/ The still discordant wav'ring multitude" (Ind. 18–19). Thus far, the opening scene would seem to stage a contrast between a composite figure, Rumour/Lord Bardolph, who converts the past into a version of the present, with all its confusion and uncertainty of outcome, and another, Morton, whose "sullen" office of relating unwelcome news transforms everything in the present into an image of the past and of loss.

Subsequent to the news of his son's death, Northumberland will hear only the sound of death (*la mort*) in Morton's voice, as his name punningly suggests. For Northumberland, Morton's tongue, far from signaling a commitment to enduring memory, sounds a death-knell to all further engagement with the world. No simple antidote to Rumour, a fixation on the past bears the risk of producing another form of oblivion. Similarly, remembrance for the King bears some resemblance to the maddening repetition of a tolling bell, and therefore (according to the Archbishop) "will he wipe his tables clean/ And keep no telltale to his memory/ That may repeat and history his loss/ To new remembrance" (4.1.201–4).[83] Memory is a type of disorder in *2 Henry IV*, of which the play explores at least three kinds: Rumour, which holds most of the territory belonging to recent events or short-term memory; the prince of long-term memory, Nostalgia for a remote and invented past; and Mourning, a fixation on an actual event that at least temporarily incapacitates memory, freezing it in a posture of grief. It is hard to locate a productive use, either personal or collective, for memory in *2 Henry IV*, one that enables characters to experience real growth based on a more or less authentic remembrance of things past.[84]

The Epilogue, like the opening scene, is informed by an implicit quarrel between rumor and historical memory. Apparently Rumour has been as resistant to perpetual banishment as Bolingbroke in *Richard II*. The Epilogue reminds the audience of an earlier performance, resulting in a debt to the audience for which the present play has been intended to serve as payment: "Be it known to you, as it is very well, I was lately here in the end of a displeasing play, to pray your patience for it and to promise you a better" (Epi. 6–8). Adopting the role of theater-historian, the Epilogue also recalls a political problem, not spelled out but apparently involving the Queen (Epi. 12–13) and attempts to correct a popular misconception, echoing the correction of error that takes place in the opening scene with the entrance of Morton: "[F]or Oldcastle died martyr, and this is not the man" (Epi. 24–25). As Melchiori notes, the Epilogue's reference to Oldcastle could serve as "an oblique reminder that the change from Oldcastle to Falstaff was forced upon the company," or, in the more widely accepted theory, "as a belated apology possibly prompted by the successful performance by the Admiral's Men late in 1599 of *I Sir John Oldcastle*."[85] In addition to a sly act of defiance and an apology, the correction may also serve to cover up the historical outrage committed by *1 Henry IV*. Unleashing more speculation than it resolves, the reference to Oldcastle seems calculated to do anything but restrain Rumor.

The epilogue plays out again at the level of theatrical memory the confrontation over historical memory in the Induction and opening scene. It brings us uncomfortably close to the beginning: awash in speculation, and ostensibly dispelling Rumour once again, only this time rumors not of Henry IV but of *Henry IV*. One might reasonably expect a history play introduced by Rumour to articulate a sharp contrast between chaotic history-in-the-making, history before confirmed facts are sorted out from false report, and a well-ordered historical memory profiting from hindsight and defining the arc of the play as a whole. Not only does the play fail to produce a vision of history purged of rumor, but the ending insinuates that rumor is the real victor in the civil wars depicted in the play, preparing the way for the masterful manipulation of collective memory by King Henry V in the play that will follow.

The *Henry IV* plays began in one of the most unsettled fields of early modern historiography, the contentious area having to do with the Lollard martyr Oldcastle. *2 Henry IV* ends with a gesture that leaves its engagement with those histories an open question, as if we merely imagined or dreamed that the Lollard knight had a part in the two plays of Henry IV. In this respect, the ending of the play recalls the epistemological play of comedies like *The Taming of the Shrew* and *A Midsummer Night's Dream*. Although *2 Henry IV* has been called "autumnal" in mood,[86] the epilogue has elicited comparisons to Rosalind's epilogue in *As You Like It*. At the end of *2 Henry IV* we cannot rule out the possibility that, like Christopher Sly, we have been thoroughly duped about what we have witnessed.

With this play's preponderance of private memories and multiple nostalgias, memory takes highly fragmented and dispersed forms, virtually opposite to the illusion of a consolidated and uniform memory in *Henry V*. Private memory may temporarily deflect attention from collective memory, as when Justice Shallow reduces the memory of the recent civil conflict to a nostalgic "list of names of West Country men who were hell-raisers with him at the Inns of court."[87] But private memory in *2 Henry IV* wears more rebellious masks as well, potentially serving to caricature the official, public memory orchestrated by the monarchy and even to serve as a dangerous remainder, unassimilable to state memory. Memory in *2 Henry IV* remains uncollected and unconsolidated, multiple, dispersed, and beyond monarchal control. Unlike *Henry V*, where the eccentric and relentless memorializing of Captain Fluellen seems safely absorbed into the fabric of national memory woven by Henry, in *2 Henry IV* the memories of figures of mnemonic excess—figures as diverse as Pistol, Morton, and Shallow—remain unincorporated into a totalizing public memory.

In *2 Henry IV* England's past is as rag-tag a thing as Falstaff's troops in *1 Henry IV*: a motley and shambling procession of personal recollections and nostalgia, false reports overseen by Rumour, grieving of an intensity that looks forward to *Hamlet*, reminiscences of *1 Henry IV*, classical reminiscences, and reminiscences of England's early theatrical history in the character of the exaggerated and exaggerating Pistol: all juxtaposed with *2 Henry's* two Henrys' strong motivations to forget and to have others forget the process by which they achieved power. The play seems as reluctant to perform its function of rehearsing, reinforcing, and consolidating the national memory as Falstaff traipsing off to battle. Incongruities between nobles' and commoners' attitudes toward the past help to explain the discrepancy between an overwhelming sense of superannuation in the play and the hope for imminent renewal that rests on the new king. *2 Henry IV*, however, does not use the former as a backdrop and pre-text, as it were, for *Henry V*. Instead, it leaves us with the uneasy sense that what looks like renewal from the nobility's perspective is in reality an Act of Oblivion (to borrow the title of the parliamentary act of 1660), not so much renewing the past as canceling it.

In *2 Henry IV* we receive a foretaste of Hal's future career as prince of forgetfulness and careful orchestrator of the national memory in *Henry V*. In a conversation bearing echoes of King John (the Bastard's "new-made honour doth forget men's names"), the Prince chastises himself for remembering first "so weak a composition" as small beer, and second, its human equivalent, Poins: "What a disgrace is it to me to remember thy name—or to know thy face tomorrow—or to take note how many pairs of silk stockings thou hast with these, and those that were the peach-coloured once—or to bear the inventory of thy shirts, as: one for superfluity, and another for use" (2.2.7–8, 11–15). Sensing his mind to be too close a record-keeper, too honest a chronicler of the humble and everyday, not unlike the Shakespeare of *2 Henry IV*, the Prince recoils at such an office. There is something princely about forgetfulness, Hal implies, although later tragedies will cast doubt on the notion: *Hamlet*, especially, but also *Coriolanus*, whose haughty protagonist's inability to recall the name of his poor benefactor hardly seems a mark of nobility. Before these will come a play, *Henry V*, in which a people's liberties to remember the past in popular, local, regional, and potentially subversive forms are largely silenced by a monarch whose ambitions to recreate and to control the nation's memory leave no place for Oldcastle/Falstaff—the Prince's former tutor in the ways of forgetfulness, whose memory he now strives to cancel—and all the historically unruly forces that so memorable and composite a character may help us to recollect.

Self-forgetfulness on the part of actors and audiences alike, *2 Henry IV* shows, is not an accidental feature, a danger to which an unwary or unusually distracted spectator might succumb, but rather an element essential to the impersonations of playacting, the absorptions of playgoing, and collective acts of historical memory alike, besieged as they are by the hazards of nostalgia. The genre of the history play, ostensibly designed to reinforce its audiences' collective memory, may be riven with contradictions, given the element of self-forgetfulness entailed by both staging and watching a play, this most skeptical of Shakespeare's histories seems to propose. The mnemonic contradictions of theater are analogous to those of national memory—a decidedly forgetful memory, as Renan articulated, like that of a history play. The genre of the history play, as it was invented in Elizabethan England, with its inevitable and sometimes breathtaking abbreviations and omissions, was well suited to participate in the invention of the English nation. But at the pinnacle of the genre—namely, Shakespeare's later history plays—it proved capable of questioning its own acts of oblivion and exploring the relation of such acts to the maintenance of power and the silencing of dissent.

4 Wars of Memory in *Henry V*

> Our souls indeed are too like filthy Ponds, wherein fish die soon, and frogs live long: Rotten stuff is remembred, memorable mercies are forgotten; whereas the soul should be as an holy Ark; the memory as the pot of Manna, preserving holy truths and special mercies.
>
> —Samuel Clarke[1]

> And finally, be of one mind, since you know that unity is the more strong, disunity is the weaker and likely soon to fall in ruin.
>
> —Elizabeth I[2]

> Unity is always effected by means of brutality.
>
> —Ernest Renan[3]

WAR AND THE CANON

"No one bored by war will be interested in *Henry V*," challenges Gary Taylor in his Oxford Shakespeare edition of the play.[4] But Shakespeare's play has found an audience with many who find military history a barren field: partly, no doubt, because not all warfare in the play is of the grisly military sort. There is, of course, the sexual skirmishing between Henry and Katherine, faintly reminiscent of *The Taming of the Shrew.* But most of the battles in the play are over memory, the importance of which to the formation and strength of a sovereign national state is evident throughout. This play, so singularly unimpressive as a representation of the epochal battle of Agincourt, is nonetheless a remarkable study of how a nation remembers.

Although the play has been regarded as "a propaganda-play on National Unity: heavily orchestrated for the brass,"[5] recent criticism has emphasized gaps and tensions within the appearance of national unity and resistances to unifying ideology, a familiar spinoff of the poststructuralist rereading of Shakespeare as "fissure king."[6] What has gone largely unremarked on both sides is the extent to which nationalist ideology and resistances to it take the form of collisions over memory. Memory is the larger, moveable battlefield to which King Henry, England, and England's last Tudor monarch were repeatedly called to arms. Collective memory is an extension of the kinds of power and even the brutality exercised in war. Wars of memory are not bloodless but intimately tied to the loss of lives and limbs. Control over how a nation remembers a momentous event like a war is almost as significant as the outcome of the war itself, given how crucial memory is for the legitimation and exercise of power.

The evidence of *Henry V* suggests that consolidation of the collective memory was becoming a timely issue in the 1590s, a period of shifting self-definition for England. According to John Guy, by the 1590s English politicians ere regularly beginning to conceptualize England as a unitary "state," a term that did not acquire its modern meaning until late in the Tudor era: "In the reigns of Henry VII and Henry VIII politicians had spoken only of 'country,' 'people,' 'kingdom,' and 'realm.'"[7] "In the older imagining of the dynastic realm," writes Benedict Anderson, "states were defined by centres, borders were porous and indistinct, and sovereignties faded imperceptibly into one another."[8] Besides being identified with a sovereign, monarchical government that "recognized no superior in political, ecclesiastical and legal matters" and which ruled over a "defined territory," the new concept of the state, according to Guy, was supported by "three underlying beliefs: (1) that humanity was divided into races or nations; (2) that the purity of the English nation would be sullied by foreign admixtures; and (3) that English language, law, and customs (including dress) were the badges of nationality."[9] The shift from dynastic realm to nation-state is apparent in differences between Shakespeare's first and second tetralogies. In the latter, as England's identity tilts toward that of a modern nation-state, memory becomes more contested and divisive an issue.[10]

Elizabethan wars of memory were fought on several fronts. The memory of the loss of Calais shortly before Elizabeth's accession remained a source of irritation throughout her reign. The subduing of local memory, either by absorption or by erasure, was an essential feature of Elizabethan policy toward Ireland. A tension between Church and nation, reflected in Henry's Crispin's Day speech, lay beneath the manipulation of calendrical memory during Elizabeth's reign, the transmutation of the holy calendar into a record of national and patriotic events. Elizabeth's wars of memory were no immediate, unqualified successes, no Agincourt. They bore a greater resemblance to the protracted and frustrating struggle that was the Hundred Years' War.

"The struggle of man against power is the struggle of memory against forgetting," Kundera's narrator recalls Mirek saying in *The Book of Laughter and Forgetting.*[11] Nowhere in the Shakespeare canon is that struggle more evident than in *Henry V*, a play illustrating the uses of forgetting for the consolidation of national memory, an essential process in the formation of the modern nation-state. The play confirms that power can usually get away with forgetting a great deal, suppressing any public memory that might challenge it, so long as it wears the cloak of remembrance, as Henry does throughout the play. In what follows I want to show that the play both mimics and to some degree undoes Henry's role as choreographer of the national memory. Just as Henry is anxious to mask the fault lines in the appearance of national unity that run throughout the play, so the play as a whole both hides and—largely by making visible the process of hiding—reveals the stress points in the sense of nationhood to which the increasingly militaristic and imperial England of the 1590s was aspiring. Besides calling attention to Henry's manipulation of the national memory, the play also stages many points of contention within Elizabethan memory. The play quietly subverts Henry's rhetoric of remembrance by building a case for Henry and his nation's debt to forgetting.

THE ROUTE TO AGINCOURT

For England's sense of nationhood in 1599, the route to Agincourt seems as significant as the rout at Agincourt. Following Hall and Holinshed, Shakespeare sets the conspiracy scene (2.2) at Southampton. But subsequent references imply that the English army embarked not at Southampton but at Dover, located at the narrowest point of the English Channel, opposite Calais. Two scenes from Act 3 that make reference to Calais introduce an element of geographical confusion that may very well have been due to an authorial memory lapse.[12] As Gary Taylor sums up the problem, contradicting the references to Southampton in Act 2, "subsequent scenes seem to envisage a voyage from Dover to Calais, then later a *retreat* from Harfleur to Calais. The geographical confusion is thus probably Shakespeare's—the more so as a compositor is unlikely to have substituted *Dover* for *Hampton*."[13] Given the play's absorption with the politics of memory, however, it is entirely possible that the confusion, rather than the result of a playwright's forgetting, amounted to an act of remembrance. Rerouting the English army through Dover and Calais rather than Southampton takes it past the city that could serve as a mnemonic for much of the vexed foreign relations of the Elizabethan era. Calais was a dubious memorial to England's international affairs, capable of evoking memories of some of England's greatest triumphs and failures.

Captured by Edward III in 1347 following the battle of Crécy, Calais was finally surrendered to the French on January 8, 1558. The last remnant of England's Continental empire was lost. Elizabeth's accession to the throne later that year inaugurated a long and fruitless obsession with repossessing Calais. Much of her reign was preoccupied with compensating for what has been described as the "degrading peace" she signed with France in April 1559, a peace that "blacken[ed] the memory of Agincourt and Crécy."[14] The "backward-looking policy of recovering Calais" dominated Elizabeth's dealings with France, although it sometimes fused with the "new-fashioned goal" of supporting the Protestant cause in France.[15]

Her famously protracted marriage negotiations with foreign princes had as one of their chief aims the return of Calais. It had been of vital importance to the English wool trade (a trade already in decline when Calais fell to the French) and continued to seem militarily strategic as a likely launching place for invasions of England by either the French or the Spanish. Elizabeth's wooing of foreign rulers, including her brother-in-law, Philip, involved negotiations for the recovery of Calais. She gave the agent of Philip's French rival, King Henry, reason to hope that she might break with Philip if only the French would return Calais to English hands. She also made one of the conditions of marriage to the duke of Alençon, the French king's brother-in-law, an alliance with France that would include repossession of Calais. The marriage of Elizabeth's cousin Mary Stuart to the dauphin François augmented English fears that Catholic France would support Mary's claim to the English throne. Because of the loss of Calais, England felt itself caught between a Scotland supported by France and a French army in control of the port opposite the narrowest point of the channel.

Throughout her reign Elizabeth was perpetually hopeful about this repossession. The eight years prior to *Henry V* saw two expeditions to France, both involving the Earl of Essex and likely to be remembered by at least some in Shakespeare's audience in 1599. In the first of these, Elizabeth came to the aid of Henry of Navarre, a Huguenot who succeeded to the French throne in 1589 owing to the assassination of Henry III. The following year Spain, in alliance with the Catholic League, invaded Brittany, calling up all the old English fears of "important Channel bases in enemy hands."[16] Another year later the twenty-six-year-old Earl of Essex came to Henry's aid in Normandy, leading a futile siege of Rouen, from which he returned in disgrace in January 1592 only "to brave a more formidable foe in Elizabeth's displeasure and sarcasm."[17] These events would themselves have recalled an earlier Elizabethan expedition to France on behalf of the Protestant cause. In 1563, during France's first war of religion, English troops entered France to help the Huguenots but were hampered by the terms under which they entered, terms that included the return of Calais and other territories. These terms actually led to an alliance of the divided French parties, who united to expel the English. The name of the treaty that marked the end of hostilities, the Treaty of Troyes (April 11, 1564), made it a potentially embarrassing recollection of the treaty signed in Act 5 of Shakespeare's play. After 1564 England's Continental ambitions were in reality dead, although Elizabeth continued to work at reversing her sister's loss of Calais.

In 1596, closer to the date of composition of *Henry V*, Calais was in danger of falling into Spanish hands as the result of a surprise attack launched by the Archduke Cardinal Albert, Philip's new governor of the Netherlands, an event that delayed a proposed expedition to Spain by Essex, Howard of Effingham, and Howard Vere. Again Essex was involved, although Elizabeth did not need any persuasion. Asked by Henry IV of France for aid, she gave the order on Good Friday for 6,000 men under Essex to be ready to embark at Dover within two days. Because she made the return of Calais a condition of aid, she lost her opportunity, and the port fell to the Spanish, renewing English fears of invasion.

In 1588 the Armada, anchored off Calais, waiting expectantly for the Duke of Parma, was attacked by English fire ships that destroyed several of the vessels and inaugurated the Armada's long and costly voyage northward around the island back to Spain. This event led to the "Thankfull Remembrance of 1588," a thanksgiving for the "Protestant Wind" that delivered the English from the fearsome Armada. The earl of Essex himself—prospective hero of the conquest of Ireland when the play premiered in 1599—helped to organize one of the events in that remembrance, a great review in the tiltyard at Whitehall.

With its passing references to Calais, references that are actually foregrounded by the geographical confusion, Shakespeare's play about the building of England's Continental empire would likely have reminded many in its audience of the ignominious loss of that empire's last fragment. For Henry within the play and Elizabeth without, reference to Calais would have nearly opposite effects. For Henry they serve as reminder of the great precedent for Agincourt, Edward III's Normandy expedition, including the victory at Crécy in 1346, remembered elsewhere in the play. Like the English army in Shakespeare's play, Edward's army found themselves blocked en route to Calais. As at Agincourt, English archers inflicted considerable damage on the French army, after which Edward's army marched triumphantly to Calais and captured it in 1347. For Elizabeth, Calais would have evoked more than anything else the immense fears and frustrations of relations with Catholic France and Spain, with the exception of the triumphant events of the Armada year, which, it has been suggested, *Henry V* as a whole commemorates.[18] But as Elizabeth's continuing preoccupation with recapturing Calais in the eleven years between the Armada and Shakespeare's *Henry V* attests, the events of 1588 off the Calais coast could not erase the more distressing memories that city evoked: its hoped-for possession seemed to Elizabeth almost a talismanic protection against foreign invasion. "Our too-much-memorable shame," Shakespeare's King Charles calls Crécy (2.4.53), the battle that led directly to English possession of Calais. Elizabeth could almost say the same of Calais, because the first twenty-five years of her reign were, as Christopher Hill notes, the "only period in English history since 1066 when the country had no overseas possessions (except Ireland)."[19] It was a circumstance that would grant Calais a symbolic importance far in excess of its strategic military one, although Elizabeth imagined this to be considerable as well. Toward the end of a long reign preoccupied with retrieving England's last Continental possession, Shakespeare's Henry fulfills Elizabeth's dream of repossession, accomplishing what Elizabeth and Essex failed to do by either political or martial means.

"TO THE ENDING OF THE WORLD"

Not only Calais but Agincourt as well, that most famous of English military victories, held an ambiguous status as a memory common to all

Englishmen and promising to bind the nation together. For one thing, in 1599 and indeed throughout the reigns of Elizabeth and her immediate predecessors (including her father's), there was no annual observance of Agincourt, in spite of Henry's boast that "Crispin Crispian shall ne'er go by/ From this day to the ending of the world/ But we in it shall be remembered" (4.3.57–9). Joel Altman writes of Henry's Crispin's Day speech as "an embracing ritual gesture" by means of which "Shakespeare has joined past to present, audience to soldiery, in an honorable fellowship transcending time and space." "Fathered" by "Harry's vile participation . . . the audience at the Curtain or, perhaps, the new Globe Theatre . . . are the lineal descendants" of Henry's soldiers.[20] In light of England's failure to mark the anniversary of its great victory with a national observance, however, it would be as apt to say that the speech marks the discontinuity of past and present. The mnemonic function of the speech in 1599 would most likely have been to remind audiences not of Agincourt, which had been "remembered" theatrically often enough in preceding years,[21] but of the absence of any national day of remembrance. The absence was necessary, perhaps, because any such observance would likely have reminded Elizabethans of eventual defeat, especially the recent loss of their last foothold in France. The far more enduring national memory was not the English victory but the eventual expulsion of the English from northern France. As historian Desmond Seward points out,

> For centuries the north-western French celebrated the expulsion of the English. Until 1735 the liberation of Paris in 1436 was celebrated annually by the "Procession of the English." The Earl of Warwick's banner, captured at Montargis in 1427, was borne in triumph through that town on the *Fête des Anglais* every year till 1792.[22]

Instead of an Agincourt Day celebrating Henry's and England's great victory, a day commemorating the martyrdom of Henry's sometime friend and nemesis Sir John Oldcastle was proposed by one of the more vigorous voices in Elizabethan England, John Foxe, as part of "a new Anglican martyrology,"[23] "a Protestant calendar in competition with the Roman Catholic practice of celebrating saints' days."[24]

Like Shakespeare's Henry, the historical Henry seems to have been more than a little preoccupied with the political function of memory. Soon after his accession to the throne, he began reviving the claims of his ancestors, which included his "ancient rights" in the duchy of Normandy, demanding the return of French territories granted to Edward III through the Treaty of Brétigny and reasserting Edward's claim to the French crown. He ordered a scroll listing the names of his soldiers, the so-called Agincourt Roll, of which Sir Harry Nicolas wrote, "It is pleasing to trace the rewards bestowed by Henry on his companions in arms at Agincourt, and the measures which he adopted to preserve their names from oblivion."[25] The future remembrance of Agincourt referred to repeatedly in the play's Crispin's Day speech was overseen in its initial stage by Henry himself, who ordered the first anniversary celebration of the battle on October 25, 1416.[26] And he clearly gave considerable thought to England's remembrance of him after his death. In his will Henry supplied carefully specified plans for his tomb and chantry chapel in Westminster. Believing that he should occupy a preeminent place among the kings of England, he chose a spot for his chapel that "dwarfed the shrine of Edward the Confessor."[27]

Similarly, Shakespearean Henry's actions are usually contingent on remembering or forgetting. Shakespeare even deploys a special word, "memorable," which Gary Taylor notes is used four times in *Henry V* and in no other play,[28] as if to underscore the king's absorption with both personal and national memory. Early in the play Henry imagines his alternatives to be "tombless, with no remembrance" (as Richard II was during the reign of his father), or to have history "with full mouth / Speak freely of our acts" (1.2.229–31). Troubled by memories of Richard and the origin of his own succession, Henry reminds his Maker, in prayers the night before Agincourt, of his public reinstatement of Richard's memory by interring him in Westminster Abbey.[29] Henry forgets Falstaff and his old tavern cronies, an action that might appear to be either a treasonous betrayal, akin to that of Cambridge, Scrope, and Grey, or a carefully plotted measure to assert the precedence of national memory over private memory. Of the leek he wears in his cap for Captain Fluellen and in remembrance of his Welsh heritage, King Henry says, "I wear it for a memorable honour" (4.7.93). And, most memorably, Henry rouses his troops before the Battle of Agincourt by depicting it as both a reenactment of England's glorious past and a capital reserve of memory on which his soldiers will be able to draw in future years. Together these instances and others assert the precedence of a consolidated national memory over several other forms that might compete with or offer resistance to it. Regional, ecclesiastical, and private forms of memory are all subdued as surely as the French army at Agincourt, although their ghosts (like those of Richard and Falstaff and like the Irish whom the Earl of Essex had been recently dispatched to subdue) remain unruly, refractory, and restive.

In spite of officialdom's extraordinary deployment of a rhetoric of remembrance in the play, reminding characters and viewers alike of the sacred, moral, and patriotic obligations to remember, *Henry V* bears more powerful testimony to the advantages of forgetting. English colonial policy and national unity are shown to be based on a pattern of forgetting disguised as remembrance. To audiences still filled with vivid memories of Falstaff, a great favorite in *1 Henry IV* (1596), *The Merry Wives of Windsor* (1597–1598), and *2 Henry IV* (1597–1598), Henry's systematic forgetting of him and his other tavern companions must have seemed powerfully contrary to their own experience. The betrayal of Falstaff, although it has received inordinate attention in criticism of the tetralogy, is not unique in the play but belongs rather to an intricate pattern of forgetting. Forgetting is not merely a lapse in personal or private obligation, a betrayal of old friends, but is intimately connected to the exercise of power. Social divisions are conveniently remembered and forgotten throughout the play. They are forgotten in the temporary brotherhood of the English army at Agincourt only to be remembered subsequently, when Henry conveniently forgets his promise, "For he today that sheds his blood with me/ Shall be my brother" (4.3.61–2). Edmund Mortimer, whose claim to the throne the traitors Cambridge, Scrope, and Grey were advancing, would have been remembered by the vast majority of Shakespeare's audience, because he inaugurates the Yorkist claim to the throne, dramatized in the popular *Henry VI* plays. But in *Henry V* he is erased. Cambridge's line indirectly pointing out his true motive—"For me, the gold of France did not seduce" (2.2.150)—is the closest the play comes to recalling the rival claimant to the English throne. As Karl Wentersdorf puts it, a "conspiracy of silence" surrounds Mortimer in the play.[30] Falstaff and Mortimer in different ways both represent the threat of internal disorder, and both are victims of the king's prodigious powers of forgetting. On a larger scale, it is all of Ireland, the play intimates, that promises to become the next victim on the chopping block of memory.

That the formation of a national identity is at least as much based on forgetting as on remembering was articulated by nineteenth-century French historian Ernest Renan in a lecture titled "What Is a Nation?' delivered at the Sorbonne in 1882. Renan was writing in opposition to ethnographers, especially the Germans who had lately "raised the banner of ethnography so high," because ethnographers too often functioned as the "advance guards of . . . expansion."[31] By contrast with ethnographic scientists, Renan emphasized that "nations are made by human will," not subject to a "naturalistic determinism" by "language, geography, race, religion, or anything else."[32] Supplementing his claim that one of the "spiritual principles" of a nation is "the possession in common of a rich legacy of memories," Renan adds important comments on the necessity of forgetting:

> If you take a city such as Salonika or Smyrna, you will find there five or six communities each of which has its own memories and which have almost nothing in common. Yet the essence of a nation is that all individuals have many things in common, and also that they have forgotten many things. No French citizen knows whether he is a Burgundian, an Alan, a Taifale, or a Visigoth, yet every French citizen has to have forgotten the massacre of Saint Bartholomew, or the massacres that took place in the Midi in the thirteenth century.[33]

Because unity is achieved only by coercion and bloodshed, according to Renan, a national narrative inevitably has its origins as much in the will to forget as in the will to preserve or remember. But a people must not only forget; they must also forget the very processes of forgetting that, according to Renan, make it a nation. *Henry V* continually and paradoxically reminds us of the communal amnesia that help to produce and support the sense of nationhood.

Renan's remarks on forgetting appear in the context of a discussion of invasions: German invasions of France and the Norman conquests, one or two generations after which "the Norman invaders no longer distinguished themselves from the rest of the population."[34] Following the lines of Renan's analysis, it would be fair to say that Henry's England owed more to the ability to forget than any country in Renaissance Europe, despite his entering upon the conquest of France under the banner of remembrance. The events of *Henry V* are to some degree a reverse or mirror image of the Norman Conquest. To the extent they called up memories of the Conquest, these events might also call up a national memory counter to Henry's. More specifically, Henry's pseudo-democratic rhetoric before the battle might evoke the historical theory that Christopher Hill has labeled the "Norman Yoke," a theory Hill summarizes as follows:

> Before 1066 the Anglo-Saxon inhabitants of this country lived as free and equal citizens, governing themselves through representative institutions. The Norman Conquest deprived them of this liberty, and established the tyranny of an alien King and landlords. But the people did not forget the rights they had lost. They fought continuously to recover them, with varying success. Concessions (Magna Carta, for instance) were from time to time extorted from their rulers, and always the tradition of lost Anglo-Saxon freedom was a stimulus to ever more insistent demands upon the successors of the Norman usurpers.[35]

To some in Shakespeare's audience, Henry's rhetoric might very well have evoked the historical myth of the Norman Yoke, inclining them to accuse Henry and Henry's England of forgetting ancient English laws and liberties. Certainly the alliance with France in the final act, although suffused with suggestions that English manners and customs will be exported to France, might imply perpetuation of an ancient betrayal of Anglo-Saxon freedom and equality. This is especially likely as Henry takes the familial rhetoric of the battle scenes, which suggests a democratic brotherhood of Englishmen akin to that envisioned by the myth of the Norman Yoke, and transfers it onto "brother France." In Act 5 Henry steals the Crispin's Day rhetoric of "we band of brothers" (4.3.60) from his soldiers as surely as his father stole the kingdom and as he himself so recently stole honor from the common soldier Williams. What is worse, he bestows the stolen tropes as a royal gift on France's ruling family. A democratic sense of brotherhood or familial connection across social classes but within national boundaries yields to a rhetoric of family tied to dynastic descent and deployed to foster solidarity within a social class and across national boundaries. In other words, Henry is willing to jettison the entire public rhetoric of nationhood when it gets in his way politically, as it does at the moment of entry into a dynastic marriage with France. The ending of the play makes clear that the rhetoric of the nation and the rhetoric of empire and dynastic descent are not always consonant. The final scene, I would submit, attempts to reconcile the rhetoric of the dynastic realm, caricatured early in the play in the lengthy speech of the archbishop of Canterbury, and the rhetoric of the nation-state, developed at length in the remainder of the play. It is an uneasy alliance, not unlike that between England and France.

Together with the extraordinary proliferation of a rhetoric of remembrance, a pattern of forgetting, unmarked of course by public rhetoric, is one of the play's main features. In Act 5 the Duke of Burgundy gives Henry a little advice about the reluctant Princess Katherine: "[F]or maids well summered and warm kept are like flies at Bartholomew-tide, blind, though they have their eyes, and then they will endure handling which before would not endure looking on" (5.2.275–8). Recall here Renan's admonition: "Every French citizen has to have forgotten the massacre of Saint Bartholomew." It would be a trumped-up charge, certainly, in 1599 to accuse a representation of the Duke of Burgundy in 1415 of willfully forgetting an event that took place in 1572, one of the most notorious bloodbaths in history. But in 1599 mention of St. Bartholomew's Day by a French character would surely have evoked for many spectators one of the most infamous days in their recent memory. Its evocation in the midst of Shakespeare's greatest speech about peace seems far from accidental, especially given a wider pattern of memories surfacing at moments that seem politically inopportune, alternately for Henry and for Elizabeth. In 1599 a character's innocent reference to Bartholomew-tide becomes a prophecy of slaughter and of war,[36] calling on an Elizabethan audience to summon its powers of forgetting, challenging it to forget the unforgettable, but reminding it of nothing so much as the very processes of forgetting. It is something (I have been arguing) that the play does repeatedly. The play is a minefield of counter-memories prepared to detonate and to disrupt the appearance of a unified public memory.

The fragility of the elaborate edifice of national memory, the construction of which has been carefully supervised by Henry, becomes apparent in the Epilogue, which removes the keystone of that edifice. When the Chorus reminds audiences of the brevity of Henry's reign and his triumph at Agincourt, the champion tamer of memory seems victim to it in the end. Furthermore, the Epilogue quietly challenges the very heroism of remembering, that second Agincourt fought by Henry, Fluellen, the Chorus, the Lord Chamberlain's Men, and the armies of their audiences. The Chorus has repeatedly suggested that the collective remembrance of author, players, and audience is as vigorous and heroic an action as were the English assaults on the French at Harfleur and Agincourt. Now the Chorus, which has been "remembering" the audience of its processes of "abridgement" (5.0.43–4) and of that which passes between acts, ends by reminding us that Henry's life, "small time" (5.3.5), was already abridged. The theater doesn't merely abridge historical processes; history shares the theater's practice of abridgement. This last sudden reminder of Henry's abbreviated career undermines our sense of the strain and heroism implicit in what have been depicted as strenuous acts of memorializing and re-presentation (just as the play can undermine the sense of heroic effort in its depiction of Agincourt), leaving the field open for an alternative sense, several times hinted at in the play, of national memory as the product of cunning and artful manipulation practiced by monarchs, conquerors, and colonizers against dissidents, the vanquished, and the colonized.

IRELAND BEWALED

On March 19, 1604, the new monarch with a slightly disheveled appearance and thick Scottish accent stepped onto the English political stage and made gestures toward stage-managing his new nation's historical and political memory when addressing his first English parliament. James began his first speech to parliament by invoking England's "late Soueraigne of famous memory," who unfortunately left James a legacy of nostalgia that would burden him throughout most of his reign. Next he invoked the longevity of his own memory, as if to rival the dead Queen and simultaneously shift attention from the object to subject of memory. Promising ever to keep alive the memory of his people's acceptance of him as her lawful successor, James left no doubt that he was no "forgetful man," as Hotspur says of Henry IV. James vowed always to recall with gratitude the readiness with which he was embraced as England's legitimate ruler:

> Shall I euer? nay, can I euer be able, or rather so vnable in memorie, as to forget your vnexpected readinesse and alacritie, your euer memorable resolution, and your most wonderfull coniunction and harmonie of your hearts in declaring and embracing mee as your vndoubted and lawfull King and Gouernour? Or shall it euer bee blotted out of my minde, how at my first entrie into this Kingdome, the people of all sorts rid and ran, nay rather flew to meet mee?[37]

One of King James VI/I's most pressing tasks was to deflect a potent, although certainly not universal, nostalgia for his cousin, the recently deceased queen. One means of doing so was to stress his descent not from Elizabeth's father but from the first Tudor monarch, Henry VII, "that King of happy memorie" who "was the first Vniter [of England], as he was also the first-ground-layer of the other Peace."[38] Remarking the parallel with Elizabeth's grandfather allowed him to represent himself as a peacemaker between Protestant and Catholic factions in Europe as a whole and as the uniter of a fractured island. Henry's marriage to Elizabeth of York marked the end of the long period of civil strife known as the Wars of the Roses; "the other Peace" refers to the Treaty of Medina del Campo with Spain in 1489. James's reference to the earlier treaty looks ahead to his own treaty with Philip III of Spain later that year (talks began in May and the Treaty of London was ratified by August 1604), concluding the expensive, twenty-year-old Spanish War. His reference to the union as a joining of two halves—both of the isle and of his life[39]—itself enacts the political movement toward absorption and erasure, as Wales, which had been politically and culturally appropriated by England largely during the reign of Henry VIII, has been effaced, made invisible in this representation of the island as of "two halves," England and Scotland. James relegated the absorption of Wales, begun by the Acts of Union of 1536 and 1543 but completed rather gradually over the course of the sixteenth century, as English laws and customs largely displaced Welsh cultural practices, to an afterthought. But for at least ten years, the absorption of Wales was continually in English minds as analogous to England's attempts to subjugate a troublesome and resistant Irish population. The addition of Wales in a gesture that both recalls and marginalizes or erases it—"Do we not remember, that this Kingdome was diuided into seuen little Kingdomes, besides Wales?"—could potentially serve as a disruptive counterexample, uneasily reminding the King's largely English audience that union with a neighboring kingdom or principality usually did, in fact, involve subjugation and suppression of one culture at the expense of another.[40]

A moment of historical transition like James's accession is both an occasion for recollection, for legitimating the present by asserting continuity with the past, as well as for forgetting, because it marks a beginning or new departure. The beginning marked by James's inaugural speech to his first parliament gestures in both directions. Transitioning to the touchy union issue, however, he suddenly inverted the values of remembrance and forgetting in one of the most telling passages of the speech. King James, like Renan, would prove keenly aware of how indebted a unified nation would be to the power to forget, although James was in favor of national expansion, Renan against.

In laying before a recalcitrant parliament the "great benefits that by that Vnion [of England and Scotland] do redound to the whole Island," James recalled a time when not only England but other great monarchies as well were "diuided, and euery particular Towne or little Countie, as Tyrants or Vsurpers could obtaine the possession, a Segniorie apart." England in particular was divided into seven Saxon kingdoms: "Do we not yet remember, that this Kingdome was diuided into seuen little Kingdomes, besides Wales? And is it not the stronger by their vnion? And hath not the vnion of Wales to England added a greater strength thereto?" Greatly exaggerating the cultural uniformity of England and Scotland, and displaying no awareness of the degree to which he seemed a foreigner to his new subjects, James asked parliament, "Hath not God first vnited these two Kingdomes both in Language, Religion, and similitude of manners?" Now they were to be united further in his royal person, "alike lineally descended of both the Crownes."[41]

Scotland and England will be joined by peaceful means, the King maintains: not "by the speare of Bellona" but by the wedding ring of *Astrea*."[42] The earlier union of England was accomplished much less peacefully: "one of them behooued to eate vp another, till they were all vnited in one."[43] But even this bellicose scenario did not result in one small kingdom imposing its culture and will upon others. Rather, the happy result was the larger and stronger monarchies of contemporary Europe, in each of which no single part claimed "priority of place":

> And yet can *Wiltshire* or *Devonshire*, which were of the *West Saxons*, although their Kingdome was of longest durance, and did by Conquest ouercome diuers of the rest of the little Kingdomes, make claime to Prioritie of Place or Honour before *Sussex*, *Essex*, or other Shires which were conquered by them? And haue we not the like experience in the Kingdom of *France*, being composed of diuers Dutchies, and one after another conquered by the sword?[44]

Recalling that James conveniently relegated Wales to the borders of his narrative, so to speak, because "Prioritie of Place" most certainly did define England's relations with Wales, it seems as if he were trying to head off any such assertion of priority in the relation between his new inheritance, England, which he himself described as the "land of promise," and the "wilderness and barren soil" of his own, relatively impoverished native land.[45]

In his next sentence James naturalizes the process of nation-building, transforming it from a contingent historical result of uncertain wars and conquest to an inevitable, natural process:

> For euen as little brookes lose their names by their running and fall into great Riuers, and the very name and memorie of the great Riuers swallowed vp in the Ocean: so by the coniunction of diuers little Kingdomes in one, are all these priuate differences and questions swallowed vp."[46]

Union, like a court of law, settles disputes among principalities, which are denigrated as "priuate differences and questions." The impermanence of the identities of "little Kingdomes" is suggested by the simile of the river, commonly associated with the passage of time as well as territorial boundaries. The sea, by contrast, is permanent and also primordial, like Britain itself, according to the myth subscribed to by James and supported by Jacobean antiquarians. James's conceit supports Adrian Poole's observation,

> Forgetting seems to require a kind of liquefaction . . . From classical antiquity onwards forgetting is associated with liquid, with the

> drugged wine that Helen serves Menelaus and their guest Telemachus in *Odyssey IV*, with the "river of unmindfulness" at the end of Plato's *Republic*, and the river Lethe of Virgil's *Aeneid VI*, from which souls must drink before they achieve reincarnation.[47]

In a startling anticipation of Ernest Renan's analysis late in the age of European nationalism, James implied, toward the very beginning of that age, that it is not so much the strengthening of collective memories as their attenuation that leads to union and produces nations.

Beneath this performance by the new monarch, one may sense two anxieties. The first is a wish to have his new subjects forget his own foreignness, his all-too-patent differences in custom and manner that separated him from both his new subjects and his predecessor, now the object of considerable nostalgia. As one biographer writes of the first impression he made on the English,

> But it must be admitted that the blood of Brute in the veins of King James was less obvious to his new subjects than something rather more recent—and more Scottish. They beheld a middle-aged Scotsman (James was approaching thirty-seven) with a broad Scots accent, a homely fellow, stocky and rather untidy, with a pleasantly convivial manner to his intimates.[48]

Neither standing on ceremony nor taking any delight in the public ceremony that Elizabeth used to such great political effect, James exhibited an "indifference to ceremonial" that soon "became public talk."[49] In his speech James insisted too much on the cultural uniformity of the two realms he commands: "Hath not God first vnited these two Kingdomes both in Language, Religion, and similitude of maners?"[50] Second, James's interweaving of the rhetoric of remembering and forgetting throughout his speech makes explicit his wish to show himself ruler of England by mastering its collective, national memory. James's speech, like Shakespeare's second sequence of history plays, may serve to remind us of the extent to which the maintenance of power depends upon a ruler's ability to govern how his people remember the past. Both confirm Foucault's assertion that "if one controls people's memory, one controls their dynamism."[51] It is an elusive control, of course, and one that James would never achieve, as his Project for Union foundered throughout his reign. England and Scotland would not become united politically until the Act of Union in 1707; until then they remained separate states despite the union of crowns.

Well before both James's advancement of the Project for Union and Shakespeare's *Henry V*, Elizabethans seemed aware of the importance of forgetting as both an instrument and an achievement of colonization. Writing specifically of the colonization of Ireland, Sir Thomas Smith summarized English aims there in 1565: "To augment our tongue, our laws, and our religion in the Isle, which three be the true bands of the commonwealth whereby the Romans conquered and kept long time a great part of the world."[52] In A *View of the Present State of Ireland* (1596), Edmund Spenser advocated policies designed both to wean the Irishman from loyalty to the head of his Sept and "in short time [to] learn quite to forget his Irish nation."[53] Like Spenser's *View* and like the speech the new king would deliver to parliament, *Henry V*, in spite of its historical theme of remembrance, makes it clear that England and Henry are just as interested in fostering a kind of cultural amnesia to help produce a union. It is equally apparent that the memories of "little brookes" and "great Riuers" will not be "swallowed vp" indiscriminately. Some will be swallowed and digested more completely than others. Specifically, it is Ireland that seems destined for sacrifice on the altar of Mnemosyne, although the largely pacified Welsh are quite explicitly admitted to the community of her votaries.

No less important to the politics of *Henry V* than England's last Continental possession is "the first English colony," as Christopher Hill calls Ireland.[54] Jonathan Dollimore, Alan Sinfield, and Philip Edwards all regard the attempt to conquer France in the play and the promised union at the end as representing "the attempt to conquer Ireland and the hoped-for unity of Britain."[55] I believe this is right, although I think Ireland is summoned even more powerfully by the example of Wales. The play offers not one but two representations of Ireland and, in a sense, two alternatives: brutal conquest *à la* France or passive absorption *à la* Wales. This double representation soothes whatever bad conscience the play might evidence regarding Ireland, as if whatever happens to Ireland is Ireland's choice.[56] Were Ireland to follow the example of Wales, it would be bribed in the currency of remembrance and allowed its own Fluellens, so long as their memories could be fitted to English memory as neatly as that of the Welsh.[57] This was an unlikely prospect given the enormous advantage England possessed with regard to Wales because of the Tudors' Welsh heritage.

"Quite unhistorically," writes Philip Edwards in *Threshold of a Nation*, "Shakespeare introduced his quartet of the Welsh Fluellen, the Irish Captain MacMorris, the Scottish Captain Jamy, and the English Gower as a tribute to the Tudor idea of Britain as a union of peoples setting out to conquer foreigners."[58] In actuality, however, there were several contingents of Irish soldiers and many Welshmen in Henry's army at Agincourt, although no Scot, according to Holinshed, except King James I of Scotland, Henry's prisoner since the age of eleven.[59] Still, Edwards is essentially right in seeing the captains as an anachronistic reference to the Elizabethan myth of an originally unified Britain that was on its way to being pieced together again.[60] Even in Elizabeth's reign, before James proclaimed himself king of Britain in 1604 and before his prolonged campaign for the Project for Union, the idea of a once-unified Britain that had been sundered by the formation of individual nations was well established. John Turner has written of the historical myths of a unified Britain, ultimately designed to legitimize the power of the Tudor monarchy: "Genealogies were constructed to derive the Tudor dynasty directly out of the line of Brutus, and ancient prophecies were interpreted to show each Tudor monarch as a second Brutus, come to reunite for ever the divided kingdoms of England, Wales and Ireland."[61] The four captains in *Henry V* bear testimony to the Elizabethans' growing conviction that the national unit was not England but England, Wales, Scotland, and Ireland.[62]

The expansion of the national unit was a timely issue in 1599, when the Elizabethan conquest of Ireland was at a turning point. The Great Irish Revolt of the 1590s was perhaps the most acute crisis that Elizabeth had to face in the latter years of her reign, following the defeat of the Armada. England was attempting to incorporate Ireland into the English administrative system as it had Wales, which, unlike Ireland, "bent before the English rather than faced them."[63] The year before the play appeared onstage, the Elizabethan conquest of Ireland suffered its most crushing setback at the Battle of Yellow Ford (August 14, 1598), when the defeat of English troops effectively collapsed English authority on the island. Later that same year the Munster plantation was overthrown by Irish rebels under the leadership of Hugh O'Neill, second earl of Tyrone. If Ireland were to slip completely out of English control, it could be used as a base for foreign attacks on England by Catholic interests, especially Spain. Ireland in the 1590s seemed a repetition of Wales in the early 1400s, and Tyrone's rebellion reminiscent in some ways of the revolt that Prince Henry had helped to quell and to which Shakespeare made repeated reference in the *Henry IV* plays, namely, the revolt of Owain Glyn Dŵr.[64] It was in an atmosphere of crisis that Robert Devereux, the second Earl of Essex, was dispatched to Ireland on March 27, 1599 to put down a virtual national revolt against English rule. This is the expedition referred to by the Chorus in what Gary Taylor identifies as "the only explicit, extra-dramatic, incontestable reference to a contemporary event anywhere in the canon."[65] In Act 5 the Chorus sets up a triple correspondence between the senators and plebeians of ancient Rome pouring forth to welcome Caesar, the similar welcome of Henry by London's citizens, and the projected welcome (on a smaller scale) of Essex returning from the Irish wars.

Henry VIII adopted the title "king of Ireland" in 1541. But loyalty to the crown was not immediate, to say the least. Only the English inhabiting the Pale around Dublin were consistently obedient, and it was left to Elizabeth to more vigorously commit resources and troops for the control of Ireland. Essex would fail miserably in his attempt at pacification and return to London in disgrace after only twenty-one weeks. Because Wales served the English as a precedent if not a model for their hoped-for annexation of Ireland, the play's references to Wales may perform a complex act of remembering and forgetting Ireland and Essex's failure to pacify it. English policy toward Ireland, like most colonial policy, was amnesiac; the play, by "forgetting" the Ireland that was its most immediate context, mimics that policy; it does not necessarily follow, however, that the play is complicit with England's nationalist ideology, because (as we have seen) it exposes the national and imperial mechanisms of forgetting.

Of Shakespeare's quartet of captains, the Welshman Fluellen and the Irishman MacMorris make the strongest impression. The two roles are in some respects equivalent. Both seem designed to elicit an often condescending affection mixed with admiration. Of MacMorris, the English Captain Gower says, "The Duke of Gloucester, to whom the order of the siege is given, is altogether directed by an Irishman, a very valiant gentleman, i'faith" (3.3.10–12), although in the next speech Fluellen will brand him an "ass" (1. 15). But Fluellen, to whom the play owes a far greater debt, is a droll mixture of fierce loyalty, explosiveness, and bookishness, always equipped with volumes of Tacitus and Plutarch, which more seriously summon the context of ancient Rome, the model for the Elizabethans' imperial vision.[66] Besides length, the critical difference between the two parts that makes them so unequal as objects of audiences' remembrance is that MacMorris may be viewed as assenting to the erasure of his nation's memory, whereas Fluellen repeatedly echoes Henry's language of remembrance.

Objecting to the military tactic advanced by MacMorris to plant mines under the besieged fortifications of Harfleur, Fluellen tries to engage MacMorris in a debate concerning military theory, in which, it is clear, he intends to display his learning in a discourse about Roman military discipline. MacMorris rebuffs him, claiming the midst of a siege "is no time to discourse" (l. 46). Patriotic feelings soon take command, as Fluellen begins, "Captain MacMorris, I think, look you, under your correction, there is not many of your nation—" (ll. 59–60). MacMorris interrupts, "Of my nation? What ish my nation? Ish a villain, and a bastard, and a knave, and a rascal. What ish my nation? Who talks of my nation?" (ll. 61–3). Philip Edwards, who argues that MacMorris's retort is usually misread, takes MacMorris to mean, "What is this separate race you're implying by using the phrase 'your nation'? Who are you, a Welshman, to talk of the Irish as though they were a separate nation from you? I belong in this family as much as you do."[67] He is not, according to Edwards, daring Fluellen to make yet another retort about his people or nation but, rather, bristling at the "sense of discrimination" implied by the Welshman's remarks, as if Ireland were "a separate nation from the great (British) nation which the Welshman apparently thought he belonged to."[68] Edwards's interpretation is consistent with the amnesiac nature of power in the play, which is shown quietly forgetting anything that might challenge it: all the more powerfully, forgetting under the cloak of a rhetoric of remembrance. But his revisionist interpretation of MacMorris's lines actually limits the play's critique of the attempt to master collective memory. It is the indeterminacy of the speech, its openness to two contradictory readings—an assertion and remembrance of MacMorris's national origins on the one hand and an erasure of those origins on the other—that is reminiscent of the nearness, even the coincidence, of remembering and forgetting in Henry's rhetoric as well as in other contemporary manipulations, such as the Elizabethan modification of the calendar. MacMorris's line may in fact caricature the forgetful memory of the play's sovereign.

The Battle of Agincourt is framed by two discourses on remembrance and the English calendar: the Crispin's Day speech at the beginning and the Welsh St. David's Day at the end. At Agincourt, Fluellen, speaking to one he considers a Welsh monarch, knows that he can demand from Henry what Fortinbras describes at the end of *Hamlet* as certain "rights of memory," not a kingdom but a national heritage. In a conversation that takes place immediately after the French herald concedes, "The day is yours," the two speak to each other as if they were partners in remembrance. Henry first mentions the famous name of Agincourt, linking it with the by now talismanic names of Crispin and Crispianus, which can hardly fail to remind us of Henry's speech four scenes earlier.

KING HENRY: Then call we this the field of Agincourt,
Fought on the day of Crispin Crispianus.

LLEWELLYN: Your grandfather of famous memory, an't please your majesty, and your great-uncle Edward the Plack Prince of' Wales, as I have read in the chronicles, fought a most prave pattle here in France.

KING HENRY: They did, Llewellyn.

LLEWELLYN: Your majesty says very true. If your majesties is remembered of it, the Welshmen did good service in a garden where leeks did grow, wearing leeks in their Monmouth caps, which your majesty know to this hour is an honourable badge of the service. And I do believe your majesty takes no scorn to wear the leek upon St. Tavy's day.

KING HENRY: I wear it for a memorable honour,
For I am Welsh, you know, good countryman. (4.7.80–94)

Fluellen adopts Henry's words "countryman" and "Welsh" in his next two speeches, a private and homespun attempt at emulating the king's vivid public rhetoric of remembrance in the Crispin's Day speech. Picking up the staff of keeper of the nation's memory, he now instructs his monarch, who, together with the archbishop, seems throughout most of the play to fulfill that function. Fluellen's allusion to Henry's great-grandfather Edward III and his victory at the Battle of Crécy, referred to and named earlier in the play by the French King Charles and characterized as "our too-much memorable shame" (2.4.53), establishes him as the king's "brother" in remembrance, the very thing Henry promises in his Crispin's Day speech. Of the many details from Henry's speech echoed by Fluellen, the feast of St. David, patron saint of Wales—devotion to whom the first Tudor monarch, Henry VII, encouraged at court[69]—recalls St. Crispin's. The exchange as a whole interweaves English and Welsh national memories, the Welsh victory over the Saxons, Crécy, Agincourt, and St. David's.[70]

Comparison between Ireland and Wales was irresistible, because, as George Macauley Trevelyan puts it, "The Tudors had solved the problem of Wales, by which the mediaeval English had been baffled only less completely than by the Irish question itself."[71] English audiences watching the *Henry IV* plays in 1596–1598, in which the Glendower rebellion figures so prominently, might easily have compared Henry IV's troubles in Wales to Elizabeth's in Ireland. Military and social conflict between the "wild Welsh" of the hills and the Marcher lords in the valleys, champions of English feudalism, extended throughout the Middle Ages. In the course of the fifteenth century, the independent power of the latter steadily eroded, partly because of the significant roles they played in the English dynastic conflict of the Wars of the Roses. By the end of the century, the English crown held most of the castles and estates of the marches. In Henry IV's lifetime, however, Wales was in a state of rebellion comparable to Ireland late in Elizabeth's reign.

Having been instrumental in the suppression of the Welsh rebellion under Glyn Dŵr and the reconquest of the Principality of Wales, Henry V had largely settled the Welsh question by the time of Agincourt. In 1415 English pacification of Wales was much farther along than the English pacification of Ireland in 1599, although jurisdiction in Wales was a welter of confusion until the 1530s, when Cromwell undertook the reform of county government in a way that impinged on the Church and the old feudal nobility but satisfied most Welsh landowners, leaving local power in the hands of landowners who served as JPs and sheriffs. An image of what the Elizabethans hoped to accomplish in Ireland, Henry's Wales is as much an allusion to the burning question of Ireland and the Essex expedition as the more explicit Chorus to Act 5 and the minor part of MacMorris. But whereas reference to Ireland in the play is almost always slant or indirect, Wales is remembered constantly in the play, in the dilated part of Fluellen and in references to Welsh military victory, St. David, and the Welsh practice of wearing the leek, in many respects the centerpiece of the final act. The attention the Welsh receive in *Henry V* is justified by the king's Welsh birth and associations and by the participation of Welsh soldiers in his army,[72] but it also flows from more contemporary springs: the Welsh background of the Tudor monarchy, the participation of Welsh soldiers in the Elizabethan pacification of Ireland, and perhaps even the substantial holdings in Wales of Robert Devereux, Earl of Essex. Both Elizabeth and Essex were known, like Henry V in Fluellen's conjecture, to wear the leek on St. David's Day.[73] But that Welsh national memory will not be allowed to proliferate unchecked is made clear by the instance of Dafydd ap Llewellyn ap Hywel, brother-in-law to the rebel Glyn Dŵr.

Dafydd ap Llewellyn ap Hywel, known in the play as Davy Gam, Esquire, was one of many Welsh soldiers in Henry's army at Agincourt and one of

England's few casualties. Gam is remembered in the abbreviated roll of the English dead following Agincourt (4.8.96).[74] That his Welsh background and his family's loyalty to Henry's father during the Glendower rebellion are forgotten (they receive no mention in the play) defines the difference between a living Welshman and a dead one. The patriotic memory of Fluellen is tolerated so long as it does not conflict with English national memory; the Welsh heritage of Davy Gam is quietly effaced, belying Henry's claim to Fluellen following the battle, "For I am Welsh, you know, good countryman." Henry's relation to Fluellen is a complex one. His practical joke at Fluellen's expense, passing off the soldier Williams's glove as belonging to the duke of Alençon, is turned upside down in more ways than one, as Fluellen is, from a certain angle, a running joke at Henry's expense. With his devoted interest in patriotic memory, Fluellen is potentially a broad caricature of Henry. But as a comic version of the national Rememberer, a Chancellor of the Exchequer of Memory, Fluellen may also serve the often parallel interests of Henry and Elizabeth by deflecting attention from the serious consequences of national memory and its manipulation: for instance, its crucial role in the subjugation of Ireland.

Tudor policy toward Ireland differed from policy toward Wales in several important respects, among them the attempt to suppress the native tongue altogether in Ireland.[75] The Church's translation of the Prayer Book and New Testament into Welsh in 1567 and of the entire Bible in 1588 counteracted the state's anglicizing policy. By contrast, the Prayer Book was not translated into Irish until the beginning of James's reign. In the Acts of Union of 1536 and 1543, the language clauses pertaining to Wales allowed the persistence of Welsh, although English was declared the language of government and the use of Welsh in education was discouraged. In addition, English laws supplanted Welsh, and English county government was imposed in all shires. Unlike their counterparts in Wales, Irish bishops were bidden to preach in English, although nine tenths of the population spoke Irish. A legislative act of 1537 was designed to impose English culture on Ireland in the forms of dress and language.[76] Both Old English and Gaelic Irish were commanded to wear English clothes and to speak English. The legislation was intended to remedy "the diversity of language, dress, and manners" among the Irish, which caused them to appear "'as it were of sundry sorts, or rather of sundry countries, where indeed they be wholly together one body.'"[77] A participant in the English war against Tyrone, Fynes Moryson expressed an extreme version of the Elizabethan attitude toward the Irish: "But all I have said hereof might well be spared, as if no other tongue were in the world I think it would never be missed either for pleasure or necessity."[78]

By 1541, when Henry VIII was no longer merely "lord" of Ireland but "king," his deputy there, Sir Anthony St. Leger, had already begun advancing a policy of anglicizing the kingdom of Ireland by incorporating Gaelic lordships through a policy of surrender and regrant.[79] In Wales, by contrast, the Tudors had the inestimable advantage of their Welsh heritage.[80] Most Welsh accepted the yoke of Tudor rule quite readily because they felt that they had placed one of their own on the throne of England, gaining their independence rather than bowing to servitude as a result of the events at Bosworth Field. Also, because he held the Marcher lordships of the Houses of Lancaster and York, Henry VII was a more powerful Marcher lord than any of his predecessors. When he set about to abolish both the Principality of Wales and the Marcher lordships, he did so in a way that brought parliamentary representation to Wales. In 1536 Henry VIII incorporated Wales into England on relatively equal terms in the first Act of Union in British history, which introduced English laws and administrative methods and also created twenty-four new seats allocated to Wales in the House of Commons.[81] Ultimately England aspired to have all Irish estates held or reconfirmed under English law, as had already been achieved in Wales. But the Irish, unlike the Welsh, were never offered incorporation on equal terms. And whereas in Wales the English government had actively tried to befriend the upper class, in Ireland the ruling families, most notoriously the Fitzgeralds of Kildare, were brutalized. Henry VIII hanged the Earl of Kildare and his five uncles at Tyburn, effectively ending the system of aristocratic home rule in Ireland. The aim of the Irish plantations was to implant a new, colonial English ruling class in Ireland to supplant the Irish families. The disastrous and expensive Ulster plantations of Sir Thomas Smith and Walter Devereux, first earl of Essex and father of Robert Devereux, were an important part of that policy and contributed significantly to the deterioration of Anglo–Irish relations.

Finally, Jesuit activity, which had been meager in Wales, was extensive in Ireland. In 1580 the Pope sponsored an invasion of Ireland, which, although successfully repulsed by the English, heightened Elizabethan fear that Ireland was the most dangerous and vulnerable point in all her dominions. In Wales the peasantry passively accepted the Dissolution of the monasteries, and the Welsh upper class, like the English upper class, actually profited by it. In Wales there was no Pilgrimage of Grace as there was in the north to protest the Dissolution. But in Ireland the Jesuits helped to fill the vacuum left by lack of English governance. Capitalizing on hatred of the English, the Jesuit missions succeeded to a large extent in overcoming local clan divisions and unifying the Irish nation. By the late 1590s Hugh O'Neill had become the credible leader of a movement for an independent Catholic Ireland. Altogether, some "thirty-five thousand English and Welsh levies were sent to Ireland between 1595 and 1601."[82]

In the midst of the conflict, *Henry V* offered the successfully incorporated Welsh as a model for the projected absorption of the Irish, although, like everything else in the play, this piece of wishful modeling of sixteenth-century Ireland after fifteenth-century Wales could be read ironically. For not only did Irish unwillingness to be subsumed into a larger Britain contrast with the relative cooperativeness of Wales, but Elizabeth's policy toward Ireland also differed from earlier policy toward Wales, especially that of her famous father, to whom she was often compared.

NATIONAL MEMORY AND THE CALENDAR

In addition to reminding the English of the loss of their foothold in France, the Crispin's Day speech might also have reminded them of a recent and ongoing national victory: the state's gradual appropriation from the Church of the means of collective memory. The battleground for this Elizabethan national victory was the calendar, another prominent site of contested memory. Elizabeth's government had considerable stakes in debates over the calendar and especially over observances of religious festivals. Although in 1536 Henry VIII had curtailed the number of holy days and stemmed the tide of saints' days, throughout Elizabeth's reign religious radicals pressed for further reforms, while many conservative churchmen, believing that reform had gone too far, persisted in the observance of abrogated days such as Corpus Christi and All Souls'.[83]

In Elizabeth's reign the ecclesiastical calendar was not the explosive affair that it would become in the Jacobean and Caroline periods. Controversy over the calendar under Elizabeth was limited by her policy, which, as in most other matters, was deliberately equivocal. Leah Marcus writes,

> When it came to the promotion and regulation of traditional pastimes, Queen Elizabeth allowed her policy to remain ambiguous and kept her personal taste in the background. The adamant Sabbatarians who unleashed the Marprelate pamphlets against plays, old pastimes, and the ecclesiastical hierarchy were able to convince themselves that the queen was on their side. Such measures as Queen Elizabeth did take for the regulation of pastimes were issued much less publicly than James I's declaration. Under James I and Charles I, however, the Elizabethan ambiguity was dispelled.[84]

Part of the ambiguity regarding festivals stemmed from Elizabeth's strategy of developing new secular and political alternatives to the festivals of the old Church year that would coexist with the religious celebrations of the English calendar, just as at her coronation she made her secular civic progress "the main event, one that completely overshadowed the sacred ritual."[85] The Elizabethan ambiguity is nowhere better exhibited than in *Henry V*, which shows a keen awareness of the usefulness of festivals and the memories they institutionalize for fostering social order and especially national cohesion.

The national devotional framework had been established by the Book of Common Prayer (1549, 1552, 1559), which greatly reduced the number of holy days and centered the calendar year more firmly on commemorating the life of Christ. One of the casualties was St. Crispin's Day, which, however, continued to be marked in black in most Elizabethan and Jacobean almanacs, and which "lingered in popular memory" during Elizabeth's reign, together with St. David's Day,[86] another feast day to which *Henry V* makes reference. To this reduced framework was added a significant innovation, as David Cressy points out: "Beginning in the last quarter of the sixteenth century, there was added to this prayer-book calendar a new national, secular and dynastic calendar centering on the anniversaries of the Protestant monarch."[87] Over the course of the next century, the calendar would change following the precedent set by the observance of Royal Accession Day on November 17, first celebrated in 1570 after the Northern Rebellion of the previous year: "Momentous episodes involving Queen Elizabeth and the Spanish Armada, the Gunpowder Plot and the fortunes of the Stuart kings, were memorialized and commemorated as signs of God's interest in his Protestant nation." Eventually, writes Cressy, "the anniversary of each monarch's accession and the recollection of famous 'deliverances' shaped a calendar unique for its patriotism and its contentiousness."[88] The reshaping of the English calendar along secular and political lines was already well under way in 1599, by which time Royal Accession Day—"a nationwide annual celebration, without precedent in early reigns"[89]—had been celebrated for nearly three decades.

Popular acceptance of a day of prayer and festivity on November 17, "the first annual concert of bells that was not tied to the Christian year,"[90] seems to have been aided by the circumstance that it fell on the former feast of St. Hugh of Lincoln. As Cressy writes, "The national dynastic observance was conveniently grafted on to a regional custom, and the ringing could simultaneously satisfy conservative religious instincts and honour the Protestant queen."[91] Furthermore, since the Reformation had erased many popular feast days from the calendar, particularly Corpus Christi with its elaborate processions and pageantry, "The rise of the Queen's Day festivities enabled these energies to be concentrated into a stream designed to glorify the monarchy and its policies."[92] But this grafting clearly did not erase the sense of competition between national ceremony and religious festival. A participant at one of the annual tilts referred to November 17 as "a holiday which passed all the Pope's holidays."[93] Objections to the Queen's Day festivities, although necessarily muted, came from both the Puritan and Catholic camps, which leveled charges of pagan idolatry. According to the Puritan malcontent Robert Wright, it had the shocking effect of deifying Queen Elizabeth.[94]

The coincidence of St. Hugh of Lincoln's feast day with Elizabeth's Accession Day made for an ambiguity that could alternately cause resentment, protect celebrants, or serve the crown. Catholics could continue to celebrate a saint's day under the guise of honoring their Protestant monarch, but they could also interpret it as part of a program for displacing or erasing Church festivals, complaining that the queen's birthday (which fell on the eve of the

Virgin Mary's nativity and exacerbated the sense of competition with it) and her "Accession Day were observed with more solemnity than the great festivals of the Church."[95] On the whole, the convergence seemed to do the cult of Elizabeth more good than harm. Conservative Anglicans harboring reservations about the extremity of reforms could satisfy their devotion to the queen and the Church simultaneously. More militant Protestants, on the other hand, could rejoice in the displacement of a popish holiday with one honoring the Protestant savior of the nation. Protestants who had formerly associated bell-ringing with saints' days could now accept bells being rung for the queen.

Elizabethans would therefore have recognized in Henry's Crispin's Day speech the situation of a major patriotic event coinciding with a religious festival.[96] Just as proponents of the queen's Accession Day capitalized on former observances of the feast of St. Hugh of Lincoln, so Henry's speech takes full advantage of this happy convergence. Overhearing the earl of Warwick wishing the English soldiers were greater in number, Henry delivers his rousing Crispin's Day speech moments before Mountjoy's final embassy to offer clemency in exchange for the king's ransom:

> This day is called the Feast of Crispian.
> He that outlives this day and comes safe home
> Will stand a-tiptoe when this day is named,
> And rouse him at the name of Crispian.
> He that shall see this day and live old age
> Will yearly on the vigil feast his neighbours
> And say 'Tomorrow is Saint Crispian.'
> Then will he strip his sleeve and show his scars,
> And say, 'These wounds I had on Crispin's day.'
> Old men forget; yet all shall be forgot,
> But he'll remember, with advantages,
> What feats he did that day. Then shall our names,
> Familiar in his mouth as household words,
> Harry the King, Bedford and Exeter,
> Warwick and Talbot, Salisbury and Gloucester,
> Be in their flowing cups freshly remembered.
> This story shall the good man teach his son,
> And Crispin Crispian shall ne'er go by
> From this day to the ending of the world
> But we in it shall be remembered. (4.3.40–59)

The speech as a whole bears testimony to the importance of controlling memory both for Henry and for the English nation in the 1590s, when England's sense of itself was shifting in imperial directions.[97] References to St. Crispin's Day chime throughout the speech as if to imitate the bell-ringing that customarily marked the observance of saints' days in early Tudor

England.[98] This extraordinary attention to the feast day of the brothers Crispin and Crispianus, Roman shoemakers who traveled through France propagating the Christian faith, may be motivated partly by the war with France, because an English victory on the feast day of two French saints would prove particularly satisfying. It serves an even more important psychological purpose in marking the coming battle (and, by implication, the current expedition to Ireland), with all the uncertainty about its outcome for the assembled troops, as remembrance. Henry's repeated references to future recollection of the battle, aided by the observance of a feast day regularly marked in black in Elizabethan and Jacobean almanacs, are consistent with his references to the event as a reenactment of past victories. Both ways of referring to the battle help impart to it the safe and settled quality of something already accomplished, preserved, sheltered, even sacralized by memory. In this respect it mimics the Epilogue, which similarly projects a dangerous military venture, Essex's expedition to Ireland, as accomplished. In both passages, the Crispin's Day speech and the Epilogue, power projects an image of itself as controlling the future, transmuting the wild and refractory into obedient subject, the uncontrollable future into memory. The irony of these attempts in *Henry V* is that the past turns out to be not an obedient kingdom but a site of struggle and contestation, the outcome of which is as uncertain as that of the anxiously awaited battle.

But the most important effect of Henry's speech is to yoke one of the most celebrated victories in English military history with the ecclesiastical calendar. *Henry V* is in many respects a calendrical play, making repeated references not only to Crispin's Day but also to Whitsuntide, St. Bartholomew's, and St. David's Day. Henry's speech at Agincourt reenacts the transformation of the calendar, which was so crucial to Elizabethan England's emerging concept of itself as a nation. Like the queen's Accession Day, Agincourt Day, as projected in Henry's speech, could be read as an aggressive displacement of a popish holiday by a secular nationalistic observance; as a piece of Elizabethan opportunism, taking advantage of an established saint's day; or as a means of simultaneously serving conservative religious instincts and nationalistic ones. Henry's speech is an attempt to weave together ecclesiastical, patriotic, and even private forms of memory into a unified and centralized national memory.

The Elizabethan policy of tampering with the liturgical calendar for national ends actually had a precedent in Henry V's reign and specifically in St. Crispin's Day. During Henry's reign, Henry Chichele, archbishop of Canterbury, established "new feasts of national and military saints," often displacing established feast days. Above all of these in importance was the new feast of "St John of Beverley, the saint especially adopted by the house of Lancaster, for whom SS Crispin and Crispinian had to make way on October 25, the anniversary of Agincourt."[99]

Like Henry's speech, the opening scene of the play echoes the Elizabethan conversion of a predominantly ecclesiastical calendar to a national, dynastic, secular one. A scene of remembrance of sorts, the bishops' colloquy gives the impression of ecclesiastical memory channeled in nationalistic directions. Like so many other moments in the play, this scene establishes the partnership between official memory and forgetting. Henry will conveniently forget the proposed law that would cause so much of the Church's wealth to be forfeit to the crown if, in addition to a healthy contribution to the war effort, the archbishop turns in a convincing exercise in historical memory that will discredit the Salic Law and thereby legitimate Henry's claim to France. Whether played comically, as in Olivier's 1944 film, or in the sinister and darkened mode of Branagh's, Act 1, scene 2, featuring Canterbury's dilated speech on the Salic Law, is an extraordinary test of an actor's memory as well as a feat of historical memory so remarkable as to seem comically overdone. It is both a metatheatrical device for calling attention to the exaggerated interest in memory shared by players and monarchs[100] and also a way of emphasizing the artful manipulation of the national memory as overseen by Henry. Canterbury's speech suggests that the Church has been relieved of its role as caretaker of the collective memory. "Awake remembrance of those valiant dead," Ely urges as he and Canterbury remind Henry of what Exeter calls "the former lions of your blood" (1.2.115,124). But although the bishops may have bought some time before their lands are transferred to the crown, the titles to collective memory have, even as they speak, been signed over to Henry and his heirs.

OLDCASTLE FORGOT

Although forgotten by the king, Falstaff does successfully compromise Henry's purified version of national memory, and in more ways than one. Soon after the Hostess's moving evocation of Falstaff's death, there follow a few scant recollections of the substantial knight, including the Boy's "Do you not remember a saw a flea stick upon Bardolph's nose, and a said it was a black soul burning in hell?" (2.3.33–4). To quote my epigraph, "Rotten stuff is remembered" by audiences of *Henry V*, muddying slightly the "memorable mercy" that was Agincourt and ensuring that not all English in 1599 would have the same memories of *Henry V* or Henry V.

Of course, if a certain uniformity of memory is the aim of all power, then anything as variously committed to memory as a play, especially a Shakespearean one, is potentially subversive, not simply and unproblematically a nationalistic orgy of remembrance. Recall that Henry wrestles with the memory of Richard II; that some in Shakespeare's audience would have remembered Edmund Mortimer, whose claim to the throne was clearly identified by Holinshed as the cause behind the conspiracy at Southampton; that the France Henry enters is a weakened one, headed by an incompetent monarch and riven by faction between the Burgundians and Orleanists, whose erasure in some sense mimics a similar erasure of faction among the

English; that Henry's claim to the French throne in Act 1 is forgotten in Act 5 and "quietly shifts to his final demand only to be named as heir"[101]; that the dispossessed Dauphin, who in all the sources is present at the Treaty of Troyes, is absent from the fifth act[102]; that Sir John Falstaff was originally called Sir John Oldcastle after the Lollard martyr, a reference whose erasure makes Henry's reign seem more devoid of internal dissent than it actually was[103]; that Sir Thomas Erpingham, whose cloak Henry borrows, was a recanted Lollard; that Oldcastle, who fought for Hal's father in France and Wales, participated in an attempt to assassinate Henry, planning to raise a rebellion in the West Country while Hotspur's son would do likewise in the North; that the Earl of Cambridge was prepared to take advantage of the Lollards' disaffection, and that letters from Scrope and Grey to the king following their arrest mention Oldcastle (although Cambridge "did not mention the most controversial aspect of his machinations, namely, his readiness to join forces with the surviving Lollard malcontents")[104]; or that Oldcastle was eventually hanged on the gallows and subsequently burned.[105] All this is quite apart from the "rotten stuff" all audiences tend to remember, like that flea on Bardolph's nose.

National memory is so selective that it may be more justly characterized as national amnesia, as Shakespeare himself would have experienced firsthand. Pressured to change the name of Oldcastle as a result of influence exerted by Oldcastle's descendants and "'others allso whoe ought to haue him in honourable memorie,'"[106] Shakespeare might have felt disposed to write a play about the machinations of public memory. In the sixteenth century the Lollard leader was variously remembered both as a proto-Protestant martyr and as a dissolute heretic. Subsequent to the name change, Taylor notes, Shakespeare plays metatheatrically on the fact of the suppression by having characters themselves momentarily forget Falstaff's name. Mistress Page asks Robin in *Merry Wives*, "What do you call your knight's name, sirrah?" (3.2.17–18). And Fluellen, in the passage comparing his king to Alexander the Great (4.7.34–41), also stumbles over the name, only to have it supplied by Gower.[107] Long before he is forgotten by his old friend the king, the original identity of this knight who seems so forgetful of his place, duties, and function has been, in turn, firmly denied and forgotten.[108] Constructed of layer upon layer of forgetting, Falstaff's character is nothing so much as a dilated figure of forgetfulness itself, its importance swelling for an England reinventing itself as a nation-state.

The extraordinary force of the epilogue to *Henry V*, which transforms Henry from vivid, bodied presence to wraith in a matter of seconds, derives in part from the speed with which Henry has joined the ranks of the ghosts he has been battling. "Thus with imagined wing our swift scene flies/ In motion of no less celerity/ Than that of thought," the Chorus had said of the play's swift changes of scene (3.0.1–3). The play's final scene change, from play to page, speech to writing, vivid oral re-presentation of history to "Our bending author," "with rough and all-unable pen"

(5.3.1–2), and from the present play to the audience's theatrical memories of the earlier *Henry VI* plays ("Which oft our stage hath shown," 5.3.13), with equal alacrity makes ghosts of us all, as Hamlet would say: author, players, historical figures, and audiences. In contrast to the ending of *Richard III,* this one looks backward, imparting the sense that this play, like its predecessors on the reign of Henry VI, has passed into history. Like a segment of history, we can now delude ourselves that we see it whole, from its genesis in our "bending author" to its recession into theatrical history and the popular memory of its audiences, although the play bears multiple reminders that the "whole" that we see is largely specious because produced by manifold excisions.

Henry V is a play about the need to unify and control the popular memory, but Shakespeare has written it (as well as its immediate predecessors) in such a way that our memories of *Henry V* (and of Henry V) are as likely to divide theater audiences as to unite, far more so than the earlier sequence of histories. In other words, the form of the play belies the thrust of its theme of national unity amidst difference. It is a play that generates unusually conflicted and opposed responses and interpretations. Mimicking the king's own manipulation of popular memory, it challenges and plays with our own memories. For instance, immediately after Henry has given the command that "every soldier kill his prisoners," in response to the sound of an alarm signaling that "the French have reinforced their scattered men" (4.6.35–7), the English captain, Gower, interprets the recent action quite differently, as if to show us not "history in the making" in the usual sense of the phrase, but rather the manufacturing of history: history being actively shaped by erroneous or misleading interpretations and judgments. Historical error, *Henry V* shows, did not have to wait for chroniclers and playwrights. It was a part of "being there," at the event itself. Gower states with utter confidence that the king's order stems from a quite different event: "'Tis certain. There's not a boy left alive, and the cowardly rascals that ran from the battle ha' done this slaughter. Besides, they have burned and carried away all that was in the King's tent: wherefore the King most worthily hath caused every soldier to cut his prisoner's throat. Oh, 'tis a gallant king!" (4.7.4–8). The gallantry of the order, of course, is contestable, but the divided memory that Gower's interpretive act imposes on audiences—in my experience, students and audience members alike recall this episode in divergent ways—is extreme. In the divided interpretations that it invites, *Henry V* reinforces the sense of the play that national unity, like the dramatic unities as well as the unity of its theater audiences, can be achieved only through the artful manipulation of memory and suppression of difference.

It is the very selectiveness of his memory or memory as denial that Henry must firmly deny. His uncle Exeter, serving as ambassador, presents a roll or document containing a genealogical table to the French King Charles, saying of his nephew's claim to the crown of France,

> That you may know
> 'Tis no sinister nor no awkward claim
> Picked from the wormholes of long vanished days,
> Nor from the dust of old oblivion raked,
> He sends you this most memorable line,
> In every branch truly demonstrative. (2.4.85–90)

Exeter distinguishes two types of memory, fragmentary and organic. The fragmentary amounts to a scrounging through the rubble heap of history for whatever scraps will substantiate a claim[109]; the organic is ostensibly whole, as the metaphors of line, tree, and branch all suggest. Only the most forgetful of readers and viewers, I submit, could mistake the national memory of Shakespeare's *Henry V* for the latter kind.

Exeter's representation of memory as whole and organic reminds me of my third epigraph, from Ernest Renan. Of course Renan is concerned with national unity, but his claim would seem to hold ramifications for other forms of unity as well. I like to imagine that Shakespeare's notorious disregard for certain kinds of unities, including the classical unities, might derive from a suspicion like Renan's that "unity is always effected by means of brutality." *Henry V* seems the product of a keen awareness that the unity of a nation or a play may be not only precarious but also specious and the result of sometimes brutal campaigns of forgetting.

5 Coda
The History Play as Palimpsest in *King John*

Shakespeare can serve to remind the English, and some others, that remembering and forgetting are as inseparable from each other as winners and losers. And that it is not always easy to tell which is which.

—Adrian Poole[1]

Critics for the most part concur in regarding *King John* as a transitional text between the two historical tetralogies.[2] Phyllis Rackin writes of "the radical separation of *King John*, the most Machiavellian of all Shakespeare's histories, from the temporal and causal chain that unites the two tetralogies."[3] A play outside the main line of succession of Shakespeare's history plays and bearing little affiliation with, or filial piety toward, historiographic sources, it is a dramaturgical bastard, so to speak, bearing a strong resemblance to its dominant figure Philip.[4]

Like Philip the Bastard, the play as a whole acts in unpredictable ways. Shakespeare's earliest history plays, set in the reign of Henry VI, depict struggles to hold onto a heroic past represented by the deceased warrior-king, Henry V. In these plays, Phyllis Rackin has shown, in her indispensable study *Stages of History*, the recurring threats to the English historical record are represented at the outset as foreign and feminine.[5] In the course of the cycle they become increasingly associated with figures who are masculine and English: the commoner Jack Cade in *2 Henry VI* and eventually the King himself, Richard III, the master at making others forget,[6] at least until the past he has attempted to suppress returns to exact its revenge in the form of his victims' ghosts, visiting him the night before the Battle of Bosworth Field. One of the lessons of *Richard III* is that however one may overmaster the living, one may never entirely subdue the dead.

Rackin has persuasively described Shakespeare's histories as being guided by a "double agenda: the historical story they tell is also a story of historiographic reproduction. Shakespeare's historical protagonists, in fact, repeatedly conceive their actions as versions of history-writing."[7] The early histories stage a battle between the production of history and its effacement. Beginning with Henry V's death, *1 Henry VI* "can be seen as a series of attempts on the part of the English to write a history that will preserve Henry's fame." In the teeth of the historicizing English, "French victories

. . . threaten to erase Henry's name from the historical record."[8] His characters' efforts to keep the past alive double the playwright's own, and in turn are doubled by his audience's struggles to make order out of, and thereby make available to memory, a dramatic structure that is "loose and episodic."[9] The loose structures of these plays require audiences to battle alongside the English armies in the plays against the enemies of memory: disorder, historical erasure, and oblivion.

In the plays that are the subject of this study, Shakespeare's second cycle and the transitional *King John*, the forces of effacement become increasingly internal to the historical memory that the English regularly fight to preserve. The power to forget and to make others forget, and the related power to revise or rewrite historical memory, increasingly become partners rather than enemies of English national identity. It is as though Shakespeare, in dramatizing two divisive historical figures who were heroes of the English Reformation, King John and Sir John Oldcastle, became increasingly aware of the centrality of historical erasure in the ongoing processes of reform in Elizabeth's reign, of the utility of forgetting in responding to the traumatic effects of the Reformation, of the importance of a collective amnesia for enhancing national unity, and of the power of the stage in contributing to the reshaping of English historical memory. As Shakespeare reworked the divisive historical materials of King John's reign, forgetting rises in stature, like an Elizabethan new-made man.

In a superb study of the roles played by remembering and forgetting in the construction of individual identity in the early modern period, Garrett Sullivan writes,

> Memory . . . is intimately linked with notions of discipline and order; forgetfulness, associated as it is with practices and physiological processes antithetical to ideals of bodily comportment, connotes idleness, sloth, lethargy, excessive sleep . . . Memory is aligned with an array of social virtues—studiousness, diligence, rigor, piety—while forgetfulness and forgetting are associated, in a range of discourses, with everything from illness to alienation from God . . . In sum, oblivion has its own forms of embodiment and social practice, ones that are coded as at best passive and at worst sinful and erosive of identity.[10]

Renaissance drama, Sullivan adds, "offers important qualifications to this characterization" of forgetting as marked by passiveness and a lack of discipline.[11] Largely because of its engagement with a figure whose recollection was "troublesome" to many in the wake of the Reformation, *King John* plays an important role in the revaluation of mnemonic values in Shakespeare's canon. If it does not straightforwardly celebrate the value of forgetting embodied in the figure of Philip the Bastard, it certainly challenges audiences to question the values they attach to memory and its occlusion.

SHIFTING ALLIANCES

Placing unusual demands upon audience's memories, *King John* is notable for what A. R. Braunmuller has called its "diffused rather than concentrated effects."[12] It tempts its audiences to forget more than it helps them to remember characters like King Philip II, who is replaced as the father-surrogate of Louis by Cardinal Pandulph. In Act 3, Philip "(quite unhistorically) loses his influence over Louis and vanishes from the play." The three principal women in the play are similarly subject to a disappearing act that tests spectators' memories: "The play's dramatic economy treats Eleanor and Constance almost as brutally as its political contrivance treats Blanche. No longer needed, all three are dismissed or forgotten."[13] *King John*'s audiences are likely to feel that, like their own memories of the play, English memory within the play is multiple and fractured. For instance, "the legacy of the great Coeur-de-lion," as Phyllis Rackin writes, "is discredited and dispersed."[14]

With its complex national politics, *King John* also challenges its audience to form permanent alliances with French or English forces. In other words, audiences experience the tenuousness of political alliances within the play through their own shifting allegiances. Equally tenuous are the affiliations of various character groupings with or against a stable English historical record. *King John* makes it unusually difficult for audiences not only to identify a political enemy but also to determine which political interests stand for, and which against, the durability of English historical memory. The nemeses of English history in the *Henry VI* plays—the combined forces of the French and the feminine—have now become its sometime defenders: a French character, the Dauphin, who anxiously promotes the mnemonic stability promised by writing, and one of the prominent women of the play, Constance. She is anything but constant in her desire for either permanent remembrance or forgetfulness, promoting her son's rights of memory while he is alive, praying for oblivion when she thinks him dead. Early modern texts, Sullivan shows, associated the devalued term forgetting with effeminization. Lethargy, a condition linked by humoral theory to the moist and cold properties of the female body, "makes the male body more like a female one."[15] More recently, Lina Perkins Wilder has explored the art of memory as a masculine discipline in Shakespeare's plays. Like Sullivan, Wilder is interested in challenges to the association of a disciplined memory with the construction of an early modern masculinity. Noting that the Hostess in *2 Henry IV*, for example, functions as the keeper of Falstaff's memory, she concludes that "here memory begins to look like a woman."[16] In the figure of the mnemonically inconstant Constance, too, memory begins to look like a woman, but, I would argue, memory of a highly particular form: her inconstant commitment to remembering resembles the anxious and conflicted allegiance to the past of a culture that, having survived the traumas of the English Reformation, could no longer afford to embrace the dominant value and discourse of remembering as it had in the not so distant past. Like the culture to which it belonged, the play as a whole is equally inconstant to the value of remembering the past. Its commitment to preserving the historical record from the forces of oblivion seems as uncertain as the audience's allegiance to England and France, as the play's later speeches, in Braunmuller's words, "increasingly obscure or confuse the combatants' legal and ethical positions."[17]

It is John and not his more sympathetic rivals Constance and Arthur who issues the most memorable injunction to remember. Insinuating to Hubert that he wishes him to do away with Arthur, John demures from fixing a reward for the deed, although he demands fixed intent from Hubert, elicited by "Remember" (3.3.69). Nevertheless, he himself will later conveniently forget his own responsibility for the murder. John's allegiance to remembering remains as slippery and ambiguous as virtually all alliances in the play. In this respect he resembles his opponent, the papal legate Pandulph, whose long and specious argument (3.1.253f.) persuades King Philip of France to break his oath to King John. Pandulph will later echo John's injunction to "remember," warning the King, "On this Ascension Day, remember well,/ Upon your oath of service to the Pope" (5.1.22–3), referring to a deal whereby in exchange for John's oath of submission, Pandulph will call off France's invasion of England. The sometime enemies Pandulph and John are both agents of oblivion deceptively wielding the language of memory.

Conversely, it is Constance, fixed (as her name implies) in a posture of grief and complaint who seems at first to align herself with the largely foreign and feminine antihistorical forces exemplified by Joan la Pucelle in *1 Henry VI*. Accused of madness by Pandulph, she protests, "I am not mad. I would to God I were,/ For then 'tis like I should forget myself./ O, if I could, what grief should I forget!" (3.4.48–50). Madness offers the tantalizing prospect of an oblivion devoutly to be wished, a consuming if not a consummation of memory. As Constance had craved self-forgetfulness, Salisbury will crave the balm of oblivion at the end of the play for his divided nation (5.2.33–9). Like shifting political allegiances in this play, there is no abiding compact between any character and either the endurance of historical memory or its cancellation.

Unlike the earlier histories, this pivotal play seems more interested in exploring the creative uses rather than the tragic consequences of forgetting. Bound to produce lapses of memory in its audiences, it is also a play about gaps in historical memory, and about the ways in which "borrowed majesty," as the French Ambassador snidely refers to King John (1.1.4), and the opportunistic self-fashioning of Philip the Bastard exploit such gaps. Perhaps it is to be expected that in a play about John's reign, Shakespeare exposed "the historical record as a fragile and dubious construct."[18] Like Oldcastle, the many-layered outrage to historical memory at the center of the second tetralogy, King John was an inherently divisive subject for Tudor historians and dramatists. "Of all the medieval kings" the one who "resisted the papacy most strongly,"[19] he became like Oldcastle a Protestant hero for many in Tudor England, largely through John Bale's play *Kynge Johan* (ca. 1539), the first English history play, and John Foxe's immensely popular and influential *Actes and Monuments* (1563). Instead of staging a confrontation between opposed royal houses as in his first tetralogy, in *King John* Shakespeare faced opposing historiographic traditions that, unlike York and Lancaster, he never successfully unites: "a protestant tradition which saw John as England's champion against interference by the Catholic powers of Europe; and an older, no less powerful tradition which saw him as a usurper who had his nephew murdered to secure his throne."[20] To retell a historical narrative of considerable controversy like the reign of King John, it was necessary to enlarge the role of what might be termed history's bastard child, oblivion. More than the usual degree of a dramatist's practice of omission or suppression was necessary in order to shape this particular subject into the form of a play.

King John shows the nearly forgotten emerging into the light of history, often through force or usurpation, and in the process taking advantage of imperfect retention of the past to advance their own interests. Both of the play's central characters, King John and Philip the Bastard, belong to the category of the "new-made," those whose authority, rank, or standing does not derive from established rules of inheritance. The Bastard is the offspring of the same coupling of remembering and forgetting that produced in the early modern period such vital possibilities for self-fashioning, as Stephen Greenblatt has shown,[21] and that, as Lawrence Stone has argued in detail, spawned widespread inflation of honors in the century leading up to the English Civil War. "Between 1540 and 1640," Stone writes,

> there steadily built up an intense acquisitive pressure for outward marks of social distinction. . . . The century witnessed changes in the composition of the English landed classes which were quite unprecedented in their scope. Families rose and fell with extraordinary rapidity, and those that rose, from yeomen to gentlemen, from gentlemen to squires and beyond, urgently demanded some open recognition of their new position.[22]

The crown's elevation of families, less common in the Elizabethan period than it was to be under the Stuarts, entailed rewriting the past on a small scale. Such families required "genealogies and titles commensurate with their wealth." Conversely, old families could be erased: "As the preamble to the patent of creation of Lord Darcy of Chiche in 1551 observed," that estate had been "almost wiped out by various chances and by death," although it was now saved from oblivion by a newly coined lord.[23]

Nearly obliterated from the historical sources Shakespeare used, appearing there "so transiently as to seem a wraith,"[24] the "virtually unhistorical"[25] Philip usurps a prominent place both in the anonymous *The Troublesome Raigne of John King of England* (1591) and Shakespeare's *The Life and*

Death of King John from the disinherited Constance and Arthur. An antihistorical figure by virtue of both his failure to be recorded in the official histories and his disputed paternity, which makes his past subject to rewriting, Philip the Bastard is newly created by Shakespeare, just as in the play he is new-made by the actions of John and Eleanor. Depending on the still disputed order of composition of *The Troublesome Raigne* and *King John*, Shakespeare either appropriates the Bastard from *Troublesome Raigne* and alters him from reluctant nobleman to the type of the contriving, upwardly mobile Elizabethan new-made man, or, if *King John* did indeed predate *Troublesome Raigne*, fashions him out of whole cloth.[26]

As the younger brother of Richard Lionheart and Geoffrey, King John, too, was at one time threatened with being forgotten by history. Nicknamed "Sans Terre" or "Lack-Land" by his parents Henry II and Eleanor of Aquitaine, John in Shakespeare's conception seems determined to inherit both space and time, land and history alike. Indeed, his claim to the throne, as against Arthur's, supported by King Philip of France, rests more on "strong possession" than right or rightful inheritance, as his mother reminds him in an aside (1.1.40). Whereas Philip the Bastard initially lays claim to the patrimony of the elder Falconbridge, King John lays claim to what might be called the patrimony of history itself, which rightfully belongs to Geoffrey's young son Arthur. *King John* does more, however, than simply show the often forgotten of history vying for a more central position and more memorable roles. It casts in a leading role not merely the (nearly) forgotten but forgetfulness itself, which, in the second tetralogy, Shakespeare increasingly reveals to be the muse of a genuinely national history.

SPACE AND TIME AS PALIMPSESTS

The relationship of Shakespeare's *King John* to the anonymous *Troublesome Raigne* has been extensively debated. In particular, the order of composition has never been decisively established. Opinions of the relationship of the two plays have ranged widely. Older theories postulated that the former was either Shakespeare's rough draft of the finished play or a bad quarto, a flawed reconstruction of Shakespeare's text. More recently E. A. J. Honigmann, L. A. Beaurline, and Brian Boyd, among others, have held that Shakespeare's play is the earlier text without maintaining that the anonymous play was a bad quarto.[27] Most critics, however, continue to regard *King John* as the later play. The anonymous author of *Troublesome Raigne* crafted a coherent narrative from the chronicle sources, a narrative shaped largely around the death of Arthur, which Shakespeare subsequently adopted, while improving the language and expanding the exploration of motives.

Beatrice Groves has recently advanced an original argument in support of this majority view by focusing on the ways in which stories are memorized and transmitted. Groves sees the stylistic differences between the two plays as issuing from "the natural process of memory and composition."[28] For instance, "the removal of 'lifeless preliminaries' [such as those in *Troublesome Raigne*] creates a more effective opening, something that is habitual in memorizing stories."[29] Groves cites psychological experiments that she sees as echoing the textual relationship between the two plays:

> *King John* and *The Troublesome Raigne* are structurally close but linguistically distinct, sharing only the occasional line or phrase. Such a textual relationship is an oddity in Shakespeare source study, but a commonplace in the study of memory. Psychological experiments have shown that while subjects can often recall the content of what they have read or seen, style and precise mode of construction are very rarely faithfully reproduced.[30]

Shakespeare's play, according to Groves, is an exercise in remembering, as evidenced by a few vestigial memories of the earlier play not fully exploited or developed in the later one: "There are . . . moments in the action of *King John* that seem to be best explained as aspects that Shakespeare remembered from *The Troublesome Raigne* but has not chosen to borrow in their entirety."[31]

Groves' intuition about the two plays being joined by "the natural processes of memory"—that is, certain characteristic ways in which memorizing an earlier story alters elements of that story—strikes me as consonant with the play's internal exploration of the social and political dimensions of remembering and forgetting.[32] I would place the emphasis, however, not on what Shakespeare selectively remembers but on the process of erasure and writing over in such a way that portions of the original, a strongly pro-Reformation text, remain visible. *King John* has the qualities of a palimpsest, a wax tablet that has been imperfectly scraped clean for reuse or a paper reclaimed for rewriting in such a way that portions of the earlier text remain legible. Beneath Shakespeare's writing may be glimpsed portions of the text he reworked. Similarly, Shakespeare's principal way of conceiving memory *within* the play is not as retrieval or recovery of the past but rather as a rewriting. Because the play's most colorful character, Philip the Bastard, bears the qualities of a palimpsest, it is fitting that the play as a whole does, too.[33] To take Groves' argument one step further, then, Shakespeare's play may be an exercise in remembering the earlier play, *The Troublesome Raigne*, that exploits the occasion to consider the way in which identities and historical memory alike bore the qualities of a palimpsest in early modern England. Shakespeare belonged to a culture for which space and time, urban spaces as well as the liturgical calendar, resembled palimpsests.

Philip serves as an apt prologue to the second sequence of history plays, which shows the past to be plural and multi-layered. In the second tetralogy, memory forms ever-closer partnerships with forgetting: in other words, Shakespeare began to represent the operations of memory for his audiences in a way that was consonant with aspects of the very city in which they dwelt. Indeed, Philip is an apt symbol of a period that saw an increased reliance on written records. "In localities throughout England," Adam Fox writes, "flexible usages were being codified into fixed form and oral traditions transmuted into written records."[34] Such growing reliance produced a growing pressure to rewrite. In a land dispute in Shropshire, "An inquisition early in the seventeenth century found that someone had erased and altered a custumal in an attempt to validate the claimed entitlements of the copyholders there."[35] According to diarist John Manningham, a law student at the Middle Temple, the antiquarian John Stow told him that in his *Survey of London* (1598), a painstaking and loving record of London's antiquities punctuated by sighs at the spoliation of many monuments by the forces of the Reformation, he deliberately omitted references to many new monuments, "because those men have bin the defacers of the monumentes of others, and soe thinkes them worthy to be deprived of that memory whereof they have injuriously robbed others."[36] The monumental face of Shakespeare's London, in other words, was a canvas on which old monuments had been partly effaced and the defacers themselves, those responsible for obliterating so much of London's and England's past, paradoxically monumentalized in their place. Stow leaves these obliterators of the past unrecorded in his *Survey*, denying those he sees as hostile to memory of London's past a memory of their own. According to Keith Thomas, the "provision of physical memorials to the dead in place of the monasteries and chantries" increased in the century following the Reformation. "Noble expenditure on such memorials is thought to have reached a peak in the forty or fifty years preceding the death of James I . . . But destruction kept pace with these new erections and the memory of the past was continually being effaced in the popular mind."[37] Still, Elizabethan London was a city whose Catholic past had been only partly erased.[38] Its monumental face bore traces of the very acts of obliteration that made it such a powerful trigger for nostalgia of the kind expressed by Stow.[39] As Steven Mullaney has written in his indispensable exploration of "the rhetoric of space" in Elizabethan London, "For Stow, London is a palimpsest of the many who have lived and died within its confines, of the people and events that were shaped by the city and that shaped it in turn, leaving the signs of their passage on its streets and conduits, its customs and rituals."[40]

In a subtly turned reading of Stow's *Survey*, Lawrence Manley shows how the nostalgic Stow, in spite of himself, managed to maintain a veneration for the past while transferring that veneration from religious to civic objects, thereby producing "an innovative civic religion" cloaked as nostalgic remembrance, "in the guise of a traditional order": "For Stowe, much of the piety that might have been reserved for religious veneration has now become invested in a civic religion based on veneration for the past."[41] Manley writes of the ongoing transformation of and displacements within London's ceremonial life, so that the Lord Mayor's "inaugural show was beginning to absorb some of the functions of the Midsummer Watch, which had in turn replaced the feast of Corpus Christi as the principal event of the civic year."[42]

Not only geographic space but ritualized time also had this palimpsest-like quality for Shakespeare and his contemporaries. David Cressy has shown at length how the development of a new Protestant calendar of national deliverance gradually displaced the older ritual calendar, with new holidays sometimes bearing preexisting calendrical associations. Even for the most radical reformers seeking to reform the old religious calendar, "it was difficult to treat the year as a neutral grid when so many of its days and seasons had religious or historical significance."[43] The traditional calendar, like the stony face of London, had been only partly effaced. The reformed calendar bore traces that might trigger either nostalgia or dangerous memories of the ritual year and of the religion that supported and was supported by it, for those inclined to make rebellious uses of the past. It was especially difficult to disentangle the agricultural calendar from the framework of the traditional Christian calendar: "The old saints' days were fondly preserved in the popular memory, governing traditional farming practices and days of markets and fairs."[44] According to Thomas,

> Almost all annual fairs . . . occurred on specific saints' days, or their eves or morrows. It was the value of such festivals for marking the days for paying rent, or carrying out other secular activities, which explains why the Elizabethan Church Calendar remained so liberally splattered with black-letter saints' days, even though they were not otherwise celebrated as holidays.[45]

Rather than a completely reformed expression of a national Protestant culture, the calendar of Elizabethan England may best be described as "layered," to adopt Cressy's term.[46] In this it resembled the half-forgotten nature of Catholicism in general, at least in the eyes of the more extreme reformers who bristled at the numerous statute Protestants in England, "those whose 'popery' was unacknowledged, half forgotten but incompletely abandoned."[47]

Elizabethan England was a period of cultural rewriting, or writing over, on a smaller scale as well: not only of monuments and the calendar but also of the very identities of individuals and families through what Philip the Bastard calls "new-made honour." Stow records a particularly intriguing instance of how "the suddaine rising of some men, causeth them to forget themselves." Surveying "Throgmorton Streete in Brodestreete warde," he comes to a house "very large and spacious, builded in the place of olde and small Tenementes." The owner of the house in question was none other than Thomas Cromwell, whom Stow describes as "Maister of the kinges

Iewell house, after that Maister of the Rols, then Lord *Cromwell* knight, Lord priuie seale, Vicker Generall, Earle of Essex, high Chamberlaine of England, &c."[48] Of course, behind that "&c" crouches Cromwell's enormous power as Henry VIII's chief minister and one of the primary architects of the English Reformation, which for Stow mark his as a career in obliteration. It is not surprising, therefore, that Cromwell's achievements trail off into a nebulous "&c" rather than reaching a triumphant conclusion. Stow's list of Cromwell's successive titles suggests a career of rising and concomitant self-forgetting, one that presumably caused him to ignore the boundaries of his land as well as those of his own person, station, and power. Stow recounts the construction of Cromwell's grand house as follows: "hee caused the pales of the Gardens adioyning to the northe parte thereof on a sodaine to bee taken downe, 22. foot to bee measured forth right into the north of euery mans ground, a line there to bee drawne, a trench to be cast, a foundation laid, and a high bricke Wall to bee builded." One of the victims of Cromwell's imperial home building was none other than Stow's father. His house was "lowsed from the ground, & bare vpon Rowlers into my Fathers Garden 22. foot, ere my Father heard thereof."[49] Although he lost thereby half of his land, Stow's father was still obliged to pay his whole rent for the year. The story of the injury done to his father and their neighbors by the chief architect of the Reformation implicitly links the erasure of property lines to those that mark identity or status: joins self-forgetting to the English Reformation's project of topographical rewriting and erasure that Stow quietly regrets in his *Survey*.

King John, a play featuring a proto-Reformation monarch and, to some of Shakespeare's contemporaries, a Protestant hero, features a character who perfectly illustrates Stow's point that "the suddaine rising of some men, causeth them to forget themselves." Unlike Stow, Shakespeare seems as ambivalent about such self-forgetfulness as he is about King John. Among other things, he seems to regard John as a partner in rewriting, erasing, and forgetting. As Shakespeare rewrites *Troublesome Raigne*, reforming many of the Reformation elements out of the play, he turns the Reformation legacy of erasure back upon the Reformation itself (or at least, its prehistory). Beneath his own palimpsest-like play, one may glimpse residues of the earlier, pro-Reformation play, as well as signs of a more ambivalent attitude toward the sixteenth-century legacy of reform. Palimpsest-like, and making a career of self-forgetting, the Bastard stands as a synecdoche for the play as a whole, for the relationship between Shakespeare's play and it source, and for the instabilities and opportunities of a century featuring widespread rewriting of both personal and collective identities.

Unlike Shakespeare's play, *Troublesome Raigne* has a stridently anti-Catholic tone. It follows the trend established by John Bale's *Kynge Johan* (c. 1538) and John Foxe's *Actes and Monumentes* (1563) in reviving the reputation of King John and rewriting him as a Protestant hero, rescuing him from the earlier, disapproving chroniclers of the Middle Ages.

Shakespeare's *King John*, therefore, with its far more neutral tone, rewrites the revisionist Protestant account of John's reign, but not in order to return him to the historical purgatory to which he had been originally assigned by medieval chroniclers. Rather, Shakespeare's rewriting acknowledges and explores the various ways in which he and his fellow playwrights were engaged in covering as well as recovering the past.

BASTARDIZING MEMORY: MINGLED LINES OF REMEMBERING AND FORGETTING

It is curious, to say the least, that a play with a disputed patrimony—is it the offspring of chronicles or of a prior play, *The Troublesome Raigne of John King of England*?—should devote so much of its own attention to the same issue, namely, the uncertain parentage of Philip the Bastard. Both *Troublesome Raigne* and *King John* feature scenes in which Philip the Bastard publicly learns his father's identity. Ed Gieskes has usefully compared the parallel recognition scenes in terms of the two Philips' attitudes toward their rise in status. *The Troublesome Raigne*'s Philip "is forced to avow his ancestry, against his better judgment, and in this involuntary manner enters the aristocracy"; Shakespeare's more complex and conniving character, by contrast, freely chooses his new identity: "His status as adopted Plantagenet is treated by the play as a vocation in our modern sense of employment."[50] This difference between reluctantly accepting and actively embracing the revelation that he is a Plantagenet and the illegitimate son of Richard Coeur-de-Lion, I would add, signals divergent ideas about the obligation to remember and the burdens placed upon the present by the past. *The Troublesome Raigne*'s Philip expresses a conservative attitude toward memory when, debating inwardly, he chastises himself for being "Forgetfull what thou art, and whence thou camst./ Thy Fathers land cannot maintain these thoughts,/ These thoughts are farre unfitting *Fauconbridge*" (*Part I,* 1.1.258–60).[51] He regards his bastardy as a blot and a cancellation, not an opportunity: "the shamefull slaunder of my parents, the dishonour of myself" (*Part I,* 1.1.89). Forgetting for the *Troublesome Raigne*'s Philip can only represent a lapse from origins and loss of identity. By contrast, Shakespeare rewrites Philip as a figure for the creative uses of rewriting his past, and in so doing, rewrites the role of forgetting itself. For Shakespeare's Philip, acknowledging his bastardy marks an opportunity for an uncertain life of service to the crown, one that holds no guarantees of financial security, unlike his previous identity as the heir of Sir Robert Falconbridge, but that may carry the prospect of advancement and untold rewards.

The evidence for the two Philips' paternal descent differs as well, in ways that are consistent with Shakespeare's accent on forgetting. Early in *Troublesome Raigne*'s recognition scene, Philip's younger brother Robert maintains that the evidence for his bastardy and relation to Richard are written plainly in his face and his body, both in motion and at rest: "looke but on *Philips* face,/ His features, actions, and his lineaments,/ And all this Princely presence shall confesse,/ He is no other but King *Richards* Sonne" (*Part I,* 1.1.168–71). Philip, however, is persuaded not by a text, even a visual one, but by a more immediate source, a voice, and in particular one that seems to have supernatural origins. Asked in the most direct manner by both John and Essex, "who was thy father?" (*Part I,* 1.1.227,231,238), Philip falls into a trance, in which he seems to repeat what the natural world utters about his parentage: "Birds, bubbles, leaves and mountaines, Eccho, all/ Ring in mine eares, that I am *Richards* Sonne" (*Part I,* 1.1.254–5).

Whereas this Philip hears voices bearing the force of divine revelation, Shakespeare's counterpart is presented as a text to be read. The Queen Mother, Eleanor, is the first to approach Philip in this manner and to read therein both visual and aural signs of her eldest son: "He hath a trick of Coeur-de-lion's face,/ The accent of his tongue affecteth him./ Do you not read some tokens of my son/ In the large composition of this man?" (I.1.85–8). The phrase "some tokens of my son" (Richard Coeur-de-lion) suggests that Shakespeare's Philip is what we might call bitextual. Both Falconbridge and Plantagenet, his palimpsest-like identity is not so easily read as Robert claims his brother to be in *Troublesome Raigne.* His face has a "trick" of Richard the Lionheart, and Eleanor's observation that "the accent of his tongue affecteth him" might suggest behavior as well as biology, conscious emulation or unconscious imitation as well as an inherited property or characteristic. His textuality seems layered, like that of a palimpsest, his identity as a Plantagenet resembling the original text to be recovered through reading beneath the overwriting or second layer of textuality, his identity as Falconbridge.

In *Troublesome Raigne*, Robert's textual metaphor for his brother derives from transparent self-interest: read my brother, he urges, he is clearly Plantagenet, all the while appearing himself to be an open book with the all too familiar motives of a brother who wishes to deprive his rival of his patrimony. Robert's textual metaphor is displaced later in the scene by the absolute certainty of revelation, a shift that is consistent with Philip's initial interest in sustaining the memory of who he is. Once confirmed a Plantagenet, as Gieskes observes, "he proceeds to behave as a person of noble descent . . . as though he had always been a member of the aristocracy."[52] In *Troublesome Raigne*, a false memory is replaced by a true one. Rather than weighing the opportunities presented by refashioning himself, this Philip does not exchange his patrimony for a career of forgetting like Shakespeare's Bastard, but rather substitutes one memory for another, without changing the value of memory itself: that is, the importance and merit of remembering and conforming to the image of who he is. *The Troublesome Raigne*'s Bastard, I would suggest, resembles a figure for the Protestant Reformation itself. Often accused by Catholic polemicists of forgetting the faith of their forebears, Protestants frequently represented the Reformation not so much as an erasure of earlier constructions of the faith as the recovery of an older and more authentic form.

Shakespeare adopts the textual metaphor that Robert deploys in *Troublesome Raigne* to persuade others of the indisputable certainty of his brother's illegitimacy, but alters it to suggest a shiver of uncertainty, opportunity, and expectation. Like a text, including the play and the chronicle sources that Shakespeare appears to have rewritten, the Bastard may continually rewrite himself as he forsakes his patrimony as the heir of a member of the gentry and enters the service of the King himself. Remarkably, he does not regard his transformation from Falconbridge to Plantagenet in terms of a recovery. Significantly, the Bastard regards his newly embraced paternity not as a revelation, a romance-like recuperation of an original, noble identity, but rather as an erasure:

> But mother, I am not Sir Robert's son,
> I have disclaimed Sir Robert and my land;
> Legitimation, name, and all is gone. (1.1.246–8)

Neither does his new identity as Plantaganet represent a stepwise advancement. His new title and rank are not merely "additions" and modifications of his identity; rather, they represent a thorough cancellation of it.[53] Not only does Shakespeare's Bastard not see his rise to Plantagenet as a restoration of an identity that had been lost, but he also relishes his newfound power to wreak havoc with others' names and identities. Erasing the paternity of Falconbridge, the Bastard gleefully imagines himself rising to a level in society where a feigned forgetfulness will be deemed a sign of power and rank if not of virtue:

> Well, now can I make any Joan a lady.
> 'Good den, Sir Richard.'—'Godamercy fellow.'
> And if his name be George, I'll call him Peter;
> For new-made honour doth forget men's names:
> 'Tis too respective and too sociable
> For your conversion. (1.1.184–9)

According to editor L. A. Beaurline, the last word, "'conversion,' probably means (1) change to something better or higher; (2) conversation."[54] The word links social courtesy with the Bastard's newly converted status. Converted through new-made honour, the Bastard will not deign to converse with those beneath him, for conversation holds a power to "convert." It is an important tool of social organization and reorganization, because to choose to converse entails a recognition of rank. The Bastard's conversion from a member of the local gentry to a member of the nobility is also marked by a change in conversation or language, as Gieskes has pointed out: Philip the Bastard exhibits "developments in his speech as he moves through *King John*."[55] It may also bear a hint of conversation's power to alter popular memory. The link between conversation and conversion is powerfully demonstrated in this play that repeatedly shows us the vulnerability of our own loyalties, whether to characters or to nations, and their tendency to be "converted" simply through speech. Like a king creating new-made honors, the converted Bastard now has the power to elevate "any Joan" to the status of a lady thanks to his own prior conversion. Like women's surnames, lower-class men's given names will lack stability in the Bastard's vision of new-found power: "And if his name be George, I'll call him Peter." Like a walking scourge of history, he may rewrite at will.

The Bastard ultimately represents the power of his author to vigorously revise chronicle histories for the stage. He signals his author's recognition of the power shared by theater companies, even while operating under the watchful eye of Sir Edmund Tilney, the Master of the Revels, to manipulate popular memory. Foucault has noted the efficacy of television and the cinema in "reprogramming popular memory, which existed but had no way of expressing itself. So people are shown not what they were, but what they must remember having been."[56] As he works with more contentious and divisive historical materials like those in *King John*, or Sir John Oldcastle in the *Henry IV* plays, Shakespeare seems increasingly aware of a similar power of the stage to reform popular perceptions of the past, of what the people remember having been.

Not so much a character with a stable identity as a figure of the power to revise the past according to one's will, the Bastard answers Hubert's question, "Who art thou?" with "Who thou wilt" (5.6.9). Having rewritten his identity, he suffers the indignity of having his own name forgotten. Blaming a lapse in memory and the darkness for his failure to recognize the Bastard, Hubert chastises himself, "Unkind remembrance, thou and eyeless night/ Have done me shame" (5.6.12–3). Far from a simple case of poetic justice, a judgment against a man who earlier announced his intent to "forget men's names," this scene reveals that the Bastard is most himself when he is forgotten. He is "who thou wilt." It is a point driven home by a previous scene that demonstrates the power of the Bastard as revisionist historian. At the climax of her scourging Austria for "fall[ing] over to my foes" (3.1.127), Constance recalls Avianus's tale of the ass wearing a lion's skin, thereby revising the commemorative function of Austria's robes, worn to recall his victory over Richard Lionheart: "Thou wear a lion's hide! Doff it for shame,/ And hang a calf's-skin on those recreant limbs" (3.1.128–9). When Austria responds, "O that a man should speak those words to me!" the Bastard takes him at his word and twice repeats Constance's line, "And hang a calf's skin on those recreant limbs" (3.1.130–1,133). Thrice enunciated, the lines function like a refrain, an emphatic verbal sign rivaling the memorable visual sign of the lion's-skin robes. After he indelibly imprints Constance's mocking line on our memories, thereby new-making Austria's identity, this figure who uses erasure to his best advantage is charged with self-forgetfulness—that is, forgetting his place—by the King. "We like not this, thou dost forget thyself" (3.1.134). Paradoxically, the King delivers this line at the very moment that, as every audience member knows, the Bastard is most pointedly himself, reinforcing our sense that the core of this new-made man's identity is a self-forgetfulness that allows him to continually refashion himself.

As psychologists' studies of memory distortion reveal, a memory's legitimacy is notoriously hard to confirm.[57] Nearly every memory, private or collective, has, like Philip, a disputable patrimony and a shadowy resemblance to its original. But it is not merely that human memory is an imperfect storage-and-retrieval system, or that forgetting represents a lapse in such a system, like an error on one's hard drive. Indeed, forgetting is in many respects constitutive of the very operations of memory. As Richard Terdiman has written of memory in the postmodern world, where the "flux of reality" has become "inexpressibly dense," "*the most constant element of recollection is forgetting*, discarding the nonretained so that retention, rememoration can occur at all."[58] Working from often contradictory chronicle sources as he dramatized the reign of King John, John Foxe's *Actes and Monumentes* as well as the internally conflicted or contradictory Holinshed's *Chronicles*, and necessarily truncating his source material in order to shape it into a two-hour play,[59] Shakespeare would have repeatedly experienced in the process of composition the need to discard "the nonretained so that retention, rememoration can occur at all." In other words, he would have been reminded by his stagecraft, from the labor of transforming chronicles into stage-plays, that the most constant element of recollection is forgetting: would have recognized in Philip the Bastard a mirror of the disputable patrimony of his own historical reenactments in his chronicle history plays. Given historiographic disputes about King John's reign, it would be nearly impossible for Shakespeare to have conceived of his play as a true and exact copy of its chronicle sources. It was perhaps the confrontation with contested interpretations of King John's reign that led Shakespeare to give the Bastard such a prominent role in his troublesome history. A walking palimpsest whose descent from Richard is written in his lineaments and only partly masked by his name and social identity, the Bastard emerges as a representation of the curious kind of memory that a chronicle history play embodies, the offspring of mingled lines of memory and forgetting.

PRIVATIZING MEMORY

When Constance and Arthur engage in recollection, they do so in the key of personal remembrance, not that of public memory. In doing so, they anticipate the gulf that will open up between public and private memory in Shakespeare's second cycle of histories. "If I were mad, I should forget my son," the Senecan heroine protests following Arthur's imprisonment (3.4.57). Saturated with grief, she is inundated with memories of her son:

> Grief fills the room up of my absent child,
> Lies in his bed, walks up and down with me,
> Puts on his pretty looks, repeats his words,
> Remembers me of all his gracious parts,
> Stuffs out his vacant garments with his form. (3.4.93–7)

Grief, as Constance imagines it, is an actor, skilled at impersonating the dead and filling both empty space and clothing with bodied presences, reanimating the absent and the lost by recalling their action, speech, look, qualities, and gestures. In *King John*, authentic and affecting memory like Constance's is precisely what is excluded from the public arena. This is decidedly not a mourning play, unlike *1 Henry VI*. Mourning is a private rather than public affair in *King John*. The memories of the legitimate heir and his mother consistently occupy the register of the private, as if to continually remind us of Arthur's exclusion from the form of collective remembrance that is history.

One would expect Arthur, as Richard Lionheart's legitimate successor, to repeatedly sound the theme of memory, but he does so only in weak, diminished, and private contexts: perhaps the keenest demonstration that Arthur has been disinherited, not only of the throne and the power it conveys but also of any claim to command public memory of the past. In jail he recalls young Frenchmen's habit of affecting melancholy—"Yet I remember, when I was in France,/ Young gentlemen would be as sad as night,/ Only for wantonness" (4.1.14–16)—and a few lines later, after realizing Hubert's purpose, to put out his eyes, he reminds us of the kindly "sick-service" performed him by a prince (4.1.52). Arthur's memories are as confined as his person. The disparity between Arthur's minute recollections and the larger frame of the play, the collective remembrance of the reign of a monarch whom many regarded as a proto-Protestant hero, is jarring. He has lost not only the throne but also a place in history. He is left outside the very community that watches him: the audiences whose assembly at theaters for remembrance of the nation's past that, as Peter Womack has suggested, served the same social ends as the traditional calendar that was being dismantled over the course of the sixteenth century: "Just at the point where the Catholic ceremonial calendar was giving way to a growing list of national celebrations and commemorations, the metropolitan theatre was seeking to draw its miscellaneous audience into a new kind of unity by rehearsing the fall and redemption of England."[60]

Only in Act 5 does control of public remembrance return to the triumphant political forces, somewhat in the manner in which they are transferred from rebel forces to royalty over the course of *1–2 Henry IV* and *Henry V*. The Dauphin, at the head of the victorious forces of invading

French and discontented English, refers to their treaty, secured in the presumably fixed form of the written word:

> My Lord Melun, let this be copied out
> And keep it safe for our remembrance;
> Return the precedent to these lords again,
> That having our fair order written down,
> Both they and we, perusing o'er these notes,
> May know wherefore we took the sacrament,
> And keep our faiths firm and inviolable. (5.2.1–7)

It is not only the throne but also the prerogative to exercise, manipulate, and control memory that must be restored to the rightful possessor or legitimate heir at the end of a Shakespearean history play. One of the more troubling things about *King John* for English audiences is memory's apparently coming to rest in the hands of its perennial enemy France: an ending more fitting, perhaps, for tragedies like *Hamlet* or *King Lear*.[61]

TWICE-TOLD TALES

Remembrance in *King John* is not the clear duty and heroic action, tantamount to Talbot's feats of war, that it is in the *Henry VI* plays. This much is evident from Lewis the Dauphin's grieving lines following the news of King John's stunning victories against the French forces: "Life is as tedious as a twice-told tale,/ Vexing the dull ear of a drowsy man" (3.4.108–9). The lines are curious within the context of a play, which presumably strives for the repetition of an extended run. This play especially, regardless of its success in repeated performances, may be suspected of twice-telling, of retelling *The Troublesome Raigne of John, King of England*. Because retelling is an essential means of preserving the past, especially in predominantly oral cultures like Shakespeare's own, and because various forms of repetition were enlisted in plays to help audiences remember key material, Lewis's lines seem a curious disparagement of the aims and practices of memory. Most chronicle history plays were twice-told tales, whose basic material was already known to audiences before coming to the theater.

Lewis's lines are not the play's last words on retelling. In fact, they serve as prologue to a curious form of repetition that will take place moments later. John, in order to bolster his claims to the throne, answer doubts about his legitimacy, and reconfirm the loyalty of the assembled nobles and bishops, re-stages his coronation. Yielding to increasing pressures, John surrenders his crown to the papal legate Pandulph, only to receive it from him again, thereby making himself a vassal of the pope. "Here once again we sit, once again crowned/ And looked upon, I hope, with cheerful eyes" (4.2.1–2). The ritual backfires, however, with some onlookers. Repetition, especially of a costly ritual, may smack of superfluity, "wasteful and ridiculous excess," according to Salisbury (4.2.16). "This 'once again,' but that your highness pleased,/ Was once superfluous," Pembroke responds to John's hopeful lines, echoing and adding to the King's superfluity by uttering the King's "once again" once again (4.2.3–4). In Pembroke's next speech superfluity expands further, as he echoes Lewis's recent sentiments about twice-told tales:

> But that your royal pleasure must be done,
> This act is as an ancient tale new told,
> And, in the last repeating, troublesome,
> Being urgèd at a time unseasonable. (4.2.17–20)

From wasteful excess, the re-coronation becomes the sign of trouble in the kingdom, disfiguring tradition: "the antique and well-noted face/ Of plain old form" (4.2.21–2). By their anxious mutual repetition of the disfiguring effects of repetition, Pembroke and Salisbury reenact the troubling act of the King's. They tell and retell the trouble with retelling, although not so as to lend such acts stability. Alternately conceived as tedious, ridiculous, wasteful, disturbing, and unseasonable, the meaning of retelling itself, it seems, never achieves the tedious predictability of the "twice-told." Pembroke's word "troublesome" directly implicates Shakespeare in the "once again" by evoking the anonymous *Troublesome Raigne* and thereby reminding us that the new play we watch unfold "is as an ancient tale new told." To retell it is itself a sign of trouble within the kingdom, Elizabeth's (where the troublesome matter of King John's reign was twice-told on stage in the same decade) as well as John's. Pembroke's line, "And, in the last repeating, troublesome," suggests an application to Shakespeare's plays as a whole. In the wake of what Patrick Collinson has termed the Second English Reformation of the 1580s, it is "unseasonable," Shakespeare seems to be acknowledging in a textual wink, to repeat the history of this troublesome proto-Reformation figure who still held the power to breed contention in the closing decade of the sixteenth century.[62]

Acts of repetition in the play frequently express a desire for political stability, but they also function as signs of an instability that the repetition is designed to stabilize or secure. The next two scenes both begin with instances of politically motivated repetition: in 5.1, Pandulph's re-crowning of John and his reference to Ascension Day, reminding the audience of Peter of Pomfret's prophecy that King John will yield up the crown before next Ascension Day in 4.2, a form of twice-telling that is anything but tedious; and in 5.2, the Dauphin's order to copy out the original draft of the treaty conditions: "My Lord Melun, let this be copied out/ And keep it safe for our remembrance" (5.2.1–2). The latter, repeated command mimics the stability imputed to the written word, for which it expresses a desire. Retelling would seem ballast against the rampant "commodity"—profit, advantage, or self-interest, "This bawd, this broker, this all-changing word" (2.1.582)—the bastard sees everywhere. "Commodity" draws from "fickle France" "his own-determined aid,/ From a resolved and honourable war,/ To a most base and vile-concluded peace" (2.1.583–6). Potentially gestures for resisting change or otherwise securing order, repeating and retelling in *King John* do not themselves remain stable in meaning, let alone serve to stabilize, as the meaning of the twice-told tale shifts wildly in the play's last two acts. The divergent comments on retelling are consistent with the spirit of *King John*: an especially troublesome retelling of a troublesome period in English history. Unlike the earlier histories, which seem secure at least in their aim of helping to perpetuate the historical record, and unlike *The Troublesome Raigne*, an exercise in patriotic Reformation history, Shakespeare's retelling seems disturbing and unseasonable, and its implications for the fledgling Protestant nation unsure.

Referring to England twice as "nation" in its final act, the play closes by suggesting the extent to which English national identity must be informed by what had seemed the enemy of the dynastic realm in the first tetralogy, the forces of memory's erosion. *King John* anticipates the argument of the second tetralogy and of King James's address to his first English parliament: that acts of oblivion are the foundation of national unity, which is built on the quicksands of forgetfulness as well as the rock of remembrance. One of the two references to the English "nation" in the fifth act is tied to the island's projected self-forgetfulness. The Earl of Salisbury, who had joined forces with Lewis the Dauphin, later returning to King John after realizing Lewis's treachery, fondly wishes for a crusade that would unite the two opposed Christian armies against a "pagan" enemy and thereby help them to forget their differences. His imagery suggests a stolen child removed and carried into self-forgetfulness:

> O nation, that thou couldst remove,
> That Neptune's arms, who clippeth thee about,
> Would bear thee from the knowledge of thyself,
> And grapple thee unto a pagan shore,
> Where these two Christian armies might combine
> The blood of malice in a vein of league
> And not to spend it so unneighborly. (5.2.33–9)

Historically the illegitimate son of Henry II, King John's half-brother Salisbury wishes for his nation an occlusion of parentage and patrimony akin to that of Philip the Bastard: a hope that would have been inconceivable within the chronicle tradition on which Shakespeare drew, a tradition which knew unequivocally how to identify memory and oblivion as friend and foe. In his *Chronicle*, Edward Hall celebrated the didactic power of memory guided by historical works like his own, to "enduce vertue, and represse vice: Thus, memorie maketh menne ded many a thousand yere *still to live as though thei were present.*"[63] The Bastard comes to suggest how memory and oblivion may be difficult to even tell apart in a play, with its commingled lines of remembering and forgetting. In *King John*, a play founded on the contested memories of opposed historiographic traditions, internal differences, more than a monarch's "troublesome reign," are what Shakespeare's play memorializes, and with those differences, the need to forget, more perdurable than any memory.

Notes

NOTES TO THE INTRODUCTION

1. Milan Kundera, *The Curtain: An Essay in Seven Parts*, trans. Linda Asher (New York: HarperCollins, 2007), 148–149.
2. Michel Foucault, "Film and Popular Memory," in *Foucault Live*, trans. John Johnston, ed. Sylvère Lotringer (New York: Semiotext(e) Foreign Agent Series, 1989), 92.
3. George Orwell, *1984* (1949; New York: Signet Classics, 1977), 35.
4. Unless otherwise noted, all citations from Shakespeare's plays refer to the individual New Cambridge Shakespeare editions, Brian Gibbons, general editor.
5. Phyllis Rackin, *Stages of History: Shakespeare's English Chronicles* (Ithaca, NY: Cornell University Press, 1990), 151.
6. Rackin, 150.
7. Mary Carruthers, *The Book of Memory: A Study of Memory in Medieval Culture* (Cambridge: Cambridge University Press, 1990), 156.
8. Keith Thomas, *The Perception of the Past in Early Modern England* (The Creighton Trust Lecture 1983) (London: University of London, n.d.), 9.
9. Ian Archer, "The Nostalgia of John Stow," in *The Theatrical City: Culture, Theatre and Politics in London, 1576–1649*, ed. David L Smith, Richard Strier, and David Bevington (Cambridge: Cambridge University Press, 1995), 31.
10. Nina Levine, "Extending Credit in the *Henry IV* Plays," *Shakespeare Quarterly* 51 (2000), 409. See also H. R. Coursen, *The Leasing Out of England: Shakespeare's Second Henriad* (Washington, DC: University Press of America, 1982); Sandra K. Fischer, "'He means to pay': Value and metaphor in the Lancastrian Tetralogy," *Shakespeare Quarterly* 40 (1989), 149–164; and Lars Engle, *Shakespearean Pragmatism: Market of His Time* (Chicago: University of Chicago Press, 1993). Other influential and important studies exploring the relation of the market and the theater include Jean-Christophe Agnew, *Worlds Apart: The Market and the Theater in Anglo-American Thought, 1550–1750* (Cambridge: Cambridge University Press, 1986), and Douglas Bruster, *Drama and the Market in the Age of Shakespeare* (Cambridge: Cambridge University Press, 1992).
11. W. H. Auden "Brothers and Others," in *The Dyer's Hand and Other Essays* (New York: Vintage Books, 1968), 220.
12. Adam Fox, *Oral and Literate Culture in England 1500–1700* (Oxford: Oxford University Press, 2000), 271.
13. Lawrence Manley, "Of Sites and Rites," in *The Theatrical City: Culture, Theatre and Politics in London, 1576–1649*, ed. David L Smith, Richard

Strier, and David Bevington (Cambridge: Cambridge University Press, 1995), 51.

14. Benedict Anderson, *Imagined Communities: Reflections on the Origins and Spread of Nationalism* (London: Verso, 1983); Richard Helgerson, *Forms of Nationhood: The Elizabethan Writing of England* (Chicago: University of Chicago Press, 1992).
15. Fox, 383. To take one example at the local level, in order to settle land disputes that greatly increased in the wake of the Reformation's dissolution of the monasteries, the number of land surveyors in Elizabethan and Jacobean England increased dramatically, as pressure mounted to produce written surveys and to rely less on memories of local customs and practices. Fox notes, surveys "presented only a snapshot of the customs as they operated at a particular moment. It froze in time what had been a highly mutable set of usages adapting year by year in response to changing conditions; it fixed in text for posterity what memory had been able to forget and circumstance to forego . . . On the one hand, written fixity may have helped to settle contention, or perhaps even to avoid it in the first place. On the other hand, all parties were now bound to a rigid system which denied the flexibility and sensitivity to change allowed in the past" (293). As written records replaced the living memory of local custom in legal disputes, "both landlords and tenants, clergymen and parishioners, corporations and citizens, engaged in the battle for documentary proof" (281).
16. Victor Mayer-Schönberger, *Delete: The Virtue of Forgetting in the Digital Age* (Princeton, NJ: Princeton University Press, 2009). See also the article by Jeffrey Rosen, "The Web Means the End of Forgetting," *The New York Times*, July 19, 2010.
17. Zenon Luis-Martinez, "Shakespeare's Historical Drama as Trauerspiel: *Richard II* and After," *ELH* 75 (2008), 685.
18. E. M. W. Tillyard, *Shakespeare's History Plays* (New York: Barnes and Noble, 1944), 289. For Tillyard *Richard II* expresses this medievalism, on the brink of passing into history, because Richard is the last of England's kings to rule "by hereditary right, direct and undisputed, from the Conqueror."
19. Anderson, 19.
20. Liah Greenfeld, *Nationalism: Five Roads to Modernity* (Cambridge, MA: Harvard University Press, 1992), 30. Many literary critics have recently supported the contention that the modern nation predates the Enlightenment. See, for example, Claire McEachern, *The Poetics of English Nationhood, 1590–1612* (Cambridge: Cambridge University Press, 1996).
21. John Guy, *Tudor England* (Oxford: Oxford University Press, 1988), 352.
22. Guy, 352; Greenfeld, 31f.
23. For example, in the first tetralogy "realm(s) appears a total of thirty-eight times by comparison with five mentions of "nation(s)." In the second tetralogy, the frequencies of the two words are nearly even: eleven for "realm(s)" and ten for "nation(s)." The dying John of Gaunt's reference to "this earth, this realm, this England," like other feudal rhetoric (e.g., his opening line, "I have, my liege"), makes him seem a superannuated figure. For a reading of this speech as a proto-nationalist performance, see McEachern, 5–6.
24. Ernest Gellner, *Encounters with Nationalism* (Oxford: Blackwell, 1994), 192–193.
25. Gellner, 192.
26. Gellner, 193.
27. Gellner, 192. Like many influential analysts of nationalism, Gellner sees the nation as a post-Enlightenment phenomenon. The process by which nation-states replaced dynastic-religious ones as the European norm took place "in

the two centuries following the French Revolution" (192). See also Gellner, *Nations and Nationalism* (Ithaca, NY: Cornell University Press, 1983); E. J. Hobsbawm, *Nations and Nationalism Since 1780: Programme, Myth, Reality* (Cambridge: Cambridge University Press, 1990); Benedict Anderson, *Imagined Communities*; and Linda Colley, *Britons: Forging the Nation, 1707–1837* (New Haven, CT: Yale University Press, 1992). The evidence presented by this book, drawn from Shakespeare's plays and their contexts, supports the view, shared by a growing number of historians and literary scholars who study the period, that the transition from dynastic realm to nation-state was well under way in early modern England. See, for instance, Peter Womack, "Imagining Communities: Theatres and the English Nation in the Sixteenth Century," in *Culture and History, 1350–1600* (Detroit: Wayne State University Press, 1992), 91–145; Richard Helgerson, *Forms of Nationhood: The Elizabethan Writing of England* (Chicago: University of Chicago Press, 1992); Claire McEachern, *The Poetics of English Nationhood, 1590–1612* (Cambridge: Cambridge University Press, 1996); Jean E. Howard and Phyllis Rackin, *Engendering a Nation: A Feminist Account of Shakespeare's English Histories* (London: Routledge, 1997), 26, 47; Michael Neill, "Broken English and Broken Irish: Nation, Language, and the Optic of Power in Shakespeare's Histories," in *Putting History to the Question: Power, Politics, and Society in English Renaissance Drama* (New York: Columbia University Press, 2000), 339–372; and Liah Greenfeld, *Nationalism: Five Roads to Modernity*. David Scott Kastan summarizes the implications of *1 Henry IV* for Elizabethan nationalism, "The unitary state, 'All of one nature, of one substance bred' (1.1.11), would be produced in opposition to an alien and barbaric 'other,' almost precisely the way an idea of an orderly and coherent English nation was fashioned in Elizabethan England largely by reference to the alterity and inferiority of the Irish" ("'The King Hath Many Marching in His Coats' or What Did You Do in the War, Daddy?" in *Shakespeare Left and Right*, ed. Ivo Kamps [New York: Routledge, 1991], 242). Geoffrey Elton writes, "The essence . . . of Tudor England, despite the unquestioned difficulties, lay in national awareness and allegiance: social and economic strains could be controlled, and even differences over religion diminished the common loyalties only for a small number of extreme Protestants and entrenched Catholics" (*The English* [Oxford: Blackwell, 1992], 130). The Tudor system worked, according to Elton, because "the rulers of the realm shared background and opinion with the rulers of the localities" (130). Thus, cultural uniformity had only to characterize the ruling classes, not to cut across social classes.

28. Ernest Renan, "What Is a Nation?" trans. Martin Thom, in Homi Bhabha, ed., *Nation and Narration* (London: Routledge, 1990), 11. Compare Nietzsche's observation eight years earlier in "On the uses and disadvantages of history for life" (1874) that "a hypertrophied virtue—such as the historical sense of our age appears to be—can ruin a nation just as effectively as a hypertrophied vice" (*Untimely Meditations*, trans. R. J. Hollingdale, introduction by J. P. Stern [Cambridge: Cambridge University Press, 1983], 60). Late nineteenth-century Europe saw a spectacular proliferation in the theorizing of forgetting. As Renan showed it to be constitutive of the nation, Freud was beginning to show that it was equally constitutive of the self, and Nietzche to prescribe it as an antidote to excessive historical consciousness. Freud's early studies on the subject include the essay "On the Psychical Mechanism of Forgetfulness" (1898), which was developed into *The Interpretation of Dreams* (1899) and *The Psychopathology of Everyday Life* (1901). For Nietzsche, it was the artist who was most disciplined in the practice of how to forget:

"Oh, how we now learn to forget well, and to be good at *not* knowing, as artists!" "Monological" art, which Nietzsche celebrated and distinguished from "art before witnesses," issues from the superior artist who has "'forgotten the world' . . . it is based *on forgetting,* it is the music of forgetting" (*The Gay Science*, trans., with commentary, by Walter Kaufmann [New York: Vintage Books, 1974], 37, 324). As if to confirm Nietzsche's thesis, for Van Gogh, too, the occlusion of memory was an essential part of artistic production. He disdained reliance on an always unreliable memory—"a disrupter, revisionist, antic colorist"—by his contemporaries who painted in their studios rather than the open air, even while he "poured out almost daily, in an extraordinary flourish of mnemonic powers, those long, detailed, closely argued letters to his brother in which he cast his recollections of the painterliness of the real world" (W. S. DiPiero, *Memory and Enthusiasm: Essays, 1975–1985* [Princeton, NJ: Princeton University Press, 1989], 117).

29. Renan, 12.
30. Ernest Gellner, *Encounters with Nationalism* (Oxford: Blackwell, 1994), 192.
31. My reasons for identifying Henry VIII, traditionally grouped with the romances, as a chronicle history play are presented in my essay "Necromancing the Past in Henry VIII," *English Literary Renaissance* 34 (2004), 359-386. *Henry VIII* develops thematically the contest between enduring memory and the threat of oblivion that pervades the histories.
32. I have written about the contested and sometimes tortured operations of memory in *The Tempest* and *Henry VIII* in "Necromancing the Past in *Henry VIII*," *English Literary Renaissance* 34, no. 3 (Autumn 2004), 359–386; and "Exporting Oblivion in *The Tempest*," *Modern Language Quarterly* 56 (1995), 111–144.
33. The metaphorical association between oblivion and death is a very common one in early modern England. See, for instance, the frontispiece and dedicatory poem to Sir Walter Raleigh's *History of the World* (1614).
34. Ian W. Archer has recently shown how the Protestant city of London produced acts of memorialization that in many ways imitated the traditional or Catholic acts they were designed to replace. "The Arts and Acts of Memorialization in Early Modern London," in *Imagining Early Modern London: Perceptions and Portrayals of the City from Stow to Strype, 1598–1720*, ed. J. F. Merritt (Cambridge: Cambridge University Press, 2001), 89–113.
35. Eric Foner, *Who Owns History? Rethinking the Past in a Changing World* (New York: Hill and Wang, 2002).

NOTES TO CHAPTER 1

1. For a classic exposition of the way that the play hollows out the belief that the king mystically joins his subjects into a single body politic, see Ernst Kantorowicz, *The King's Two Bodies: A Study in Medieval Political Theology* (Princeton, NJ: Princeton University Press, 1957), 24–41.
2. Mary Carruthers, *The Book of Memory: A Study of Memory in Medieval Culture* (Cambridge: Cambridge University Press, 1990), 156.
3. Carruthers, 9.
4. Eamon Duffy, *The Stripping of the Altars: Traditional Religion in England, 1400–1580* (New Haven, CT: Yale University Press, 1992), 338. In an essay on "The Arts and Acts of Memorialization in Early Modern London," Ian Archer has shown that a "culture of commemoration" was not entirely swept away by the Protestant Reformation: "[T]he commemoration of benefactors

in the post-Reformation period was often expressed in forms which owed much to the supposedly displaced Catholic forms." *Imagining Early Modern London: Perceptions and Portrayals of the City from Stow to Strype, 1598–1720*, ed. J. F. Merritt (Cambridge: Cambridge University Press, 2001), 91.

5. See Phyllis Rackin, *Stages of History: Shakespeare's English Chronicles* (Ithaca, NY: Cornell University Press, 1990), 77–78; James Bulman, "*Henry IV, Parts 1 and 2*," in *The Cambridge Companion to Shakespeare's History Plays* (Cambridge: Cambridge University Press, 2002), 165: "Hal does not come by legitimacy through blood or lineage; rather, like new-made gentry in Elizabethan England who bought their coats of arms, he must *earn* it."
6. Isabel Karremann describes Richard's lines at 3.3.147–54, in which he "'rehearses' his abdication speech in the circle of his supporters," as "an inverse coronation ceremony which at the same time doubles as a ritual of saintly investiture," astutely concluding that "Richard's lament brings about his erasure from official history only to reinstate his memory on a mythical scale." "Rites of Oblivion in Shakespearian History Plays," *Shakespeare Survey* 63 (2010), 30.
7. As many historians have argued recently, the sense of detachment from and loss of a medieval past was not exclusive to recusant Catholics. As Alison Shell writes, "[T]here was no necessary correspondence in early modern England between Catholicism and nostalgia for medievalism." *Oral Culture and Catholicism in Early Modern England* (Cambridge: Cambridge University Press, 2007), 89.
8. In a provocative reading, David Norbrook comments on how the play's opening line has distracted critics and lead to a whole tradition of misguided, nostalgic readings of the play: "The play's opening line can put us on the right track. But all too often it has put us on the wrong track," spawning readings of the play and the tetralogy as a whole "as expressing nostalgia for a lost social unity." Reading the play largely from the perspective of the Essex party, Norbrook argues that "if the Elizabethans did feel nostalgic for the medieval past," it was not for absolutism; rather, "they feared its recurrence." A growing number of antiquarians looked back to the Middle Ages not for its mystical monarchism but for its aristocratic constitutionalism, for aristocratic agency and "constitutional precedents for challenges to royal power." "'A Liberal Tongue': Language and Rebellion in *Richard II*," in *Shakespeare's Universe: Renaissance Ideas and Conventions, Essays in Honor of W. R. Elton* (Aldershot, UK: Scholar Press, 1996), 37–51, esp. 37–39. I fully concur with Norbrook's criticism of readings of the play as expressing a nostalgia for "an archaic hieratic political order that has so swayed some critics" (46), but the play does engage with powerful nostalgias, which are difficult to ignore and which seem to me much broader than a desire to bring back an "aristocratic constitutionalism." I would describe the play as providing both a genealogy and an anatomy of nostalgia; it its peculiar power lies largely in its exploring the relation between nostalgia and the sense of traumatic historical rupture.
9. For "presence" in the sense of "royal presence," see, e.g., 1.3.248 and 1.3.288.
10. Unless otherwise noted, all citations from the plays refer to the individual New Cambridge Shakespeare editions, Brian Gibbons, general editor.
11. Though forgotten in *Richard II*, Mortimer's claim will be resurrected in *1 Henry IV*.
12. Bertie Wilkinson, *Constitutional History of Medieval England, 1216–1399*, 3 vols. (London: Longmans, Green, 1948–1952), 2: 130.
13. Clare Carroll, *Circe's Cup: Cultural Transformations in Early Modern Ireland* (Critical Conditions: Field Day Essays and Monographs) (Notre Dame, IN: University of Notre Dame Press, 2001), 18.

14. Judith Butler, "Primo Levi for the Present," in *Re-Figuring Hayden White* (Stanford, CA: Stanford University Press, 2009), 296, 298.
15. Butler, 296.
16. The atmosphere of concealment at the beginning of *Richard II* bears comparison to Freud's theory of repression, about which Derrida notes Freud's stressing "that what is most interesting in repression is what one does not manage to repress." Jacques Derrida, *Archive Fever: A Freudian Impression*, trans. Eric Prenowitz (Chicago: University of Chicago Press, 1996), 61.
17. Thomas Nashe, *The Unfortunate Traveller and Other Works*, ed. J. B. Steane (London: Penguin Books, 1972), 113.
18. Cited in Annabel Patterson, *Censorship and Interpretation: The Conditions of Writing and Reading in Early Modern England* (Madison: The University of Wisconsin Press, 1984), 47. More recently, Richard Dutton discusses the Bishops' Order in *Licensing, Censorship, and Authorship in Early Modern England* (New York: Palgrave, 2000).
19. Lateness is also the prevailing condition at the beginning of Shakespeare's first sequence of histories. Henry V's coffin traverses the stage in the first scene of the play. England's heroic past is both tantalizingly close and painfully remote, irrevocably beyond reach. But the opening of *Richard II* serves up a different sense of coming too late. At the beginning of *1 Henry VI* we know exactly what we have missed; at the opening of *Richard II* we only sense that something is missing that prevents our full understanding. In the later play it is our sense that we have entered the historical record "too late," that the re-presentation of Richard's reign needs to have begun at an earlier point, that prevails. In the later play we do not know what we are missing, only that we seem to be lacking vital information about Richard, Mowbray, Bolingbroke, and the murdered Thomas Woodstock, Duke of Gloucester.
20. Editors of the recent Revels edition of the play, Peter Corbin and Douglas Sedge, argue that it "as written, and perhaps staged, some time before 1595." *Thomas of Woodstock: or, Richard II, Part I* (Manchester, UK: Manchester University Press, 2002), 4,8. Macdonald P. Jackson has recently challenged the traditional view that *Woodstock* predates *Richard II* by presenting textual evidence that it was written after Shakespeare's play, in "Shakespeare's *Richard II* and the Anonymous *Thomas of Woodstock*," *Medieval and Renaissance Drama in England* 14 (2001), 17–65.
21. Nick de Somogyi, *The Life and Death of King Richard the Second* (The Shakespeare Folios) (London: Nick Hern Books, 2003), xxx; Charles R. Forker, ed., *King Richard II*, Arden Third Series (London: Thomson Learning, 2002), 144–152.
22. The recurring suspicion that yesterday lies beyond recall serves to remind us of the strenuous nature of the collective enterprise shared by playwright, actors, and audiences, one that Richard himself deems impossible: that of bidding the past return. Within the play, John of Gaunt in his swansong poignantly calls back the yesterday of his father Edward's England, reflecting the playwright's task of calling back Richard's England, with its faith in the efficacy of ritual and the unchallenged sanctity of the divine office of king, into the realpolitik of the Elizabethan present. The latter's image in the play is what Fitzwater christens "this new world" over which Bolingbroke presides (4.1.78). The play conveys the sense that it is late in history: too late for the Middle Ages and their secure ritual, which have given way to the insecurities of governance by policy rather than divine right. But Shakespeare, the Lord Chamberlain's Men, and their audiences do bid time return in a manner that accentuates that the monarch they rescue from oblivion stands helpless and paralyzed before the same task. Richard's failure to accomplish what

the Lord Chamberlain's Men performed on a daily basis serves to distance audiences from Richard and deepen his sense of isolation. Richard becomes isolated not only politically but also theatrically, from the very troupe of actors and their audiences who together rescue his reign from what Nashe colorfully termed "the grave of oblivion."

23. Furthermore, comedy allows for the circularity of yesterday returning. In pardoning the Duke and Duchess of York's son, the treasonous Aumerle, the King effectively "bids time return," undoing Aumerle's signing of the document swearing his resolve to help kill the king at Oxford.
24. Nick de Somogyi, ed., *The Life and Death of King Richard the Second* (The Shakespeare Folios) (London: Nick Hern Books, 2003), 177, n. 5.
25. Advice about optimal months for bloodletting was often included in almanacs of the period. Andrew Gurr notes that "doctors" can mean "Learned men, including astrologers," as well as physicians. Commenting on the relative merits of the Quartos' "month" and the Folio's "time," Gurr notes, "F's reading normalizes, but reduces what is probably Richard's joke about astrological influence in medicine" (63).
26. See Morris Palmer Tilley, *A Dictionary of the Proverbs in England in the Sixteenth and Seventeenth Centuries* (Ann Arbor: University of Michigan Press, 1950), F597, "Forgive and forget," 236.
27. Avishai Margalit, *The Ethics of Memory* (Cambridge, MA: Harvard University Press, 2002), 203.
28. Margalit, 196–197.
29. Margalit, 197.
30. Margalit, 205.
31. Margalit, 208.
32. Granted, the revolt took place sixteen to eighteen years before the events represented in *Richard II* (1397–1399). Still, Shakespeare and his contemporaries frequently telescoped history to juxtapose or even fuse historical events widely separated in time.
33. Annabel Patterson, *Reading Holinshed's Chronicles* (Chicago: University of Chicago Press, 1994), 193.
34. Raphael Holinshed et al., *The Chronicles of England, Ireland, and Scotland*, 3 vols. (London, 1587), 437.
35. Holinshed, 430.
36. Holinshed, 429.
37. Holinshed, 430.
38. Patterson, 193–194.
39. Holinshed, 432.
40. Steven Justice, *Writing and Rebellion: England in 1381* (The New Historicism: Studies in Cultural Poetics 27) (Berkeley: University of California Press, 1994), 48.
41. Justice (145) notes that at Bocking, on June 2, 1381, the rebels swore an oath "that they wanted no law in England except for ones proposed by themselves."
42. Justice, 48.
43. Similarly, *Henry VIII* will pit the upstart Wolsey, undisputed master of the realm of orality, against a written, documentary culture that will lead to his downfall and that will be associated with royal power toward the end of that play.
44. Naomi Conn Liebler, "The Mockery King of Snow: *Richard II* and the Sacrifice of Ritual," in *True Rites and Maimed Rites: Ritual and Anti-Ritual in Shakespeare and His Age*, ed. Linda Woodbridge and Edward Berry (Urbana: University of Illinois Press, 1992), 231.

45. For an extensive discussion of the relation between memory and history, see Jacques LeGoff, *History and Memory*, trans. Steven Rendall and Elizabeth Claman (New York: Columbia University Press, 1992); and Raphael Samuel, *Theatres of Memory*, vol. 1: *Past and Present in Contemporary Culture* (New York: Verso, 1994), ix–x. Samuel argues that memory ("subjective, a plaything of the emotions, indulging its caprices, wallowing in its own warmth") and history are "dialectically related." Memory is decidedly not history's "negative other." LeGoff, conversely, challenges the view of those who would privilege memory as "more authentic, 'truer' than history, which is presumed to be artificial and, above all, manipulative of memory." For LeGoff, the discipline of history is nourished my memory and in turn nourishes it, entering "into the great dialectical process of memory and forgetting experienced by individuals and societies" (xi).
46. The most recent entry in the debate is based on computer analysis, and ascribes 40 percent of the play to Shakespeare, and 60 percent to Thomas Kyd. See the account of Brian Vickers' evidence in Thomas Merriam, "Marlowe vs. Kyd as Author of *Edward III* I.i, III, and V," *Notes and Queries* 56 (2009), 549–551.
47. Phyllis Rackin, *Stages of History: Shakespeare's English Chronicles* (Ithaca, NY: Cornell University Press, 1990).
48. In producing history plays, Shakespeare spanned the two positions, those of Richard and of Gaunt and York. Responding to the marketplace's self-renewing hunger for novelty, Shakespeare in his chronicle histories satisfied that appetite in the form of new versions of the old.
49. Even his idiosyncratic way of imagining his own memorial, his grave, confirms his overriding interest in the vanities to which York alludes. He details for Aumerle the series of exchanges he will make—jewels for rosary, palace for hermitage, "gay apparel" for "almsman's gown," elaborately ornamented goblets "for a dish of wood," a scepter for palmer's staff, subjects for a pair of saints' statues, a kingdom for a grave—in such a way that makes the relics of a humble and holy life seem like baubles, only less colorful and dazzling than those of a king. Next, in discussing how they might dig their own graves—an apt emblem for Richard throughout the play—Richard proposes, "Or shall we play the wantons with our woes/ And make some pretty match with shedding tears,/ As thus to drop them still upon one place/ Till they have fretted us a pair of graves/ Within the earth, and therein laid?" (3.3.147–68). Not only does he carry to the grave his unregenerate taste for what York terms "vanity," but he also imagines himself digging his own grave by shedding a prodigious quantity of self-pitying tears, a veritable wanton soup.
50. Gurr, 108.
51. Harry Berger, Jr., *Imaginary Audition: Shakespeare on Stage and Page* (Berkeley: University of California Press, 1989), 51–52. Berger notes that "the same problem affects Richard's relation to the divine Father who authorizes the patriarchal ideology of kingship. This appears in the mocking irony of his setting himself up as Christ, coming down like Phaeton, and playing the role of a Faustus forced to organize and stage-manage his own damnation" (52).
52. The mirror that Richard requests, so that he may read his own face rather than the articles of deposition presented to him by Northumberland, reflects a new, politically self-conscious idea of kingship, to be realized more fully in Bolingbroke and his son. Theirs will be a kingship of the "self-born," of those who theatrically reflect and re-create themselves more or less independently of ancestral models. In Shakespeare's next chronicle play, Bolingbroke will counsel Hal in the economics of theatrical husbandry. Frugal management

of his kingly presence, with full attention to timing, entrances, exits, and visual aspects like gesture (*1 Henry IV*, 3.2.39–91), will ensure continued power. Hal, it is well known, will revise this model of the self-born king with spectacular success. In his charismatic presence it is easy to forget that he inherited the model from his father, who in turn had it from Richard. Although he has no direct descendants, the self-involved Richard generates a line of the "self-born," a dynasty of kings who must resort to strategies of self-legitimation because legitimation through ancestry remains blocked, raising too many risky and contentious questions following the deposition and murder of Richard.

53. On biblical comparisons in *Richard II*, see Kantorowicz, 34–35.
54. Michael McGiffert, "God's Controversy with Jacobean England," *The American Historical Review* 88 (1983), 1153.
55. More specifically, she has appropriated for the crown a biblical figure, Adam, who was frequently invoked for revolutionary, progressive ends.
56. See the discussion in Kantorowicz, 34–35.
57. John J. Joughin, "Shakespeare's Memorial Aesthetics," in *Shakespeare, Memory and Performance*, ed. Peter Holland (Cambridge: Cambridge University Press, 2006), 54.
58. Karremann, 31.
59. See D. Plunket Barton, *Links between Shakespeare and Ireland* (Dublin: Talbot Press, 1919); cited in O'Neill, 110.
60. Andrew Murphy, *But the Irish Sea Betwixt Us: Ireland, Colonialism, and Renaissance Literature* (Lexington: University Press of Kentucky, 1999), 113.
61. Murphy, 114; see also Philip Edwards, *Threshold of a Nation: A Study in English and Irish Drama* (Cambridge: Cambridge University Press, 1979), 74; and Michael Neill, "Broken English and Broken Irish: Nation, Optic, and the Language of Power in Shakespeare's Histories," *Shakespeare Quarterly* 45 (1994), 14.
62. Christopher Highley, *Shakespeare, Spenser, and the Crisis in Ireland* (Cambridge: Cambridge University Press, 1997), 64.
63. Stephen O'Neill, *Staging Ireland: Representations in Shakespeare and Renaissance Drama* (Dublin: Four Courts Press, 2007), 104.
64. O'Neill, 110.
65. Neill, 11.
66. Carroll, 1.
67. Rackin, 121.
68. Rackin, "The Role of the Audience in Shakespeare's *Richard II*," *Shakespeare Quarterly* 36 (1985), 262.
69. O'Neill refers to the "similarity in both scale and purpose between the Ricardian and Elizabethan campaigns in Ireland—a similarity which endows Elizabeth's reputed identification with King Richard an additional resonance" (111). Joan Fitzpatrick conjectures that the omission of the Irish wars testifies to Ireland's being "a dangerous subject for writers in Elizabethan England." *Shakespeare, Spenser, and the Contours of Britain: Reshaping the Atlantic Archipelago* (Hatfield, UK: University of Hertfordshire Press, 2004), 89.
70. Andrew Hadfield, "'Hitherto she ne'er could fancy him': Shakespeare's 'British' Plays and the Exclusion of Ireland," in *Shakespeare and Ireland: History, Politics, Culture*, ed. Mark Thornton Burnett and Ramona Wray (London: Macmillan, 1997), 49.
71. Mary installed the largely Catholic Anglo-Irish landlords known as the "Old English." Elizabeth's Protestant English plantation settlers came to be known as the "New English."

72. See also the excellent discussion in O'Neill, 107–111, on the relation between Richard's and Elizabeth's Irish policies.
73. Edmund Spenser, A *View of the Present State of Ireland,* ed. W. L. Renwick (London: Scholartis press, 1934), 201.
74. Spenser, 201.
75. Spenser, 201.
76. Spenser, 90–91.
77. Spenser, 83–84.
78. For a brilliant, detailed, and wide-ranging exploration of the idea of forgetting oneself in early modern drama, see Garrett A. Sullivan, Jr., *Memory and Forgetting in English Renaissance Drama* (Cambridge: Cambridge University Press, 2005).
79. Edward S. Casey, *Remembering: A Phenomenological Study* (Bloomington: Indiana University Press, 1987), 12. Casey cites Karl Kerényi, "Mnemosyne-Lesmosyne. On the Springs of 'Memory' and 'Forgetting,'" *Spring* (1977), 120–130.
80. See Jennifer Summit's recent study, *Memory's Library: Medieval Books in Early Modern England* (Chicago: University of Chicago Press, 2008): "Memory is a library—or so it was conventionally figured by premodern writers" (1).
81. *Wilson's Arte of rhetorique, 1560*, ed. George Herbert Mair (Oxford: Clarendon Press,1909), 209.
82. Edward Hall, *The Union of the Two Noble and Illustrate Families of Lancastre and Yorke* (1542), v–vi. For further instances of the dominant early modern retrieval model of memory, see the discussion of memory as treasurer (Pierre de la Primaudaye) and as "faithfull secretarie" (M. Andreas Laurentius) in Sullivan, 26–27.
83. John Frow, *Time and Commodity Culture: Essays in Cultural Theory and Postmodernity* (Oxford: Clarendon Press, 1997), 225.
84. Carruthers, 29. Frow thinks a variation of this model is "still the predominant metaphor in contemporary cognitive psychology, although it is now based more explicitly in the model of the electronic-storage and random-access retrieval of coded information" (227). Richard Terdiman makes a similar distinction between two views of memory: as "reproduction" and as "representation." The former, associated with the classical memory arts, seeks exact duplication of texts that have been deposited in the memory; the latter, a transformative rewriting of the text "hat makes it available for rereading. The point is crucial: the texts of memory are not *copies* but *representations*. They are always already overwritten *by the process of writing itself*." *Present Past: Modernity and the Memory Crisis* (Ithaca, NY: Cornell University Press, 1993), 58, 109. Anne Whitehead presents a useful summary of Frow and Terdiman's innovations within the historical sweep of developing ideas of memory in *Memory* (The New Critical Idiom Series) (London: Routledge, 2009), 48–50.
85. Frow, 226–227. That Frow oversimplifies the retrieval system of memory can be gleaned by the substantial work of Mary Carruthers on memory in the medieval period, particularly *The Craft of Thought: Meditation, Rhetoric, and the Making of Images, 400–1200* (Cambridge: Cambridge University Press, 1998), especially 82–96, in which she discusses medieval anxieties about the power of memory to produce disorder.
86. Frow, 228–229.
87. Frances A. Yates, *The Art of Memory* (London: Routledge and Kegan Paul, 1966).

88. Two recent studies have linked early modern stages with trauma: Thomas P. Anderson, *Performing Early Modern Trauma from Shakespeare to Milton* (Aldershot, UK: Ashgate, 2006); and Patricia Cahill, *Unto the Breach: Martial Formations, Historical Trauma, and the Early Modern Stage* (Oxford: Oxford University Press, 2008). However, both of these discuss trauma in relation to events located in the past, rather than "in the dialogical continuum that necessarily includes the present in the constitution of any 'past,'" as James Siemon notes in a recent paper ("Dead Men Talking?: Elegy, Trauma, Irony and the History Play" [unpublished paper], Shakespeare Association of America, 2010). Neither do they discuss trauma as the source for the particular kind of historical consciousness that comes to define the second tetralogy. See also Zenón Luis-Martínez's splendid recent reading of the play as an instance of what Walter Benjamin called *Trauerspiel*: "Shakespeare's Historical Drama as *Trauerspiel*: *Richard II*—and After," *English Literary History* 75 (2008), 673–705.
89. Hayden White, *The Content of the Form: Narrative Discourse and Historical Representation* (Baltimore, MD: The Johns Hopkins University Press, 1987), 68.
90. White, 70–71.
91. Richard T. Vann, "The Reception of Hayden White," *History and Theory* 37 (1998), 158.
92. Friedrich Schiller, *Two Essays by Friedrich Schiller: "Naïve and Sentimental Poetry" and "On the Sublime"* (Milestones of Thought in the History of Ideas), trans. Julias A. Elias (New York: Frederick Ungar Publishing Co., 1966), 205. Cited in White, 68–69.
93. Schiller, 210.
94. White, 73.
95. White, 72. Another theorist of history, a student of Hayden White, and a prominent interpreter and commentator on his work, Hans Kellner situates "the historical sublime" within the context of White's thought as a whole in his excellent article on "Hayden White" in *The Johns Hopkins Guide to Literary Theory & Criticism*, ed. Michael Groden and Martin Kreiswirth (Baltimore, MD: The Johns Hopkins University Press, 1994), 728–729. See also Kellner, "Beautifying the Nightmare: The Aesthetics of Postmodern History," *Strategies: A Journal of Theory, Culture, and Politics* 4–5 (1991), 289–313; and Kellner, "However Imperceptibly: From the Historical to the Sublime," *PMLA* 118 (2003), 591–596. Both of the latter essays show the connection between the historical sublime and François Lyotard's theorizing about postmodernism.
96. F. R. Ankersmit, *Sublime Historical Experience* (Cultural Memory in the Present) (Stanford, CA: Stanford University Press, 2006), 321.
97. Ankersmit, 322.
98. Ankersmit, 322.
99. Ankersmit, 323.
100. Ankersmit, 324.
101. Ankersmit, 325.
102. Ankersmit, 351. According to Ankersmit, "[M]odern historical consciousness came into being in sixteenth-century Italy" (356). The Renaissance demarcates "our own modern identity from that of the Middle Ages and . . . the loss of the latter identity still resonates in our own" (360).
103. Ankersmit, 322.
104. Ankersmit, 333. It is easy to grant that individual historians like Machiavelli or Guicciardini could have a sublime historical experience, one of irreparable

rupture, disorientation and tragic loss of the kind described by Schiller, but one might question, with reviewer Torbjörn Gustafsson Chorell, whether whole "civilizations, cultures and societies can be said to have sublime experiences" (Torbjörn Gustafsson Chorell, "Frank Ankersmit and the Historical Sublime," *History of the Human Sciences* 19 [2006], 95). In response to such skepticism, one might adopt, with Hans Kellner, the more flexible term "community" as the collective subject that experiences traumatic events (Hans Kellner, "Ankersmit's Proposal: Let's Keep in Touch," *CLIO* 36 [2006], 90).

105. J. F. Merritt, "Introduction: Perceptions and Portrayals of London 1598–1720," in Merritt, ed., 4. Elsewhere he refers to it as a "traumatic interruption" in the city of London's history (6). In the same volume, Ian Archer refers to "the Reformation traumas" (95). Merritt also shows that a series of later editors of Stow, beginning with Anthony Munday, emphasized continuity with the past rather than rupture, "adjusting Stow's message to suit the changing Protestant city. Stow's first editor, Anthony Munday, for example, found it possible to engage with the medieval past while placing it in a triumphalist celebration of continuity with the present" (5). See Merritt, "The Reshaping of Stow's 'Survey': Munday, Strype, and the Protestant City," in Merritt, 52–88.
106. Keith Thomas, *The Perception of the Past in Early Modern England* (The Creighton Trust Lecture 1983) (London: University of London, n.d.), 9.
107. Cited in Cathy Shrank, *Writing the Nation in Reformation England, 1530–1580* (Oxford: Oxford University Press, 2004).
108. Thomas, 14.
109. Eamon Duffy, "The Conservative Voice in the English Reformation," in Simon Ditchfield, ed., *Christianity and Community in the West: Essays for John Bossy* (Aldershot, UK: Ashgate, 2001), 104.
110. Susan Brigden, *New Worlds, Lost Worlds: The Rule of the Tudors, 1485–1603* (New York: Viking Press, 2000), 362.
111. Ian Archer, "The Nostalgia of John Stow," in *The Theatrical City*, ed. David L. Smith, Richard Strier, and David Bevington (Cambridge: Cambridge University Press, 1995), 31, 32–33.
112. Patrick Collinson, "John Stow and Nostalgic Antiquarianism," in Merritt, ed., 37. Collinson notes, as an "exception to prove the rule," the case of William Lambarde, a zealous Protestant antiquarian who, rather than "compensating for a present which had deprived him of his past . . . was creating for himself his own instant heritage" (38).
113. Adam Fox, *Oral and Literate Culture in England 1500–1700* (Oxford: Oxford University Press, 2000), 242.
114. Alison Shell, *Oral Culture and Catholicism in Early Modern England* (Cambridge: Cambridge University Press, 2007), 5.
115. Kellner, "Ankersmit's Proposal," 90.
116. Ankersmit, 344.
117. Kantorowicz, 37.
118. William Camden, *Britannia* (1607), trans Philemon Holland, "The Author to the Reader."
119. Duffy, "The Conservative Voice," 95.
120. In a perceptive reading of York's position as akin to that of "the writer, who only comments on action rather than undertake any himself" in a treacherous situation or "treasonous environment," Rebecca Lemon writes that "his is the fate of Catholic fathers such as Tresham and Percy, whose sons turn traitor by participating in the Essex Rebellion, and later the Gunpowder Plot. Equally, his struggle anticipates [John] Hayward's, whose loyal support for

the crown converts to tragic condemnation when the political environment radically changes." *Treason by Words: Literature, Law, and Rebellion in Shakespeare's England* (Ithaca, NY: Cornell University Press, 2006), 77.

121. Thomas, 10.
122. Felicity Heal notes, "Archbishop Cranmer recognized that the reform movement had to be temporally located in the past as a way of defending it against the charges of novelty and subjectivism. Hence his appeal to the Fathers and Christian antiquity, constructing the church of the early centuries as witness to the truths of the Gospel, with the apostolic age itself as 'the golden time.'" "Appropriating History: Catholic and Protestant Polemics and the National Past," in *The Uses of History in Early Modern England*, ed. Paulina Kewes (San Marino, CA: Huntington Library, 2006), 108.
123. See Alexandra Walsham, *Church Papists: Catholicism, Conformity and Confessional Polemic in Early Modern England* (Woodbridge, NY: The Boydell Press for the Royal Historical Society, 1993), for an important discussion of this extensive group of outwardly conforming Catholics in the period.
124. Duffy, "The Conservative Voice," 103.
125. On the growth of elegy in the period, and its relation to the Reformation's destruction of formal, ritualized means for the living to remain connected with the dead, see Scott Wayland, "Religious Change and the Renaissance Elegy," *English Literary Renaissance* 39 (2009), 429–459.
126. Patrick Collinson, "Merry England on the Ropes: The Contested Culture of the Early Modern English Town," in *Christianity and Community in the West: Essays for John Bossy*," ed. Simon Ditchfield (Aldershot, UK: Ashgate, 2001), 141.
127. Huston Diehl, *Staging Reform, Reforming the Stage: Protestantism and Popular Theater in Early Modern England* (Ithaca, NY: Cornell University Press, 1997), 4.
128. A. G. Dickens, *The English Reformation* (New York: Schocken Books, 1964).
129. David Cressy, *Birth, Marriage, and Death: Ritual, Religion, and the Life-Cycle in Tudor and Stuart England* (Oxford: Oxford University Press, 1997), 476–477.
130. Walsham, 7.
131. Peter Marshall, "Introduction," *The Impact of the English Reformation* (London: Arnold, 1997), 5.
132. Marshall, 5.
133. Walsham, 102.
134. William Fulke, *A Retentive to Stay God Christians, in True Faith and Religion, against the Motives of Richard Bristow* (London, 1580), 126. Cited in Walsham, 102.
135. Christopher Haigh, "The Church of England, the Catholics and the People," in Marshall, 236.
136. Fox writes, "The dedication of parish churches was certainly one factor which helped to keep the legendary deeds of patron saints in mind long after they had ceased to be actively recounted in pulpit and chronicle" (234).
137. Christopher Haigh, *English Reformation: Religion, Politics, and Society under the Tudors* (Oxford: Oxford University Press, 1993), 280.
138. Haigh "The Church of England, the Catholics and the People," 253–254. For a criticism of this view and Haigh's reference to his coinage "parish Anglicans" as "spiritual leftovers," see Judith Maltby, "'By this book': Parishioners, the Prayer Book and the Established Church," in Marshall, 257–278, especially 258–259: "The continued authorisation and use of some

pre-Reformation practices no more invalidates the label 'Protestant' in England than it does for many of the areas of the Lutheran Reformation where, by Genevan standards of reform, an unjustified number of pre-Reformation ceremonies were retained as well. Dr. Haigh, like many of the historians he is critical of, allows 'Geneva' to fix the goal posts of Protestantism."

139. Collinson, 141–142.
140. Patrick Collinson, "From Iconoclasm to Iconophobia: The Cultural Impact of the Second English Reformation," in Marshall, 282. See also Collinson, *The Birthpangs of Protestant England: Religious and Cultural Change in the Sixteenth and Seventeenth Centuries* (The Third Anstey Memorial Lectures in the University of Kent at Canterbury, May 12–15, 1986) (New York: St. Martin's Press, 1988).
141. Collinson, "From Iconoclasm to Iconophobia," 283.
142. Collinson, "From Iconoclasm to Iconophobia," 300.
143. Collinson, *Birthpangs*, 94.
144. Diehl, 3, 5. See also Adrian Streete, *Protestantism and Drama in Early Modern England* (Cambridge: Cambridge University Press, 2009). Jeffrey Knapp sees Shakespeare's theater as participating in the reform of older church practices, particularly the rite of communion. Persistently seeing the "mass entertainment of the theater" through the lens of "the communal partaking of Christ's body and blood," Shakespeare offered his audiences "unbloody versions of sacrifice": "By taking the place of the Corpus Christi plays, which had themselves shifted the celebration of Christ's sacrifice from the altar to the open air, Shakespeare's Lancastrian cycle as he seems to have understood it helped liberate communion from the Catholic monopoly on it so that the impact of Christ's sacrifice could be seen to pervade everywhere." *Shakespeare Only* (Chicago: The University of Chicago Press, 2009), 116–117.
145. Fox, 255.
146. For exceptions, see J. P. Kenyon, ed., *The Stuart Constitution: Documents and Commentary*, 2nd ed., (Cambridge: Cambridge University Press, 1986), 344.
147. Kenyon, 340.
148. See Tim Harris, *Politics under the Later Stuarts: Party Conflict in a Divided Society 1660–1715* (London: Longman, 1993); and Kevin Sharpe and Stephen Zwicker, eds., *Politics of Discourse: The Literature and History of Seventeenth-century England* (Berkeley: University of California Press, 1987), 6–10 (Sharpe and Zwicker) and 230f. (Zwicker).
149. Kenyon, 340.
150. Kenyon, 342.
151. Walsham, 8.
152. P. L. Hughes and J. F. Larkin, eds., *Tudor Royal Proclamations*, 3 vols. (New Haven, CT: Yale University Press, 1964–1969), 2: 128.
153. Kenyon, 341.
154. Harris, 38.
155. J. R. Jones, *Country and Court: England, 1658–1714* (The New History of England) (Cambridge, MA: Harvard University Press, 1978), 134–135.
156. Kantorowicz, 41.
157. Two years earlier, in 1599, Sir John Hayward had dedicated to Essex his *Life of Henry IV*, including an account of Richard's reign that caused him to be imprisoned in the Tower for "allegedly inviting the Earl to look for parallels in his own condition." Odai Johnson, "Empty Houses: The Suppression of Tate's *Richard II*," *Theatre Journal* 47 (1995), 507.
158. Johnson, 507.
159. Johnson, 510.

160. Johnson, 510.
161. Nahum Tate, *The History of King Richard the Second*, "Epistle Dedicatory" (1681; rpt. London: The Cornmarket Press, 1969), sig A1.
162. Johnson, 514.
163. Johnson, 510.
164. Tate, sig. A1.
165. David Cressy, *Bonfires and Bells: National Memory and the Protestant Calendar in Elizabethan and Stuart England* (Berkeley: University of California Press, 1989); Ronald Hutton, *The Rise and Fall of Merry England: The Ritual Year 1400–1700* (Oxford: Oxford University Press, 1994).
166. Jones, 134.
167. David Harris Willson, *James VI and I* (New York: Oxford University Press, 1956), 250–251.
168. *Constitutional Documents of the Reign of James I*, ed. J. R. Tanner (Cambridge: Cambridge University Press, 1930), 32.

NOTES TO CHAPTER 2

1. *Selected Poems and Letters of Emily Dickinson*, ed. Robert N. Linscott (New York: Random House, 1959), 19.
2. Ernest Renan, "What Is a Nation?" trans. Martin Thom, in *Nation and Narration*, ed. Homi K. Bhabha (London: Routledge, 1990), 11.
3. In her recent study *Shakespeare's Memory Theatre: Recollection, Properties, and Character*, Lina Perkins Wilder refers to the "innate memorability" of Falstaff (Cambridge: Cambridge University Press, 2010), 92.
4. Eamon Duffy, "The Conservative Voice in the English Reformation," in *Christianity and Community in the West: Essays for John Bossy*, ed. Simon Ditchfield (Aldershot, UK: Ashgate, 2001), 95. Duffy uses the phrase in the context of his discussion of Sir Thomas More's treatise *The Supplication of Souls*.
5. Shakespeare recreates the figure of Oldcastle with extraordinary although not unprecedented license. Kristen Poole persuasively links Falstaff with earlier anti-Martinist representations, both in pamphlets and on stage, and these characteristically took considerable license with their subjects. "Saints Alive! Falstaff, Martin Marprelate, and the Staging of Puritanism," *Shakespeare Quarterly* 46 (1995), 47–75. See Annabel Patterson, "Sir John Oldcastle as Symbol of Reformation Historiography," in *Religion, Literature, and Politics in Post-Reformation England, 1540–1688*, ed. Donna B. Hamilton and Richard Strier (Cambridge: Cambridge University Press, 1996), 6–26, and *Reading Holinshed's Chronicles* (Chicago: University of Chicago Press, 1994), 128–153, for detailed analyses of various early historical approaches to Oldcastle. For an excellent discussion of how John Foxe, in his Protestant martyrology *Acts and Monuments* (1563), erased the tension between Oldcastle as traitor and as martyr, see David Scott Kastan, "'Killed with Hard Opinions': Oldcastle and Falstaff and the Reformed Text of *1 Henry IV*," in *Shakespeare after Theory* (London: Routledge, 1999), 98. Kastan notes how Foxe records Edward Hall's deletion, in his *The Union Of The Two Noble And Illustre Famelies Of Lancastre And Yorke* (1548), of reference to Oldcastle's participation in a conspiracy against Henry V. After reading an account by Foxe's friend, the radical evangelical preacher John Bale, Hall "rased and cancelled all that he had written before against Sir John Oldcastle and his fellows" (Foxe, *Acts and Monuments*, ed. Josiah Pratt, in *The Church Historians of England* [London: Seeleys, 1855], vol.

3, 377–378). Margaret Aston observes that Bale grasped that "the exile of the papacy from England meant the ending of a whole historical tradition" and "the need to reshape and rewrite English chronicles with a new, reformist outlook" (*Lollards and Reformers: Images and Literacy in Late Medieval Religion* [London: The Hambledon Press, 1984], 235). Of King John and King Henry VIII, Roy Battenhouse writes, "John and Henry had become, in Protestant apologetic, the two chief heroes of English nationalism, simply because each had asserted his independence of the pope. There were some Protestants who likened John to the Israelite Moses who defied Pharaoh, and Henry to a Joshua who led the people to a land of milk and honey; others said John was like a David fighting Goliath the Pope and that Henry was like Solomon who built the Lord's house" (*Shakespeare and English History: Interdisciplinary Perspectives,* ed. Ronald G. Schafer [Indiana: Indiana University of Pennsylvania, 1976], 102).

6. If it seems far-fetched to compare a political uprising of disaffected nobles with historiographical conflict driven by religious differences and passions, it is important to recall that the Percies' rebellion might very well have evoked for Shakespeare's audiences historical memories of religious rebellion in their own time. As Christopher Highley notes, "The Percies of *1 Henry IV* are the ancestors of Thomas Percy, seventh earl of Northumberland, who in 1572 had been executed for the leading part he had played in the abortive Northern Rebellion, a regional uprising that had aimed at restoring Catholicism and establishing Mary Stuart as Elizabeth's successor . . . Thomas's brother Henry had pursued the same objectives, and in 1585 he died in the Tower, suspected of plotting against Elizabeth's life." "Wales, Ireland, and *1 Henry IV,*" *Renaissance Drama*, n.s., 21 (1990), 96. On Falstaff as an antihistorical figure, see Phyllis Rackin, *Stages of History: Shakespeare* 's *English Chronicles* (Ithaca, NY: Cornell University Press, 1990), 203.
7. As Jeffrey Knapp has recently written, "The comparison between the king [Henry V] and the playwright" is sometimes explicit in the second tetralogy, as in the epilogue to *Henry V.* "Since Hazlitt's time at least, commentators have seen Hal's career path from libertinism to godliness as a kind of autobiographical fantasy for his author." Knapp astutely observes that the analogy between king and author "constituted a rivalry as much as an equation," a point of view with which my reading of the tetralogy concurs. *Shakespeare Only* (Chicago: University of Chicago Press, 2009), 113–114.
8. Phyllis Rackin calls Falstaff the "chief inheritor in the second tetralogy of Joan's antihistorical legacy." *Stages of History: Shakespeare's English Chronicles* (Ithaca, NY: Cornell University Press, 1990), 203.
9. Robert C. Jones notes that no one in the play, including King Henry, Hal, and Hotspur, cites any historical model of heroism: "*1 Henry IV* is unique among the plays of the second tetralogy (indeed, in the entire series of histories) in its total abstinence from any recollection of the valiant dead." *These Valiant Dead: Renewing the Past in Shakespeare's Histories* (Iowa City: University of Iowa Press, 199l), 101.
10. Christopher Ivic makes this point in "Reassuring Fratricide in *1 Henry IV,*" in *Forgetting in Early Modern English Literature and Culture: Lethe's Legacies*, ed. Christopher Ivic and Grant Williams (Routledge Studies in Renaissance Literature and Culture) (London: Routledge, 2004), 103.
11. See Philip Schwyzer, *Literature, Nationalism and Memory in Early Modern England and Wales* (Cambridge: Cambridge University Press, 2004) for a persuasive argument that the nation that so many writers, including Shakespeare, helped imagine into existence in the sixteenth century was not England but Britain. Schwyzer extends to the early modern period what Raphael

Samuel and others have identified as an important trend in historiography of the past twenty-five years: the rediscovery "of a more pluralist conception of the national past, replacing an Anglocentric by a 'four nations' or 'British' perspective, 'breaking down the barriers between England, Ireland, Scotland and Wales.'" Samuel, "Four Nations History," in *Theatres of Memory*, vol. 2, *Island Stories: Unravelling Britain* (London: Verso, 1998), 21. Samuel cites Rees Davies, "In Praise of British History," *The British Isles, 1100–1500: Comparisons, Contrasts and Connections*. ed. Rees Davies (Edinburgh: J. Donald, 1988), 23.

12. Two texts in particular might be described as Protestant hagiographies of Oldcastle: John Bale's *A Brefe Chronycle Concernynge The Examinacyon and Death of the Blessed Martyr of Christ syr Johan Oldecastell the Lord Cobham* (1544) and John Foxe's *Actes and Monumentes* (1563).
13. Among the many commentaries on the name change, see David Scott Kastan, "'Killed with Hard Opinions': Oldcastle and Falstaff and the Reformed Text of *1 Henry IV*," in *Shakespeare after Theory* (London: Routledge, 1999), 93–106; Jonathan Goldberg, "The Commodity of Names: 'Falstaff' and 'Oldcastle' in *1 Henry IV*," in *Reconfiguring the Renaissance: Essays in Critical Materialism*, ed. Jonathan Crewe (Lewisburg, PA: Bucknell University Press, 1992), 76–88; E. A. J. Honigmann, "Sir John Oldcastle: Shakespeare's Martyr," in *"Fanned and Winnowed Opinions": Essays Presented to Harold Jenkins*, ed. John W. Mahon and Thomas A. Pendleton (London: Routledge, 1987), 118–132; Gary Taylor, "William Shakespeare, Richard James and the House of Cobham," *Research in English Studies*, n.s., 38 (1987), 334–354; and Taylor, "The Fortunes of Oldcastle," *Shakespeare Survey* 38 (1985), 85–100. In the Oxford collected works, Taylor famously restored the name of Oldcastle to *1 Henry IV*, although in the Oxford paperback edition, David Bevington reverses Taylor's editorial decision. See Stanley Wells and Gary Taylor, *William Shakespeare: A Textual Companion* (Oxford: Clarendon Press, 1987), 330; David Bevington, ed., *Henry IV, Part 1* (Oxford: Oxford University Press, 1987), 108.
14. David McKeen, *A Memory of Honour: The Life of William Brooke, Lord Cobham*, vol. 2 (Salzburg: Universität Salzburg, 1986), 652–654.
15. McKeen, 652.
16. Gary Taylor, "William Shakespeare, Richard James, and the House of Cobham," *Review of English Studies* 38 (1987), 334–354, esp. 347–349; Robert J. Fehrenbach, "When Lord Cobham and Edmund Tilney 'were att odds': Oldcastle, Falstaff, and the Date of *1 Henry IV*," *Shakespeare Studies* 18(1986), 87–101, esp. 95–96.
17. See Gary Taylor, "The Fortunes of Oldcastle," *Shakespeare Survey* 38 (1985), 86.
18. See Melchiori, 10. This story of a courtier chastised for forgetting his place during a court performance of a play resembles moments in Shakespeare when the action of watching a play or otherwise playing the spectator to a scene that is staged for one's benefit produces a lapse of memory. In *The Tempest*, Prospero, who frequently lectures others on the duties and responsibilities of owning and managing a memory, temporarily forgets the plot against his life when entertaining his daughter and future son-in-law with a masque. The aristocratic lovers who watch *Pyramus and Thisby* seem to have forgotten their own recent escapades in the woods, which seem curiously like the ludicrous theatrical material they are so quick to mock. And in an early modern enactment of false memory syndrome, the goal of the acting troupe in *The Taming of the Shrew* is to make the sodden Christopher Sly entirely forget who he is. At the same time, the play slyly tests audiences' memories,

because Sly does not return at the end of the play, and our interpretation of what we have just witnessed depends on whether we happen to remember the play's outer frame and its curious absence at the end.

19. Thomas Fuller, *The Church History of Britain* (London, 1655), Book 4, 168.
20. Fuller, *The Worthies of England*, ed. John Freeman (London: George Allen & Unwin, 1952), 408. Many Shakespearean editors take the resemblance between the historical Sir John Fastolfe and Falstaff to be largely coincidental or casual at best. Needing another name owing to the censoring of "Oldcastle," Shakespeare remembered the cowardly knight from *I Henry IV*, Sir John Fastolfe (or Falstaff in some editions), whose retreat at Patay (near Orléans) resulted in great losses to the English. Mutschmann and Wentersdorf, however, argue that the substitute name was anything but casual. Indeed, the choice of "another highly esteemed Protestant aroused the anger of the Puritans still more" (H. Mutschmann and K. Wentersdorf, *Shakespeare and Catholicism* [New York: Sheed and Ward, 1952], 348). Jessie Crosland, a biographer of Fastolfe, makes a convincing case for an underlying resemblance between the very different personalities of the dramatic character and his historical namesake: "'[T]hat villainous, abominable misleader of youth, that old, white-bearded satan' in whose pouch were found 'two gallons of sack to one halfpennyworth of bread,' and the discreet, watchful, cantankerous lord of the manor who kept his young dependants busy translating pious works and ruled his household with the strictest economy, often amounting to meanness" (Crosland, *Sir John Fastolfe: A Medieval 'Man of Property'* [London: Peter Owen, 1970], 65). For Crosland the resemblance goes well beyond the name. The common element is self-love, which expressed itself in the dramatic character as "perpetual gaiety"; in the historical figure, as "unkindness and covetousness" (69). Crosland concludes, "If it were a question of sacrificing their lives for the sake of an uncertain victory, or even a noble defeat, they were both of the same opinion, so well expressed in Falstaff's well-known phrase when accused of lack of courage: 'the better part of valor is discretion.' . . . A certain self-centredness determined the actions of both . . . for it is clear that to both Fastolfe and Falstaff their private affairs were of much greater importance and interest than the troublous state of things around them, and it is perhaps this similarity in the fundamental make-up of the two men which has led to the confusion between them, rather than just a certain similarity of name" (65, 68). Falstaff arguably has as many links to the historical Sir John Fastolfe as to Sir John Oldcastle. Fastolfe very likely had a connection to the household of Thomas Mowbray, Duke of Norfolk, like Falstaff, who purportedly served as page to Norfolk (13–14). But unlike his dissolute theatrical counterpart, Fastolfe was a military man of long and distinguished service. Serving in Henry's army at Harfleur, Fastolfe was made lieutenant to the new governor of the town, the King's uncle, Exeter, following the city's surrender. He also distinguished himself at Agincourt. For an account of Fastolfe's military career in France, see Francis Gies, *The Knight in History* (New York: Harper and Row, 1984), 169–187. At the time of his death he owned the Boar's Head tavern in Southwark (see K. B. McFarlane, *England in the Fifteenth Century: Collected Essays,* intro. G. L. Harriss [London: The Hambledon Press, 198 l], 171, 187). During the siege of Verneuil, Fastolfe found on the field of battle a wounded Duc d'Alençon, son of the man whom Henry slew at Agincourt. Fastolfe took him captive and, like Pistol, hoped for handsome profit from his prisoner. Like Pistol, he was disappointed, although for reasons more reminiscent of Hotspur's quarrel with Bolingbroke. His ransom was claimed by the king (Crosland, 26). Falstaff's relation to the historical Fastolfe seems more metonymic than

metaphoric, as perhaps befits a character who may be taken as a figure for early modem realism itself. Fastolfe belonged to the leading gentry of the day, a group of men "who sought promotion and wealth through attendance at court and in Parliament, or who reached eminence through military offices—men who returned to their estates only when too old to defend castles and lead troops" (G. E. Mingay, *The Gentry: The Rise and Fall of a Ruling Class* [London: Longman, 1976], 39). Although not a parliament man himself, his chief heir, John Paston, served two terms as knight of the shire (Gies, 192). Fastolfe was of that class that benefitted most from the gradual shift in economic resources and political power away from the Church and the great landlords in the course of the sixteenth century and the first decades of the seventeenth, a shift alluded to many times in Shakespeare's history plays.

21. See Annabel Patterson, "Sir John Oldcastle as Symbol of Reformation Historiography," esp. 9–10, on this question.
22. *The Oldcastle Controversy,* ed. Peter Corbin and Douglas Sedge (Manchester, UK: Manchester University Press, 1991), 206. Subsequent citations from both *Sir John Oldcastle, Part 1* and *The Famous Victories of Henry the Fifth* refer to this edition.
23. Corbin and Sedge, 3.
24. This prediction was recorded by the monk Walsingham as evidence of the Lollards' religious mania, as Annabel Patterson shows, although it was omitted by the more impartial Holinshed. "Sir John Oldcastle as Symbol of Reformation Historiography," 19.
25. Robert Weimann, *Author's Pen and Actor's Voice: Playing and Writing in Shakespeare's Theatre*, ed. Helen Higbee and William West (Cambridge: Cambridge University Press, 2000), 102.
26. James Shapiro, *A Year in the Life of William Shakespeare, 1599* (New York: Harper Collins, 2005), 40.
27. Bernard Spivack, *Shakespeare and the Allegory of Evil* (New York: Columbia University Press, 1958), 203–204, 394.
28. Corbin and Sedge, 2.
29. *1 Sir John Oldcastle* also divides Shakespeare's original name for the character from the new, Sir John Oldcastle from Sir John Falstaff. The King in an aside refers to "Falstaff, the villain" as "so fat he cannot get on's horse" (X.53–4), whereas the play as a whole represents Oldcastle as a virtuous and pious Lollard who does not let his religious convictions interfere with loyalty to the King.
30. See, for instance, S. Schoenbaum, *Shakespeare:* A *Documentary Life* (Oxford: Clarendon, 1975), 144; Robert J. Fehrenbach, 'When Lord Cobham and Edmund Tilney 'were at odds': Oldcastle, Falstaff, and the Date of *1 Henry IV*," *Shakespeare Studies* 18 (1986), 92.
31. Of the many critics who endorse this view, Alice-Lyle Scoufos has performed the most extensive analysis, in *Shakespeare* 's *Typological Satire: A Study of the Falstaff-Oldcastle Problem* (Athens: Ohio University Press, 1979). The Elizabethan Lords Cobham were descended from Oldcastle by marriage.
32. Herbert Weil and Judith Weil, eds., *The First Part of King Henry the Fourth* (The New Cambridge Shakespeare Edition) (Cambridge: Cambridge University Press, 1997), Introduction, 36. All citations from *1 and 2 Henry IV* refer to the New Cambridge Shakespeare Editions of the plays.
33. Weil and Weil, 36.
34. Kastan, 99.
35. Kastan, 100.
36. Poole, 62–63. Poole's analysis of Falstaff as a revival of the Marprelate controversy does not address the special problems that arise when this carnivalesque

Martinist figure is positioned not in a popular anti-Martinist lampoon but at the center of a chronicle history play. Placed in the service of history, a grotesque representation borrowed from England's recent culture war bears the power to reorient not only the public memory of the martyr/heretic Oldcastle but also the very role of public memory in the history plays.

37. Poole, 68. Poole sees the same ambivalence informing other stagings of Martinism besides Shakespeare's: "[I]n a debate where laughter becomes the ammunition for attacking political targets, to laugh *with* Martin even as he is supposed to be laughed *at* suggests—or could lead to—sympathies with his antiepiscopalian politics. In the roar of communal laughter, it becomes impossible to distinguish anti-Martinist from antiprelatical sentiment. Indeed, the same chuckle at Martin's stage antics could be simultaneously at and with Martin—or, what amounts to the same thing, at and with the city magistrates leading the attack" (72).
38. Dewey D. Wallace, Jr., "George Gifford, Puritan Propaganda and Popular Religion in Elizabethan England," *The Sixteenth Century Journal* 9 (1978), 41. Alexandra Walsham discusses Gifford's assault on "statute Protestants" in her important study *Church Papists: Catholicism, Conformity, and Confessional Polemic in Early Modern England* (Woodbridge, NY: The Royal Historical Society/The Boydell Press, 1993), 100–106.
39. Wallace, 48.
40. Duffy, 95. The description occurs in the context of a discussion of Sir Thomas More's treatise *Supplication of Souls* (1529).
41. Walsham, 29.
42. Walsham, 29–30.
43. Joseph Puterbaugh, "'Your Selfe Be Judge and Answer Your Selfe': Formation of a Protestant Identity in Conference Betwixt a Mother and a Devout Recusant and Her Sonne a Zealous Protestant," *The Sixteenth Century Journal* 31 (2000), 425–426.
44. Walsham, 105.
45. George Gifford, *Countrie Divinitie*, sigs. A2v–3r. Cited in Walsham, 106.
46. Robert Greene, *Groats-Worth of Witte and The Repentance of Robert Greene*, ed. G. B. Harrison, Elizabethan and Jacobean Quartos (New York: Barnes and Noble, 1966), 45–46.
47. Stephen Greenblatt, *Will in the World: How Shakespeare Became Shakespeare* (New York: W. W. Norton, 2004), 219.
48. Greenblatt, 219. To be sure, he doesn't claim Greene as sole model for Falstaff. The comic types of the braggart soldier and the parasite, together with the morality play's Vice figure and the hypocritical Puritan, also lend features to Shakespeare's roguish buffoon (220).
49. The phrase stands out in a series of speeches in which Hotspur otherwise uniformly couples an epithet with "king": "this unthankful King," "this subtle King," "this proud King" (1.3.134,159,167,182). One can apparently be subtle, unthankful, and proud and remain a king, but to be "forgetful"—to have forgotten the powerful nobles who helped him gain the throne—necessitates symbolic dethronement. This implication of Hotspur's speech is belied by a number of later plays—especially *Henry V, The Tempest,* and *Henry VIII*— that define princely power in terms of the power to erase or obliterate the past.
50. Jones, 110.
51. The gloss is that of Herbert and Judith Weil, 138.
52. The anonymous *Famous Victories* also invokes the more lopsided numbers. The Earl of Oxford reports, "There are of the French army slain above ten thousand, twenty-six hundred whereof are princes and nobles bearing

banners; besides, all the nobility of France are taken prisoners. Of your majesty's army are slain none but the good Duke of York, and not above five or six and twenty common soldiers" (XV.4–8). Shakespeare's play, unlike *Famous Victories*, provides a sly comment for these outrageous numbers in the form of Falstaff's loose accounting practices.

53. See Felicity Heal and Clive Holmes, *The Gentry in England and Wales, 1500–1700* (Stanford, CA: Stanford University Press, 1994), 34–37; A. R. Wagner, *English Genealogy*, 2nd ed. (Oxford: Oxford University Press, 1972), 358–366; and Michael Maclagan, "Genealogy and Heraldry in the Sixteenth and Seventeenth Centuries," in *English Historical Scholarship in the Sixteenth and Seventeenth Centuries*, ed. Levi Fox (London: Oxford University Press for the Dugdale Society, 1956).
54. The resurrection of Falstaff, an event stuffed with meaning, resonates with the history of the historical figure Oldcastle. According to one of the earliest chroniclers to mention Oldcastle, the monk Walsingham, at his execution Oldcastle promised his followers that he would be resurrected in three days. Although he used other details from Walsingham, Holinshed left out this one, which for Walsingham indicated Oldcastle's fanaticism; Stow included it, however, in his *Annales of England*. See Patterson, 152, and Alice-Lyle Scoufos, *Shakespeare's Typological Satire: Study of the Falstaff-Oldcastle Problem* (Athens: Ohio University Press, 1979), 109.
55. Thomas Nashe, *The Unfortunate Traveller and Other Works*, ed. J.B. Steane (Harmondsworth, UK: Penguin Books, 1972), 112–113.
56. Renan, 11.
57. *The Discourses of Niccolò Machiavelli*, trans. Leslie J. Walker, intro. Cecil H. Clough (London: Routledge, 1975), 1: 462.
58. Machiavelli, *The Discourses*, 463.
59. Machiavelli, *The Discourses*, 461. See also the excellent commentary and rhetorical analysis of Sebastian de Grazia, *Machiavelli in Hell* (Princeton, NJ: Princeton University Press, 1989), 260–264.
60. David Riggs, *Shakespeare's Heroical Histories: Henry VI and Its Literary Tradition* (Cambridge, MA: Harvard University Press, 1971), 141.
61. Highley, 92.
62. Highley describes this as "a virulently misogynist variation on the commonplace identification of Welsh and Irish as equally bestial languages" (92).
63. Highley, 94. Lisa Hopkins notes "the persistent Tudor construction of [the Welsh and the Irish] as similar," "Neighborhood in *Henry V*," in *Shakespeare and Ireland: History, Politics, Culture*, ed. Mark Thornton Burnett and Ramona Wray (London: Macmillan, 1997), 17. Londoners in Elizabethan England had similar expectations of exotic otherness from Welsh and Irish visitors. David Quinn writes that "every man from Ireland was regarded as somewhat outlandish and expected to speak, like many of the Welsh who also came to Elizabethan England, an unintelligible tongue." *The Elizabethans and the Irish* (Ithaca, NY: Cornell University Press, 1966), 160.
64. Highley, 96–97.
65. In his 1604 speech to parliament, King James, by contrast, spoke of the natural geographical unity of England and Scotland: "one Island . . . of it selfe by nature so indiuisible, as almost those that were borderers themselues on the late Borders, cannot distinguish, nor know, or discerne their owne limits" (135).
66. Eamon Duffy, "Bare Ruined Choirs: Remembering Catholicism in Shakespeare's England," in *Theatre and Religion: Lancastrian Shakespeare*, ed. Richard Dutton, Alison Findlay, and Richard Wilson (Manchester, UK: Manchester University Press, 2003), 45–46; the emphasis is Duffy's.

67. Duffy, 46.
68. Duffy, 46.
69. Patterson, 135.
70. *The Works of John Donne, in Six Volumes*, ed. Henry Alford (London: John W. Parker, 1839), 4: 334–335. For extensive and compelling commentary on the sermon and its intellectual contexts, see Garrett A. Sullivan, Jr., *Memory and Forgetting in English Renaissance Drama: Shakespeare, Marlowe, Webster* (Cambridge: Cambridge University Press, 2005), 67–73, and William Engel, *Mapping Mortality: The Persistence of Memory and Melancholy in Early Modern England* (Amherst: University of Massachusetts Press, 1995), 66.
71. Corbin and Sedge, 6.
72. Weil and Weil, 107.
73. Weil and Weil, 95.

NOTES TO CHAPTER 3

1. Maurice Blanchot, *The Infinite Conversation* (Theory and History of Literature, v. 82), trans. Susan Hanson (Minneapolis: University of Minnesota Press, 1993), 385.
2. *The Works of Francis Bacon*, ed. James Spedding, (Boston: Brown and Taggard, 1860), 12: 273.
3. Adam Fox, *Oral and Literate Culture in England 1500–1700* (Oxford: Oxford University Press, 2000), 222.
4. Martin Heidegger, *What Is Called Thinking?*, trans. J. Glenn Gray (New York: Harper and Row, 1968), 11.
5. Harry Berger, Jr. "On the Continuity of the *Henriad*: A Critique of Some Literary and Theatrical Approaches," in *Shakespeare Left and Right*, ed. Ivo Kamps (New York: Routledge, 1991), 227, 36. For Berger it is especially the last two plays of the sequence that "are haunted by the figure of 'the times deceas'd.'"
6. Jonathan Crewe, "Reforming Prince Hal: The Sovereign Inheritor in *2 Henry IV*," *Renaissance Drama*, n.s., 21 (1990), 238: "[O]ur critical tendency to elide or 'forget' *2 Henry IV* in this tetralogy, at the same time critically and affectively privileging *1 Henry IV*."
7. On the relation between lethargy and forgetfulness, see the excellent essay by Garrett Sullivan, Jr., "Lethargic Corporeality On and Off the Early Modern Stage," in *Forgetting in Early Modern English Literature and Culture: Lethe's Legacies*, ed. Christopher Ivic and Grant Williams (Routledge Studies in Renaissance Literature and Culture) (London: Routledge, 2004), 41–52.
8. I concur with James Bulman's assessment that *Part 2* has "more ambitious aims" than *Part 1*. "*Henry IV, Parts 1 and 2*," in *The Cambridge Companion to Shakespeare's History Plays*, ed. Michael Hattaway (Cambridge: Cambridge University Press, 2002), 167.
9. *Ben Jonson*, ed. Ian Donaldson (The Oxford Authors) (Oxford: Oxford University Press, 1985), 551.
10. Adrian Poole, "Laughter, Forgetting and Shakespeare," in *English Comedy*, ed. M. Cordner, P. Holland, and J. Kerrigan (Cambridge: Cambridge University Press, 1994), 92.
11. Zackariah Long, "'Unless you could teach me to forget': Spectatorship, Self-Forgetting, and Subversion in Antitheatrical Literature and *As You Like It*," in *Forgetting in Early Modern English Literature and Culture: Lethe's Legacies*, ed. Christopher Ivic and Grant Williams (Routledge Studies in Renaissance Literature and Culture) (London: Routledge, 2004), 151; see also the

excellent study by Garrett Sullivan, Jr., *Memory and Forgetting in English Renaissance Drama* (Cambridge: Cambridge University Press, 2005), especially 40f.

12. Of course, a whole theatrical genre, the backstage drama, challenges this premise and a clear-cut distinction between onstage and offstage identities.
13. All citations from *2 Henry IV* and *1 Henry IV* refer to The New Cambridge Shakespeare editions of the play, ed. Giorgio Melchiori (1989), and Herbert Weil and Judith Weil (1997), respectively.
14. On Falstaff as Lord of Misrule, see C. L. Barber, *Shakespeare's Festive Comedy: A Study of Dramatic Form and Its Relation to Social Custom* (Princeton, NJ: Princeton University Press, 1959), 192–221; and François Laroque, *Shakespeare's Festive World: Elizabethan Seasonal Entertainment and the Professional Stage*, trans. Janet Lloyd (Cambridge: Cambridge University Press, 1991), 224.
15. The relation between drama and the marketplace in early modern England has been extensively explored over the past two decades. See Jean-Christophe Agnew, *Worlds Apart: The Market and the Theater in Anglo-American Thought, 1550–1750* (Cambridge: Cambridge University Press, 1986); Douglas Bruster, *Drama and the Market in the Age of Shakespeare* (Cambridge: Cambridge University Press, 1992), and Jean Howard, *The Stage and Social Struggle in Early Modern England* (New York: Routledge, 1994).
16. Fox, 227. Not only individuals but whole towns indulged in this reinvention of the past in the form of written "charter myths" that "certain towns fabricated in support of their antiquity and venerability" and that would subsequently enter a popular oral tradition (230).
17. Bulman, 168.
18. A. Poole, 94.
19. Melchiori, 174.
20. Even this reference is reminiscent of *1 Henry IV*, specifically Falstaff's self-comparison to an apple-john at 3.3.3: "I am withered like an old apple-john."
21. Bulman, 169.
22. See the discussion of forgiving and its relation to forgetting in Avishai Margalit, *The Ethics of Memory* (Cambridge, MA: Harvard University Press, 2002), 183–209.
23. Melchiori, 99.
24. Ronald Hutton, *The Rise and Fall of Merry England: The Ritual Year, 1400–1700* (Oxford: Oxford University Press, 1994), 89.
25. Hutton, 106. Other historians have stressed the importance of economic, social, and political factors in the decline of festivity, although Hutton sees the reforming zeal of radical Protestantism as the main engine of change in the observance of the ritual year. For an excellent review of contrasting positions on this subject, see Phebe Jensen, *Religion and Revelry in Shakespeare's Festive World* (Cambridge: Cambridge University Press, 2008), 7–8.
26. Hutton, 89.
27. Patrick Collinson, "Merry England on the Ropes: The Contested Culture of the Early Modern English Town," in *Christianity and Community in the West: Essays for John Bossy*," ed. Simon Ditchfield (Aldershot: Ashgate, 2001), 138.
28. Collinson, 135, 141.
29. Collinson, 135.
30. Collinson, 139.
31. John Stow, *A Survey of London*, 2 vols., ed. Charles Lethbridge Kingsford (Oxford: Clarendon Press, 1908), 1: 91. For excellent accounts of the currents

of nostalgia in Stow's *Survey*, see Ian Archer, "The Nostalgia of John Stow," in *The Theatrical City*, ed. David L. Smith, Richard Strier and David Bevington (Cambridge: Cambridge University Press, 1995), 16–34; Patrick Collinson, "John Stow and Nostalgic Antiquarianism," in *Imagining Early Modern London: Perceptions and Portrayals of the City from Stow to Strype, 1598–1720*, ed. J. F. Merritt (Cambridge: Cambridge University Press, 2001), 27–51; and Jean Howard, *Theater of a City: The Places of London Comedy, 1598–1642* (Philadelphia: University of Pennsylvania Press, 2007), 51.

32. "Merry" occurs twenty times; "merrily," twice.
33. Hutton, *The Rise and Fall*, 19. For a discussion of the early modern observance of Shrovetide, see also David Cressy, *Bonfires and Bells: National Memory and the Protestant Calendar in Elizabethan and Early Stuart England* (Berkeley: University of California Press, 1989), 18–19; and Hutton, *The Stations of the Sun: A History of the Ritual Year in Britain* (Oxford: Oxford University Press, 1996), 151–168.
34. Cressy, 18.
35. Hutton, *The Rise and Fall*, 19.
36. Cressy, 19.
37. Beatrice Groves, *Texts and Traditions: Religion in Shakespeare 1592–1604*, Oxford English Monographs (Oxford: Clarendon Press, 2007), 129. See François Laroque, *Shakespeare's Festive World: Elizabethan Seasonal Entertainment and the Professional Stage*, trans Janet Lloyd (Cambridge: Cambridge University Press, 1991), 207–211, and "Shakespeare's Battle of Carnival and Lent: The Falstaff Scenes Reconsidered (1 & 2 Henry IV)," in *Shakespeare and Carnival: After Bakhtin*, ed. Ronald Knowles (London: Macmillan, 1998), 83–96.
38. The phrase apparently first appeared in print in Gifford's *Dialogue between a Papist and a Protestant* (1582), although Alexandra Walsham conjectures that "its oral currency probably predates its appearance on record." *Church Papists*, 9, n. 15.
39. A number of recent historians and literary critics have produced a body of significant work that shows the persistence of attachment to older forms of ritual and belief in early modern England, widening the definition of "Catholicism" in the period. Walsham's *Church Papists* has been seminal, as is that of Michael Questier, *Conversion, Politics, and Religion in England, 1580–1624* (Cambridge: Cambridge University Press, 1996). More recent work includes Arthur Marotti, *Religious Ideology and Cultural Fantasy: Catholic and Anti-Catholic Discourses in Early Modern England* (South Bend, IN: University of Notre Dame Press, 2005); Arthur Marotti, ed., *Catholicism and Anti-Catholicism in Early Modern English Texts* (New York: St. Martin's, 1999); Alison Shell, *Catholicism, Controversy and the English Literary Imagination, 1558–1660* (Cambridge: Cambridge University Press, 1999); and Shell, *Oral Culture and Catholicism in Early Modern England* (Cambridge: Cambridge University Press, 2007).
40. Alexandra Walsham, *Church Papists: Catholicism, Conformity and Confessional Polemic in Early Modern England* (Woodbridge, NY: The Royal Historical Society/The Boydell Press, 1993), 103.
41. Walsham, 104.
42. See the excellent discussion in Dewey D. Wallace, Jr., "George Gifford, Puritan Propaganda and Popular Religion in Elizabethan England," *The Sixteenth Century Journal* 9 (1978), 27–49. The other aspects of "countrie divinitie," in Gifford's view, are a proneness to superstition, a resentment by the "common sort" toward the interference of the more extreme Puritan clergy in their lives, and pelagianism.

43. Cited in Wallace, 32.
44. Cited in Alison Shell, *Oral Culture and Catholicism in Early Modern England* (Cambridge: Cambridge University Press, 2007), 4.
45. Cited in Wallace, 31, 35.
46. Cited in Wallace, 36.
47. Wallace, 41.
48. George Gifford, *A Briefe Discourse of Certaine Points of the Religion, Which Is among the Common Sort of Christians, Which May Be Termed the Countrie Divinitie. With a Manifest Confutation of the Same, after the Order of a Dialogue* (1581; rpt. London, 1598), 9.
49. Arthur Dent, *The Plaine Mans Path-Way to Heaven* (1601; rpt. London, 1610), 126.
50. Wallace, 41.
51. Wallace 48. On the latter, see Keith Thomas, *Religion and the Decline of Magic: Studies in Popular Beliefs in Sixteenth and Seventeenth Century England* (Oxford: Oxford University Press, 1971). Numbered among these folk-religious practices are witchcraft beliefs. Scott McGinnis writes that the laity's attachment to cunning folk and other witchcraft beliefs formed part of a more general challenge to Protestant reformers, who "faced the predicament of trying to displace what they saw as foolish superstitions held by the common sort." Scott McGinnis, "'Subtiltie' Exposed: Pastoral Perspectives on Witch Belief in the Thought of George Gifford," *The Sixteenth Century Journal* 33 (2002), 674.
52. Michael McGiffert, "God's Controversy with Jacobean England," *The American Historical Review* 88 (1983), 1153–1154.
53. *The Marprelate Tracts [1588–1589]* (Menston, England: The Scolar Press, 1967), *Hay Any Worke for Cooper*, 3–4. Kristen Poole refers to an anti-Marprelate stage attack known as "The Maygame of Martinism," in which "Martin appears crossdressed as Maid Marian with a cloth covering his beard; still the object of laughter, Martin becomes a participant in communal festival." "Saints Alive!: Falstaff, Martin Marprelate, and the Staging of Puritanism," *Shakespeare Quarterly* 46 (1995), 63.
54. On the demise of Robin Hood plays and pastimes in the early Tudor era, see Hutton, 31–33 and 66–67.
55. Orson Welles, in an interview with Juan Cobos and Miguel Rubio, "Welles and Falstaff," *Sight and Sound* 35 (1966), 159. Cited in Bridget Gellert Lyons, ed., *Chimes at Midnight* (New Brunswick, NJ: Rutgers University Press, 1988), 4.
56. Svetlana Boym, *The Future of Nostalgia* (New York: Basic Books, 2001), xiii.
57. The English word "lethal," from the Latin word meaning "deadly, fatal," became associated in LL with Greek *lethe,* forgetfulness and with *lethe hydor*, the mythological "water of oblivion" in Hades, causing the form of the L word, *letalis*, to acquire an "h" in LL, to become *lethalis*. The LL form and its English descendant both attest to a long-established association of memory with the perpetuation of life and forgetfulness with death.
58. C. L. Barber, *Shakespeare's Festive Comedy: A Study of Dramatic Form and its Relation to Social Custom* (Princeton, NJ: Princeton University Press, 1959), 192–213, links *1 Henry IV* to festive social custom, and Falstaff in particular with the "gay eating and drinking of Shrove Tuesday and Carnival" (213). Barber sees *2 Henry IV*, on the other hand, with putting the spirit of Carnival, as embodied in Falstaff "on trial" (213–221). Festivity seems to be already in the process of passing in *1 Henry IV*. Among other indicators, Hal's soliloquy in 1.2 already spells the death-knell of the festive world.

59. Hutton, 68.
60. See Maurice Hunt, "The Hybrid Reformations of Shakespeare's Second Henriad," Chapter Two of *Shakespeare's Religious Allusiveness: Its Play and Tolerance* (Aldershot, UK: Ashgate, 2004), 19–40.
61. Patrick Collinson observes, "Later ages placed Merry England in the very years in which Stow [c. 1525–1605] lived and constructed his largely mythical London": namely, Elizabethan England. "John Stow and Nostalgic Antiquarianism," in *Imagining Early Modern London: Perceptions and Portrayals of the City from Stow to Strype, 1598–1720*, ed. J. F. Merritt (Cambridge: Cambridge University Press, 2001), 27. Himself an inveterate revisionist, Shakespeare's Falstaff, I would argue, plays a huge role in this historical revisionism, this transformation of the Elizabethan period from a time of nostalgia for its "merrier," pre-Reformation past to an object of nostalgia as it became synonymous with "merry England."
62. For the cult of medievalism, replete with a nostalgia for chivalric ideals, that flourished in Elizabeth's court, see Frances A. Yates, *Astraea: The Imperial Theme in the Sixteenth Century* (London: Routledge and Kegan Paul, 1975), 88–111; Roy Strong, *The Cult of Elizabeth: Elizabethan Portraiture and Pageantry* (Berkeley: University of California Press, 1977); Richard Helgerson, *Forms of Nationhood: The Elizabethan Writing of England* (Chicago: The University of Chicago Press), 50; and Bulman, 159. Bulman astutely sees Hal not only wresting the medieval code of chivalry from Hotspur but also subsequently revising it, appropriating it for a "new nationalism: chivalry is thus contained within a political context that eschews heroic individualism" (165).
63. Melchiori, 188.
64. K. Poole, 65.
65. Marjorie Garber, *Shakespeare after All* (New York: Pantheon Books, 2004), 360.
66. Tobias Döring argues suggestively that plays provided "cultural substitutes" for the "rites of active commemoration" that were proscribed by the Reformation. Specifically, English history plays produced "new, though transformed, continuities between the living and the dead." *Performances of Mourning in Shakespearean Theatre and Early Modern Culture* (Early Modern Literature in History) (Houndsmills, UK: Palgrave Macmillan, 2006), 69.
67. Michel Foucault, "Film and Popular Memory," in *Foucault Live*, trans. John Johnston, ed. Sylvère Lotringer (New York: Semiotext(e) Foreign Agent Series, 1989), 92.
68. Alison Shell, *Oral Culture and Catholicism*, 22.
69. Fox, 221–222.
70. Boym, 13.
71. Wordsworth, "Ode: Intimations of Immortality from Recollections of Early Childhood," l. 54.
72. That may be the deeper significance of Falstaff's reference to the Prince as "A good shallow young fellow" (2.4.193): as expressing a collective wish that the Prince might share a bit of Shallow's fondness, rather than simply regarding the past as carefully contrived prologue to his triumphal entry onto the stage of history and politics.
73. Melchiori, 121.
74. Shankar Raman, "Marking Time: Memory and Market in *The Comedy of Errors*," *Shakespeare Quarterly* 56 (2005), 178.
75. Michael Kammen, *Mystic Chords of Memory* (New York: Knopf, 1991), 688.
76. Boym, xv.
77. See Charles Hobday, "Clouted shoon and leather aprons: Shakespeare and the egalitarian tradition," *Renaissance and Modern Studies* 23 (1979), 68 for a discussion of the subversive force of the adjective "merry."

78. Fox, 354–355.
79. Fox, 359.
80. Melchiori, 15–16. Melchiori is following C. Walter Hodge's suggestion as to how the opening might have been staged.
81. Melchiori, 17.
82. Nell Quickly's name registers the riot and festivity of comedy in several ways. Quickly may suggest "quick-lie," as several critics have argued—in other words, a profession like that of Doll Tearsheet—in addition to the alacrity with which a tavern hostess (and a comedy) must work. Along the same lines, "Nell," her name in *Henry V*, may suggest the festivity of bell-ringing as well as the passing of that festivity marked by Falstaff's "chimes at midnight."
83. That memory is not simply an antidote to Rumour is also quietly suggested by Northumberland's lines soon after Morton's initial entrance, comparing the pallid messenger to a famous classical ghost:

    Even such a man, so faint, so spiritless,
    So dull, so dead in look, so woe-begone,
    Drew Priam's curtain in the dead of night,
    And would have told him half his Troy had burnt:
    But Priam found the fire ere he his tongue,
    And I my Percy's death ere thou report'st it. (1.1.70–5)

    Anticipating by the look on Morton's face the news of the death of brother and son and the collapse of the rebel initiative, Northumberland has recourse to a classical precedent, in part, it might seem, to seek refuge from this incredibly tense moment in the recesses of the distant past. But Northumberland's allusion to Troy, while dignifying the rebel cause, does not allay the anxieties about memory unleashed at the outset by Rumour. In New Cambridge editor Giorgio Melchiori's gloss, these lines are "a confused classical reminiscence: it was not Priam but Aeneas who had a night vision of Hector's ghost announcing the burning of Troy" (Melchiori, 64). The distant past, it seems, no less than the present and recent past, is not safe from Rumour or false report.
84. Jones writes that the play presents only "a range of unpromising attitudes toward the past" (124).
85. Melchiori, 188.
86. Jones, 112.
87. Zvi Jagendorf, "The Life of Memory: The Experience of the Past in Shakespeare's History Plays," *Hebrew University Studies in Literature and the Arts* 4, no. 2 (1976), 53. According to Jagendorf, Shakespeare in the second tetralogy "penetrates beyond" the orthodoxy of providential history of the first tetralogy, "towards both a political and an intimate and personal assessment of how memory affects action" (46–47). I would argue instead that memory becomes largely a private issue in the second tetralogy because it is memory, together with all that it implies, that is recalcitrant, rebellious, scattered, and difficult to subdue to the purposes of the nation-state. In the first tetralogy, on the other hand, memory is the slender thread that ties the English soldiers in France to their identities as Englishmen.

NOTES TO CHAPTER 4

1. Samuel Clarke, *A True and Full Narrative of Those Two Never to Be Forgotten Deliverances: The One from the Spanish Invasion in 88. The Other from the Hellish Powder Plot* (London, 1671), sigs. A3v–A4.
2. Elizabeth I, Speech at Oxford University, 1592, in George P. Rice, Jr., *The Public Speaking of Queen Elizabeth: Selections from Her Official Addresses* (New York: Columbia University Press, 1951), 100.

3. Ernest Renan, "What Is a Nation?" (1882), trans. Martin Thom, in *Nation and Narration*, ed. Homi K. Bhabha (London: Routledge, 1990), 11.
4. The Oxford Shakespeare *Henry V*, ed. Gary Taylor (Oxford: Clarendon Press, 1982), 1; quotations of the play follow this edition.
5. A. P. Rossiter, "Ambivalence: The Dialectic of the Histories," in *Talking of Shakespeare*, ed. John Garrett (London: Hodder and Stoughton, 1954), 165.
6. A. L. Morton has dubbed Shakespeare's attempt to represent a unified British nation through the four captains the "climax of absurdity"; see "Shakespeare's Historical Outlook," *Zeitschrift für Anglistik und Amerikanistik* 12 (1964): 229–243, esp. 239. John Jump, by contrast, sees the play as an eloquent celebration of the idea of national unity; see "Shakespeare and History: The T. H. Searls Memorial Lecture, University of Hull, 1974," *Critical Quarterly* 17 (1975): 233–244. On the question of national unity in the play, see also Ludwig Borinski, "Shakespeare's Conception of History," *Bulletin de la faculté des lettres de Strasbourg* 43 (May–June 1965): 835–854; Albert C. Labriola, "'This Sceptered Isle': Kingship and the Body Politic in the Lancastrian Tetralogy," in *Shakespeare and English History: Interdisciplinarv Perspectives*, ed. Ronald G. Shafer (Indiana: Indiana University of Pennsylvania, 1976), 45–64; and Karen Hermassi, *Polity and Theater in Historical Perspective* (Berkeley: University of California Press, 1977). Hermassi argues that the play shows royal power to be "defective and illegitimate," and that "its exercise . . . always culminates in divisions" (103). More recent criticism offers more complex views of the play as engaging with discrepant ideologies and dramatizing efforts to contain opposition or resistances to ideology. See Stephen Greenblatt, "Invisible Bullets: Renaissance Authority and Its Subversion," reprinted in *Political Shakespeare*, ed. Jonathan Dollimore and Alan Sinfield (Ithaca, NY: Cornell University Press, 1985), 18–47; Leonard Tennenhouse, "Strategies of State and Political Plays: *A Midsummer Night's Dream, Henry IV, Henry V, and Henry VIII*," also in *Political Shakespeare*, 109–128; Jonathan Dollimore and Alan Sinfield, "History and Ideology: The Instance of *Henry VIII*," in *Alternative Shakespeares*, ed. John Drakakis (London: Methuen, 1985), 206–227; Graham Holderness, *Shakespeare's History* (Dublin: Gill and Macmillan, 1985), *Shakespeare Recycled: The Making of Historical Drama* (Hemel Hempstead, UK: Harvester Wheatsheaf, 1992), esp. 178–210, and "'What ish my nation?': Shakespeare and National Identities," *Textual Practice* 5 (1991), 74–93; and Christopher Pye, *The Regal Phantasm: Shakespeare and the Politics of Spectacle* (London: Methuen, 1990), 13–42. After defining ideology as the representation of "sectional or class interests as universal ones," Dollimore and Sinfield state that even in this play where it is often assumed that "Shakespeare is closest to state propaganda, the construction of ideology is complex—even as it consolidates, it betrays inherent instability" (211). Taylor in his introduction states that the play "advances dialectically: no sooner is a unity established than we are made aware of what the unity excludes" (71). Joel Altman focuses on various kinds of "participation" that structure the play, including the Chorus' invitations to the audience to participate by piecing out the imperfections of the play; Henry's "'participating' himself" with the vile," allowing himself . . . to be partaken of, taken apart by, a people who will not be able to digest him"; and the "participation . . . of the French-cum-Irish—which is the more horrific version of 'vile participation' that energizes this play." Altman's reading addresses the ambiguity of the play by referring it to "the ambivalent public response to Elizabeth's own imperial enterprise." According to Altman, Shakespeare "fashion[ed] a passionately imperialist drama

that soberly, even cynically, led its audience to question the values it represented and to embrace them nonetheless" ("'Vile Participation': The Amplification of Violence in the Theater of *Henry V*," *Shakespeare Quarterly* 42 [1991], 5, 8, 19, 21). In "Broken English and Broken Irish: Nation, Language, and the Optic of Power in Shakespeare's Histories" (*Shakespeare Quarterly 45* [1994]: 1–32), Michael Neill explores the tensions in England's policies toward Ireland and the "shift in English attitudes toward Ireland over the course of the sixteenth century" (4): "Essential to the formation of English identity," the Irish "also threatened it . . . While the ideology of national difference required that the Irish be kept at a distance and stigmatized as a barbaric Other, the practicalities of English policy more and more pressingly required that Ireland be absorbed within the boundaries of the nation-state" (3). My reading of *Henry* V is consistent with that developed in Neill's essay; where we differ is in focus. I try to place the absorption of Ireland in relation to a wide-ranging policy of orchestrated oblivion that helped fashion the developing Tudor nation-state and to a recurring number of challenges to Elizabethan attempts to govern the collective memory.

7. John Guy, *Tudor England* (Oxford: Oxford University Press, 1988), 352. See also Quentin Skinner, *The Foundations of Modern Political Thought*, 2 vols. (Cambridge: Cambridge University Press, 1978), 2: 349–358.
8. Benedict Anderson, *Imagined Communities: Reflections on the Origin and Spread of Nationalism*, rev. ed. (London: Verso, 1991), 19.
9. Guy, 352.
10. Much political theory argues that nationalism is a strictly post-Enlightenment phenomenon. I concur with those who believe that early forms of nationalism are to be found in early modern England. See Neill, "Broken English and Broken Irish," 2, n. 4; Claire McEachern, "*Henry V* and the Paradox of the Body Politic," *Shakespeare Quarterly* 45 (1994): 33–56, esp. 35, n. 10; and Liah Greenfeld, *Nationalism: Five Roads to Modernity* (Cambridge, MA: Harvard University Press, 1992).
11. Milan Kundera, *The Book of Laughter and Forgetting*, trans. Michael Henry Heim (New York: Alfred A. Knopf, 1981), 3. In *The Art of the Novel* (trans. Linda Asher [New York: Grove Press, 1988]), Kundera glosses the remark (which he says is often "cited as the book's message") as follows: "This Mirek who is struggling with all his might to make sure he is not forgotten (he and his friends and their political battle) is at the same time doing his utmost to make people forget another person (his ex-mistress, whom he's ashamed of). Before it becomes a political issue, the will to forget is an anthropological one: man has always harbored the desire to rewrite his own biography, to change the past, to wipe out tracks, both his own and others" (131).
12. The Boy makes reference to Nim and Bardolph, "sworn brothers in filching, and in Calais they stole a fire shovel" (3.2.43–4); Henry refers to a proposed retreat or retirement from Harfleur to Calais in a speech to his uncle Exeter (3.3.136).
13. Taylor, ed., 3.Chorus 4n.
14. Lacey Baldwin Smith, *Elizabeth Tudor: Portrait of a Queen* (Boston: Little, Brown, 1975), 100.
15. John Guy, *Tudor England* (Oxford: Oxford University Press, 1988), 268.
16. G. R. Elton, *England under the Tudors*, 3rd ed.(London: Routledge, 1991), 380.
17. Elton, 381. Henry ended the internal opposition to him by renouncing his religion in July 1593.
18. See James Shapiro, "Revisiting *Tamburlaine: Henry V* as Shakespeare's Belated Armada Play," *Criticism* 31 (1989): 351–366.

19. Christopher Hill, *Reformation to Industrial Revolution: A Social and Economic History of Britain 1530–1780* (London: Weidenfeld and Nicolson, 1967), 13.
20. Joel B. Altman, "'Vile Participation': The Amplification of Violence in the Theater of *Henry V*," *Shakespeare Quarterly* 42 (1991): 1–32, esp. 16. Altman convincingly demonstrates a possibility for shame inherent in the speech as well, but it is not a historical shame relating to France; rather, it is the potential shame of "stay-at-homes during the queen's Irish war," including players and their audiences. The opportunity of "participating the King and his French enterprise would have an enormous appeal" for them (17), even though the Crispin's Day speech would uncomfortably remind them that they lie abed while others fight.
21. *The Famous Victories of Henry the Fifth: Containing the Honourable Battell of Agincourt: As It Was Plaide by the Queenes Maiesties Players* was a widely popular play, possibly performed in two parts and frequently staged by the Queen's Men in the 1580s, although not published until 1598, when it was probably printed in order to capitalize on the popularity of Shakespeare's Henry plays.
22. Desmond Seward, *Henry V: The Scourge of God* (New York: Viking Press, 1988), 220.
23. David McKeen, A *Memory of Honour: The Life of William Brooke, Lord Cobham*, 2 vols. (Salzburg: Institut für Anglistik and Amerikanistik, Universität Salzburg, 1986), 1: 22.
24. *The Oldcastle Controversy: Sir John Oldcastle, Part I and The Famous Victories of Henry V,* ed. Peter Corbin and Douglas Sedge (Manchester, UK: Manchester University Press, 1991), 2.
25. Nicholas Harris Nicolas, Esq., *The History of the Battle of Agincourt; and of the Expedition of Henry the Fifth into France . . .* (London: Apollo Press, 1827), 166.
26. "And while proceedings in the same parliament continued and there came round in due course the feast of Saints Crispin and Crispinian [25 October], on which feast, the year before, God had shown His clemency to England in her resistance to the rebellious people of France at Agincourt, the king, not unmindful of God's goodness, renewed praises to Him in the hymn *Te Deum laudamus,* which was solemnly chanted in his chapel before Mass" *Gesta Henrici Quinti: The Deeds of Henry the Fifth,* trans. Frank Taylor and John S. Roskell (Oxford: Clarendon Press, 1975), 178–179.
27. Margaret Wade Labarge, *Henry V: The Cautious Conqueror* (London: Secker and Warburg, 1975), 188.
28. Taylor, ed., 2.4.53n. The *Oxford English Dictionary* (2nd ed., prepared by J. A. Simpson and E. S. C. Weiner, 20 vols. [Oxford: Clarendon Press, 1987]) cites *Henry V* as the first instance of "memorable" in the "rare" sense, "easy to be remembered" (9: 594).
29. Guilt issuing from memory of Richard supplies Henry with a powerful motive to manipulate memory. Sanford Sternlicht, in "The Making of a Political Martyr-Myth: Shakespeare's Use of the Memory of Richard II in *1 & 2 Henry IV* and *Henry V*" (*Ball State University Forum* 12 [Spring 1971]: 26–38), discusses ways in which the various memories of the martyred King Richard II influence characters' thought and action and also ways in which the conspiracy plot in *Henry V* evokes memories from the earlier plays.
30. Karl P. Wentersdorf, "The Conspiracy of Silence in *Henry V*," *Shakespeare Quarterly* 27 (1976): 264–287. Deliberately omitted, according to Wentersdorf, are details of family ties and political motives linking the conspirator Cambridge to Mortimer, as well as any discussion of the dynastic question,

which would, of course, reflect on Henry's claim to England as well as France. Wentersdorf asserts that a sensitive spectator could not fail to see the implications of what is unspoken, hushed up by Henry and Shakespeare in this scene.

31. Renan, 16.
32. Ernest Gellner, "Nationalism and the Two Forms of Cohesion in Complex Societies," in *Culture, Identity, and Politics* (Cambridge: Cambridge University Press, 1987), 6–28, esp. 8.
33. Renan, 11.
34. Renan, 11.
35. Hill, "The Norman Yoke," *in Puritanism and Revolution: Studies in Interpretation of the English Revolution of the 17th Century* (London: Secker and Warburg, 1958), 50–122, esp. 57.
36. The St. Bartholomew's Day Massacre lived in the memory of many Elizabethans, although occupying futurity for all the play's characters. The same may be said of the Chorus's reference to the earl of Essex's imminent arrival, al least in productions of the play following his ignominious return in the autumn of 1599: an unpleasant Elizabethan memory is cast in the play as a future event. Lawrence Danson has postulated that the premiere of *Henry V* might have taken place in the new Globe Theatre in the late summer of 1599, *after* it became clear that the Essex expedition was in shambles: "The Essex allusion does not rule out a date of composition in late August or early September. Such a pluckily defiant reference to temporary English setbacks could have been mighty cheering in that summer, a time enlivened anyway by the inauguration of the most splendid theatre ever built to celebrate the English in England" ("*Henry V*: King, Chorus, and Critics," *Shakespeare Quarterly* 34 [1983]: 27–43, esp. 27). Whether or not this is the case, in the majority of Elizabethan performances of the play, Essex's return from Ireland would occupy that same indeterminate historical space as Bartholomew-tide—between memory and prophecy.
37. James I, *The Political Works of James I*, ed. Charles Howard Mcllwain (Cambridge, MA: Harvard University Press, 1918), 269. D. R. Woolf notes that James's political works cite "'the late Queene here of famous memory, who was my God-mother,'" no less than eleven times, "far more than any other monarch" ("Two Elizabeths? James I and the Late Queen's Famous Memory," *Journal of Canadian History* 20 [1985]: 178). Woolf argues against the prevailing view that James was burdened throughout his own reign by the people's memory of Elizabeth's.
38. King James VI and I, *Political Writings*, ed. Johann P. Sommerville (Cambridge: Cambridge University Press, 1994), 134. This identification with Henry VII would prove to be consistent with his plans to have himself buried next to Henry VII in Westminster and to remove Elizabeth "from under the altar of the Henry VII Chapel Abbey" and relocate her body "in the marginal space of the north aisle." Julia M. Walker, "Bones of Contention: Posthumous Images of Elizabeth and Stuart Politics," in *Dissing Elizabeth: Negative Representations of Gloriana* (Durham, NC: Duke University Press, 1992), 252–253. See also Walker, "Reading the Tombs of Elizabeth I," *English Literary Renaissance* 26 (1996): 510–530; and Michael Dobson and Nicola J. Watson, *England's Elizabeth: An Afterlife in Fame and Fantasy* (Oxford: Oxford University Press, 2002), 46.
39. King James VI/I, 137.
40. See Highley, 91–114.
41. King James VI/I, 135.
42. King James VI/I, 137.

43. King James VI/I, 136.
44. King James VI/I, 136–137.
45. Cited in Antonia Fraser, *King James* (New York: Alfred A. Knopf, 1974), 92.
46. King James VI/I, 137.
47. Adrian Poole, "Laughter, Forgetting, and Shakespeare," in *English Comedy*, ed. Michael Cordner, Peter Holland, and John Kerrigan (Cambridge: Cambridge University Press, 1994), 94.
48. Fraser, 94.
49. Fraser, 94.
50. King James VI/I, 135.
51. Michel Foucault, "Film and Popular Memory," in *Foucault Live*, trans. John Johnston, ed. Sylvère Lotringer (New York: Semiotext(e) Foreign Agent Series, 1989), 92.
52. Quoted in Mary Dewar, *Sir Thomas* Smith: A *Tudor Intellectual* in *Office* (London: The Athlone Press. 1969), 157.
53. Edmund Spenser, *A View of the Present State of Ireland*, ed. W. L. Renwick (Oxford: Clarendon Press, 1970), 156.
54. Hill, *A Nation of Change and Novelty: Radical politics, Religion and Literature in Seventeenth-Century England* (London: Routledge, 1990), 147.
55. Jonathan Dollimore and Alan Sinfield, "History and Ideology: The Instance of *Henry V*," in *Alternative Shakespeares*, ed. John Drakakis (London: Methuen, 1985), 206–227, esp. 225; Philip Edwards, *Threshold of a Nation: A Study in English and Irish Drama* (Cambridge: Cambridge University Press, 1979), 74–86.
56. As Dollimore and Sinfield note, in 1599 Elizabeth received assurance from Lancelot Andrewes, in the manner of Henry from the archbishop, that the Irish conflict was a "war sanctified" (212).
57. There were significant pockets of resistance in Wales and sympathy for the Irish during Elizabeth's reign. As Christopher Highley notes, several Elizabethan writers "were convinced that the common people of Wales were sympathetic toward and in collusion with the Irish rebels" ("Wales, Ireland, and *I Henry IV*," *Renaissance Drama*, n.s., 21 [1990]: 91–114, esp. 91).
58. Edwards, 74.
59. See the New Cambridge *King Henry V*, ed. Andrew Gurr (Cambridge: Cambridge University Press, 1992), 68.
60. Shakespeare is also not quite as anachronistic as Edwards claims. Unity of the nation, the theme of many sermons preached during Henry's reign, was almost as important a concern in his reign as it was to be in Elizabeth's. See Christopher Allmand, *Henry V* (Berkeley: University of California P, 1992), 404–425.
61. John Turner, "*King Lear*," in *Shakespeare: The Play of History*, ed. Graham Holderness, Nick Potter, and John Turner (Iowa City: University of Iowa Press, 1987), 89–118, esp. 92.
62. See Edwards, 74.
63. David Beers Quinn, *The Elizabethans and the Irish* (Folger Monographs on Tudor and Stuart Civilization) (Ithaca, NY: Cornell University Press, 1966), 9.
64. On Glyn Dŵr's rebellion and Henry's "exaggerated" contribution to English victory, see T. B. Pugh, *Henry V and the Southampton Plot of 1415* (Wolfboro Falls, NH: Alan Sutton, 1988), 29–48. On the relation of Glendower and O'Neill, see Highley, passim.
65. Taylor, ed., 7. "The General of our gracious Empress . . . from Ireland coining" (5.Chorus 30–31) is usually regarded as a reference to Essex, although

David Bevington has suggested that the line may refer to Lord Mountjoy, appointed as Essex's successor in Ireland. *Tudor Drama and Politics* (Cambridge, MA: Harvard University Press, 1968), 20.

66. On Fluellen and MacMorris, especially in connection with other stage representations of the Welsh and Irish, see Frederick J. Harries, *Shakespeare and the Welsh* (London: T. Fisher Unwin, 1919); Arthur E. Hughes, *Shakespeare and His Welsh Characters* (Devizes: George Simpson, 1919): W. F. P. Stockey, *King Henry the Fifth's Poet Historical* (London: Heath Cranton, 1925), which devotes an entire chapter to MacMorris ("The Irish in *Henry V*," 71–92); and David J. Baker. "'Wildehirissheman': Colonialist Representation in Shakespeare's *Henry V*," *English Literary Renaissance 22* (1992): 37–61.
67. Edwards, 75–76.
68. Edwards, 75–76. For a representative of the more traditional interpretation, see Quinn, who says MacMorris's speech shows "that his loyalties to the English Crown do not submerge his own" (161).
69. See Ralph A. Griffiths and Roger S. Thomas, *The Making of the Tudor Dynasty* (New York: St. Martin's Press, 1985), 197.
70. Gower also helps forge links between Wales and official memory when he challenges Pistol, "Will you mock at an ancient tradition, begun upon an honourable respect and worn as a memorable trophy of predeceased valour . . . ?" (5.1.63–6).
71. George Macauley Trevelyan. *History of England* (1926; rpt. London, New York, and Toronto: Longmans, Green, 1947), 358. For a recent discussion of the parallelism of Wales and Ireland in *1 Henry IV*, see Highley, passim.
72. Many of Henry's Welsh soldiers at Agincourt had fought with him to quell the Glendower rebellion, and some had even fought with Glendower. Henry declared a general amnesty to all rebel Welshmen who would join his campaign. On the Welsh background of the Tudors, see Griffiths and Thomas, 193–198.
73. Taylor, ed., 4.7.96–8n.
74. Davy Gam's family remained loyal to Henry's father throughout the rebellion (Taylor, ed., 4.8.102n), and Gam himself was knighted by Henry as he lay dying on the field of battle.
75. For an important discussion of the development of Tudor policy toward Ireland, focusing on Spenser's *View of the Present State of Ireland,* see Nicholas Canny, "Edmund Spenser and the Development of an Anglo-Irish Identity," *Yearbook of English Studies* 13 (1983): 1–19; Ciaran Brady, "Spenser's Irish Crisis: Humanism and Experience in the 1590s," *Past and Present* 111 (1986): 17–49; and the Canny/Brady debate in *Past and Present* 120 (1988): 201–215. According to Canny, Spenser's *View* lays out a plan for "bringing the population of Ireland to an acceptance of English language, law, customs and religion" ("Debate: Spenser's Irish Crisis," 202). Even a reformer like Sir William Herbert, who advocated "training missionaries to preach in the Irish language and . . . translating the Bible and religious discourses into Irish" did so in order to promote English civility among the Irish. Once that civility was achieved, the Irish "would abandon their native language in favour of that of the conqueror" (Canny, "Edmund Spenser and the Development of an Anglo-Irish Identity," 10–11). For an extensive study of Tudor policy toward Ireland, see Steven G. Ellis, *Tudor Ireland: Crown, Community, and the Conflict of* Cultures, *1470–1603* (London: Longman, 1985).
76. For a discussion of this act and of English disturbance over the Irish "mantle" specifically, see Ann Rosalind Jones and Peter Stallybrass, "Dismantling Irena: The Sexualizing of Ireland in Early Modern England," in *Nationalisms*

and Sexualities, ed. Andrew Parker et al. (New York: Routledge, 1992), 157–171.

77. T. W. Moody's *New History of Ireland*, quoted in Guy, 359.
78. Fynes Moryson, *An Itinerary* (London, 1617); Irish material collected in C. Litton Falkiner, *Illustrations of Irish History and Topography, Mainly of the Seventeenth Century* (London: Longmans, Green, 1904), 317.
79. See Guy, 358.
80. The Tudor dynasty was actually founded through the liaison of a young Welsh squire at Agincourt, Owen Tudor, with the widowed Katherine of Valois following the death of Henry V. The first Tudor monarch, Henry VII, was one quarter Welsh and educated in Wales. His patronage of Welsh rhymsters and harpists exceeded that of his predecessors. See Griffiths and Thomas, 195.
81. Further legislation in 1543 introduced common law into Wales; see the concise discussion in Guy, 173–175.
82. Guy, 365.
83. See David Cressy, *Bonfires and Bells: National Memory and the Protestant Calendar in Elizabethan and Stuart England* (Berkeley: University of California Press, 1989), 7.
84. Leah Marcus, *The Politics of Mirth: Jonson, Herrick, Milton, Marvell, and the Defense of Old Holiday Pastimes* (Chicago: University of Chicago Press, 1986), 4.
85. Richard C. McCoy, "'Thou Idol Ceremony': Elizabeth I, *The Henriad,* and the Rites of the English Monarchy," in *Urban Life in the Renaissance*, ed. Susan Zimmerman and Ronald F. E. Weissman (Newark: University of Delaware Press, 1989), 240–266, esp. 244.
86. Cressy, "Foucault, Stone, Shakespeare and Social History," *English Literary Renaissance* 21 (1991): 121–133, esp. 132.
87. Cressy, *Bonfires and Bells*, xii.
88. Cressy, *Bonfires and Bells*, xiii. For detailed discussions of "the day of remembrance of her highness' coronation," see Roy C. Strong, "The Popular Celebration of the Accession Day of Queen Elizabeth I," *Journal of the Warburg and Courtauld Institutes* 21 (1958): 86–103; Strong, *The Cult of Elizabeth: Elizabethan Portraiture and Pageantry* (London: Thames and Hudson, 1977); and Cressy, *Bonfires and Bells*, 50–66. For commemoration of the Armada victory, which more than one critic has taken to be one of the functions of *Henry V*, see Cressy, *Bonfires and Bells*, 110–129. Deliverance from the Armada was not observed on a separate day but rather became incorporated into celebration of Elizabeth's accession. For *Henry V* as an Armada play, see James Shapiro, "Revisiting *Tamburlaine: Henry V* as Shakespeare's Belated Armada Play," *Criticism* 31 (1989), 351–366.
89. Cressy, *Bonfires and Bells*, 50.
90. Cressy, *Bonfires and Bells*, 50–51.
91. Cressy, *Bonfires and Bells*, 51. Cressy notes that interpretation varied with locale, with some local records noting expenses for observances of St. Hugh's Day, others for coronation day.
92. Strong, "The Popular Celebration of the Accession Day of Queen Elizabeth I," 91.
93. Frances A. Yates, "Elizabethan Chivalry: The Romance of the Accession Day Tilts," *Journal of the Warburg and Courtauld Institutes* 20 (1957), 4–25, esp. 14.
94. See Strong, "The Popular Celebration of the Accession Day of Queen Elizabeth I," 100.
95. Strong, "The Popular Celebration of the Accession Day of Queen Elizabeth I," 100.

96. According to Cressy, "Henry's speech is clearly dramatic invention, an anachronistic projection onto the early fifteenth century of late Elizabethan values. But Shakespeare's notion that the holy calendar could serve as a perpetual patriotic mnemonic record accords with other cultural developments of the late sixteenth century" ("Foucault, Stone, Shakespeare and Social History," 132).
97. See Edwards, 66–109.
98. G. Wilson Knight has suggested that the play on the saint's name "most excellently suggests, without forcing, the word 'Christian'" *The Sovereign Flower: On Shakespeare* as *the Poet of Royalism* ... (London: Methuen, 1958), 169.
99. Jeremy Catto, "Religious Change under Henry V," in *Henry V: The Practice of Kingship*, ed. C. L. Harriss (Oxford: Oxford University Press, 1985), 97–115, esp. 107 and 108.
100. John Kerrigan makes the keen observation that Hamlet' interest in the players derives largely from the fact that "they make remembrance their profession" (122).
101. Gurr, 23.
102. See Gurr, 23. Gurr points out other odd omissions in Shakespeare's play, such as any reference to Henry's famous innovation in the conduct of warfare, "the archers and the hedge of stakes that protected them from the French cavalry" (29).
103. The Lollard rising and the Southampton plot were the two major crises in Henry V's reign, both threatening the religious and political unity of his people. Both were marked by personal betrayals, those of Oldcastle and Scrope, both friends from Henry's youth.
104. Pugh, 166–168 and 126.
105. Gurr's introduction to the New Cambridge Shakespeare edition of the play usefully summarizes Shakespeare's omissions from his sources (22–23 and 28ff).
106. Dr. Richard James (1592–1638), in a biography of "Sir Jhon Oldcastel," quoted in Taylor, "The Fortunes of Oldcastle," *Shakespeare Survey* 38 (1985): 85–100, esp. 86.
107. See Taylor, "The Fortunes of Oldcastle," 96.
108. Jonathan Goldberg notes of Falstaff (in the context of a response to the Oxford Shakespeare substitution of Oldcastle for Falstaff), "From the start, he desires another name . . . From the start, he has many names . . . Sir John does not seem to have a proper name. What it is has been forgotten." "The Commodity of Names: 'Falstaff' and 'Oldcastle' in *1 Henry IV*," *Bucknell Review* 35, no. 2 (1992): 76–88, esp. 80.
109. The words "picked" and "raked" imply search and selection, according to Dover Wilson (quoted in Taylor, ed., 2.4.86,87nn).

NOTES TO CHAPTER 5

1. Adrian Poole, "Laughter, Forgetting, and Shakespeare," in *English Comedy*, ed. Michael Cordner, Peter Holland, and John Kerrigan (Cambridge: Cambridge University Press, 1994), 98.
2. See, for example, Virginia Mason Vaughan, "Between Tetralogies: *King John* as Transition," *Shakespeare Quarterly* 35 (1984), 407–420. Robert C. Jones, *These Valiant Dead: Renewing the Past in Shakespeare's Histories* (Iowa City: University of Iowa press, 1991), 46–68, argues that *King John* is transitional largely in respect of its realism.

3. Rackin, *Stages of History: Shakespeare's English Chronicles* (Ithaca, NY: Cornell University Press, 1990), 54–55.
4. See Rackin, "Anti-Historians," 341: Philip "dominates a play which is unique among Shakespeare's English histories for its own separation from the temporal and genealogical claims that unites the two tetralogies and its own lack of historical authority. *King John* has the flimsiest of relationships to its historiographic sources." Peter Womack provocatively likens the social and cultural position of Shakespeare's theater to that of the Bastard: "Like Faulconbridge, this theatre has not been *given* a birthright to the community to which it truly belongs. It has to reach it through 'the hazard of new fortunes.'" "Imagining Communities: Theatres and the English Nation in the Sixteenth Century," in *Culture and History 1350–1600: Essays on English Communities, Identities and Writing*, ed. David Aers (Detroit, MI: Wayne State University Press, 1992), 115.
5. Phyllis Rackin, *Stages*, 148–157. See also her "Anti-Historians: Women's Roles in Shakespeare's Histories," *Theatre Journal* 37 (1985), 329–344.
6. Isabel Karremann describes Richard III as "the prince of forgetting," one whose "actions are wholly oriented toward the present, dismissing the past and his responsibility for it out of hand." "Rites of Oblivion in Shakespearian History Plays," *Shakespeare Survey* 63 (2010), 27.
7. Rackin, *Stages*, 61.
8. Rackin, "Anti-Historians," 331.
9. Phyllis Rackin, *Stages*, 55. In the plays of the first tetralogy, Rackin argues, historical causation and dramatic structure becomes loosened because Shakespeare eschews a providential view of history for a Machiavellian one: "A providential view of history constructs an unbroken chain of historical causation, but a Machiavellian view interrupts that chain, constructing each age as unique, the product of Fortuna, or accident, and individual will" (54). By contrast, Rackin sees a providential version of history operating in the second tetralogy, a view with which I strongly disagree, as my reading of those plays in subsequent chapters will make clear.
10. Garrett Sullivan, *Memory and Forgetting in English Renaissance Drama: Shakespeare, Marlowe, Webster* (Cambridge: Cambridge University Press, 2005), 39–40.
11. Sullivan, 42.
12. Braunmuller, "Introduction," 79.
13. Braunmuller, 62, 64.
14. Rackin, *Stages of History*, 185.
15. Sullivan, 32.
16. Lina Perkins Wilder, *Shakespeare's Memory Theatre: Recollection, Properties, and Character* (Cambridge: Cambridge University Press, 2010), 101, 104.
17. A. R. Braunmuller, "Introduction" to *The Life and Death of King John*, The Oxford Shakespeare (Oxford: Clarendon Press, 1989), 40.
18. Rackin, 330.
19. F. J. Levy, *Tudor Historical Thought* (San Marino, CA: The Huntington Library, 1967), 93.
20. R. B. Parker, "Introduction" to *Coriolanus* (The World's Classics) (Oxford: Oxford University Press, 1994), 10.
21. Stephen Greenblatt, *Renaissance Self-Fashioning: From More to Shakespeare* (Chicago: University of Chicago Press, 1980).
22. Lawrence Stone, *The Crisis of the Aristocracy, 1558–1641*, abridged ed. (Oxford: Oxford University Press, 1967), 38.
23. Stone, 37.

24. A. R. Braunmuller, "*King John* and Historiography," *ELH* 55 (1988), 313.
25. Braunmuller, "Introduction," 69.
26. According to Braunmuller, no persuasive historical models have been identified for the Bastard, although literary models were available (313).
27. E. A. J. Honigmann, *Shakespeare's Impact on His Contemporaries* (London: Macmillan, 1982), 57–60; *King John*, ed. L. A. Beaurline (The New Cambridge Shakespeare) (Cambridge: Cambridge University press, 1990), 210; and Brian Boyd, "*King John* and *The Troublesome Raigne*: Sources, Structure, Sequence," *Philological Quarterly* 74 (1995), 37–56. The anonymous 1591 play has been long regarded as a principal source for Shakespeare's play, although some critics now argue that Shakespeare's play itself was a source for *The Troublesome Raigne*, sometimes likened to a bad quarto, and which contains echoes of other works by Shakespeare as well as works by Marlowe and Peele. For contrasting views on the relation between the two plays, see L. A. Beaurline's "Introduction" to The New Cambridge Shakespeare edition of the play (1990) and A. R. Braunmuller's "Introduction" to his Oxford Shakespeare edition (1989), 17f.
28. Beatrice Groves, "Memory, Composition, and the Relationship of *King John* to *The Troublesome Raigne of King John*," *Comparative Drama* 38 (2004), 278.
29. Groves, 278.
30. Groves, 277.
31. Groves, 280; she cites nineteenth-century commentator Edward Rose's examples of "the Bastard's bitterness at Blanche's betrothal and his taunting of Lewis" as "a vestigial memory of *The Troublesome Raigne* in which Blanche had been promised to the Bastard" (280).
32. Groves herself does not make this connection between memory as a compositional aspect of Shakespeare's play an the play's internal wrestling with remembering, forgetting, and the politics of identity.
33. In a letter to his friend Sir Henry Goodyer, John Donne used a similar metaphor to describe the various impressions made upon the conscience by conflicts between the traditional and reformed religions, that of a coin that had been re-stamped: "You will seldome see a Coyne, upon which the stamp were removed, though to imprint it better, but it looks awry, and squint. And so, for the most part, do mindes which have received divers impressions." As Donne's recent biographer John Stubbs remarks, "These words probably refer to Tobie Mathew, Goodyer's friend, now in exile in France; but it is unlikely that Donne would have denied that he too was one of the diversely influenced minds he describes here." *John Donne: The Reformed Soul* (New York: W. W. Norton, 2007), 267–268.
34. Adam Fox, *Oral and Literate Culture in England 1500–1700* (Oxford: Oxford University Press, 2000), 289.
35. Fox, 288.
36. *The Diary of John Manningham*, ed. Robert Parker Sorlien (Hanover, NH: The University Press of New England, 1976), 154.
37. Keith Thomas, *Religion and the Decline of Magic* (Oxford: Oxford University Press, 1971), 604.
38. To take one example, Ian Archer notes, "The iconoclasm of the Reformation had not completely obliterated the record of earlier donors to the church, as Stow regularly records the arms of key benefactors to pre-Reformation church building." "The Arts and Acts of Memorialization in Early Modern London," in *Imagining Early Modern London: Perceptions and Portrayals of the City from Stow to Strype, 1598–1720*, ed. J. F. Merritt (Cambridge: Cambridge University Press, 2001), 99–100.

39. Andreas Huyssen has recently used the palimpsest as a metaphor for cities struggling with questions of public memory and forgetting in the face of traumatic experiences, particularly Berlin, in *Present Pasts: Urban Palimpsests and the Politics of Memory* (Stanford: Stanford University Press, 2003). See especially 72–84.
40. Steven Mullaney, *The Place of the Stage: License, Play, and Power in Renaissance England* (Chicago: The University of Chicago Press, 1988), 15.
41. Lawrence Manley, "Of Sites and Rites," in *The Theatrical City: Culture, Theatre and Politics in London, 1576–1649*, ed. David L Smith, Richard Strier, and David Bevington (Cambridge: Cambridge University Press, 1995), 53.
42. Manley, 48.
43. David Cressy, *Bonfires and Bells: National Memory and the Protestant Calendar in Elizabethan and Stuart England* (Berkeley: University of California Press, 1989), 14.
44. Cressy, 15.
45. Thomas, 618.
46. Cressy, 14. He goes on to note that one's experience of the calendrical year varied according to one's locality, status, and situation in life: "A grain-growing yeoman knew rhythms different from those experienced by an upland herdsman . . . Civic officials, country lawyers, Whitehall courtiers, and ceremonial clergymen each had a different perspective on time and a different involvement in its rhythms" (14).
47. Alexandra Walsham, *Church Papists: Catholicism, Conformity and Confessional Polemic in Early Modern England* (Woodbridge, NY: The Royal Historical Society/The Boydell Press, 1993), 103.
48. John Stow, *A Survey of London*, with introduction and notes by Charles Lethbridge Kingsford, 2 vols. (Oxford: Clarendon Press, 1908), 1: 179.
49. Stow, 1: 179.
50. Edward Gieskes, "'He is but a bastard to the time': Status and Service in *The Troublesome Raigne of John* and Shakespeare's *King John*," *ELH* 65 (1998), 779–780.
51. All citations from the anonymous *The Troublesome Raigne of John, King of England, Parts I and II* refer to the facsimile edition of the First Quarto (1591; rpt. London: C. Praetorius, 1888).
52. Gieskes, 779.
53. Gieskes observes that, unlike his Shakespearean counterpart, *The Troublesome Raigne*'s Philip exhibits an essentialist idea of charactery (779).
54. See L. A. Beaurline's note in The New Cambridge Shakespeare edition of the play (Cambridge: Cambridge University Press, 1990), 71.
55. Gieskes, 787.
56. Michel Foucault, "Film and Popular Memory," in *Foucault Live*, ed. Sylvère Lotringer, trans. John Johnston, Semiotext(e) Foreign Agents Series (New York: Semiotext(e), 1989), 92.
57. See Daniel Schachter, *Searching for Memory: The Brain, The Mind, and the Past* (New York: Basic Books, 1996), 98–133.
58. Richard Terdiman, *Present Past: Modernity and the Memory Crisis* (Ithaca, NY: Cornell University Press, 1993), 22. The italics are Terdiman's.
59. In the case of *King John*, Shakespeare's prominent omissions include the legend of Robin Hood and Magna Carta. Of course, *The Troublesome Raigne* also omits these materials, choosing to focus, like Shakespeare's play, on questions of the relation of the English sovereign to the papacy and the legitimacy and succession that bore such resonance with questions about Queen Elizabeth's legitimacy and her anxieties about the rival claimant, her cousin

Mary, Queen of Scots. Given the still disputed order of composition, it is impossible to state unequivocally that the original historical simplifications were Shakespeare's.

60. Womack, 136–137.
61. At the end of *Hamlet* public memory also falls into foreign hands. Fortinbras, claiming certain "rights of memory" (rights of inheritance) also symbolically lays claim to rights *over* memory. Demonstrating the regularity with which history is written by the victors, Fortinbras, as his last gesture, rewrites the public memory of Prince Hamlet for the few Danes left standing, casting him in his own image as a soldier.
62. Patrick Collinson, "From Iconoclasm to Iconophobia: The Cultural Impact of the Second English Reformation," in *The Impact of the English Reformation*, ed. Peter Marshall (London: Arnold, 1997), 282.
63. Edward Hall, *The Union of the Two Noble and Illustrate Families of Lancastre and Yorke* (1542), v–vi. For further instances of the dominant early modern retrieval model of memory, see the discussion of memory as treasurer (Pierre de la Primaudaye) and as "faithfull secretarie" (M. Andreas Laurentius) in Sullivan, 26–27.

Bibliography

Aers, David, ed. *Culture and History, 1350–1600.* Detroit: Wayne State University Press, 1992.

Agnew, Jean-Christophe. *Worlds Apart: The Market and the Theater in Anglo-American Thought, 1550–1750.* Cambridge: Cambridge University Press, 1986.

Allmand, Christopher. *Henry V.* Berkeley: University of California Press, 1992.

Altman, Joel. "'Vile Participation': The Amplification of Violence in the Theater of *Henry V.*" *Shakespeare Quarterly* 42 (1991): 1–32.

Anderson, Benedict. *Imagined Communities: Reflections on the Origins and Spread of Nationalism.* London: Verso, 1983.

Anderson, Thomas P. *Performing Early Modern Trauma from Shakespeare to Milton.* Aldershot, UK: Ashgate, 2006.

Ankersmit, F. R. *Sublime Historical Experience.* Stanford, CA: Stanford University Press, 2006.

Ankersmit, F. R., Ewa Domanska, and Hans Kellner, eds. *Re-Figuring Hayden White.* Stanford, CA: Stanford University Press, 2009.

Archer, Ian W. "The Arts and Acts of Memorialization in Early Modern London." In *Imagining Early Modern London: Perceptions and Portrayals of the City from Stow to Strype, 1598–1720*, ed. J. F. Merritt. Cambridge: Cambridge University Press, 2001: 89–113.

———. "The Nostalgia of John Stow." In *The Theatrical City: Culture, Theatre and Politics in London, 1576–1649*, ed. David L Smith, Richard Strier, and David Bevington. Cambridge: Cambridge University Press, 1995: 17–34.

———. *The Pursuit of Stability: Social Relations in Elizabethan London.* Cambridge: Cambridge University Press, 1991.

Aston, Margaret. *Lollards and Reformers: Images and Literacy in Late Medieval Religion.* London: The Hambledon Press, 1984.

Auden, W. H. *The Dyer's Hand and Other Essays.* New York: Vintage Books, 1968.

Baker, David J. *Between Nations: Shakespeare, Spenser, Marvell and the Question of Britain.* Stanford, CA: Stanford University Press, 1997.

———. "Off the Map: Charting Uncertainty in Renaissance Ireland." In *Representing Ireland: Literature and the Origin of Conflicts, 1534–1660*, ed. Brendan Bradshaw, Andrew Hadfield, and Willy Maley. Cambridge: Cambridge University Press, 1993: 76–92.

———. "'Wildehirissheman': Colonialist Representation in Shakespeare's *Henry V.*" *English Literary Renaissance* 22 (1992): 37–61.

Baldo, Jonathan. "'A rooted sorrow': Scotland's Unusable Past." In *Macbeth: New Critical Essays*, ed. Nick Moschovakis. New York and London: Routledge, 2008: 88–103.

———. "Exporting Oblivion in *The Tempest*." *Modern Language Quarterly* 56 (1995): 111–144.
———. "Forgetting Elizabeth in *Henry VIII*." In *Resurrecting Elizabeth I in Seventeenth-Century England*, ed. Elizabeth H. Hageman and Katherine Conway. Madison, NJ: Fairleigh Dickinson University Press, 2007: 132–148.
———. "Necromancing the Past in *Henry VIII*." *English Literary Renaissance* 34 (2004): 359–386.
Barber, C. L. *Shakespeare's Festive Comedy: A Study of Dramatic Form and Its Relation to Social Custom*. Princeton, NJ: Princeton University Press, 1959.
Berger, Harry, Jr. . *Imaginary Audition: Shakespeare on Stage and Page*. Berkeley: University of California Press, 1989.
———. "On the Continuity of the *Henriad*: A Critique of Some Literary and Theatrical Approaches." In *Shakespeare Left and Right*, ed. Ivo Kamps. New York: Routledge, 1991: 225–240.
Bergeron, David M. "*Richard II* and Carnival Politics." *Shakespeare Quarterly* 42 (1991): 33–43.
Bevington, David. *Tudor Drama and Politics*. Cambridge, MA: Harvard University Press, 1968.
Bhabha, Homi, ed. *Nation and Narration*. London: Routledge, 1990.
Blinde, Loren M. "Rumored History in *2 Henry IV*." *English Literary Renaissance* 38 (2008): 34–54.
Blustein, Jeffrey. *The Moral Demands of Memory*. Cambridge: Cambridge University Press, 2008.
Borinski, Ludwig. "Shakespeare's Conception of History." *Bulletin de la faculté des lettres de Strasbourg* 43 (May–June 1965): 835–854.
Boyd, Brian. "*King John* and *The Troublesome Raigne*: Sources, Structure, Sequence." *Philological Quarterly* 74 (1995): 37–56.
Boym, Svetlana. *The Future of Nostalgia*. New York: Basic Books, 2001.
Bradshaw, Brendan, Andrew Hadfield, and Willy Maley, eds. *Representing Ireland: Literature and the Origin of Conflicts, 1534–1660*. Cambridge: Cambridge University Press, 1993.
Bradshaw, Brendan, and John Morrill, eds. *The British Problem, c. 1534–1707: State Formation in the Atlantic Archipelago*. New York: St. Martin's Press, 1996.
Brady, Ciaran. "Spenser's Irish Crisis: Humanism and Experience in the 1590s." *Past and Present* 111 (1986): 17–49.
Brady, Ciaran, and Nicholas Canny. "Debate: Spenser's Irish Crisis." *Past and Present* 120 (1988): 201–215.
Braunmuller, A. R. "*King John* and Historiography." *ELH* 55 (1988): 309–332.
Brigden, Susan. *New Worlds, Lost Worlds: The Rule of the Tudors, 1485–1603*. New York: Viking, 2000.
Bruster, Douglas. *Drama and the Market in the Age of Shakespeare*. Cambridge: Cambridge University Press, 1992.
Bulman, James C. "*Henry IV, Parts 1 and 2*." In *The Cambridge Companion to Shakespeare's History Plays*, ed. Michael Hattaway. Cambridge: Cambridge University Press, 2002: 158–176.
Burnett, Mark Thornton, and Ramona Wray, eds. *Shakespeare and Ireland: History, Politics, Culture*. London: Macmillan, 1997.
Butler, Judith Butler. "Primo Levi for the Present." In *Re-Figuring Hayden White*, ed. Frank Ankersmit, Ewa Domanska, and Hans Kellner. Stanford, CA: Stanford University Press, 2009: 282–303.
Cahill, Patricia. *Unto the Breach: Martial Formations, Historical Trauma, and the Early Modern English Stage*. Oxford: Oxford University Press, 2008.

Canny, Nicholas. "Edmund Spenser and the Development of an Anglo-Irish Identity." *Yearbook of English Studies* 13 (1983): 1–19.

Carroll, Clare. *Circe's Cup: Cultural Transformations in Early Modern Writing about Ireland*. Notre Dame, IN: University of Notre Dame Press, 2001.

Carruthers, Mary. *The Book of Memory: A Study of Memory in Medieval Culture*. Cambridge: Cambridge University Press, 1990.

———. *The Craft of Thought: Meditation, Rhetoric, and the Making of Images, 400–1200*. Cambridge: Cambridge University Press, 1998.

Casey, Edward S. *Remembering: A Phenomenological Study*. Bloomington: University of Indiana Press, 1987.

Catto, Jeremy. "Religious Change under Henry V." In *Henry V: The Practice of Kingship*, ed. C. L. Harriss. Oxford: Oxford University Press, 1985: 97–115.

Cavanagh, Dermot, Stuart Hampton-Reeves, and Stephen Longstaffe, eds. *Shakespeare's Histories and Counter-Histories*. Manchester, UK: Manchester University Press, 2006.

Chapman, Alison A. "Whose Saint Crispin's Day Is It? Shoemaking, Holiday Making, and the Politics of Memory in Early Modern England." *Renaissance Quarterly* 54 (2001): 1467–1494.

Chorell, Torbjörn Gustafsson. "Frank Ankersmit and the Historical Sublime." *History of the Human Sciences* 19 (2006): 91–102.

Collinson, Patrick. *The Birthpangs of Protestant England: Religious and Cultural Change in the Sixteenth and Seventeenth Centuries* (The third Anstey memorial lectures in the University of Kent at Canterbury, May 12–15, 1986). Houndmills, Basingstoke, UK: Macmillan, 1988.

———. "From Iconoclasm to Iconophobia: The Cultural Impact of the Second English Reformation." In *The Impact of the English Reformation, 1500–1640*, ed. Peter Marshall. London: Arnold, 1997: 278–308.

———. "John Stow and Nostalgic Antiquarianism." In *Imagining Early Modern London: Perceptions and Portrayals of the City from Stow to Strype, 1598–1720*, ed. J. F. Merritt. Cambridge: Cambridge University Press, 2001: 27–51.

———. "Merry England on the Ropes: The Contested Culture of the Early Modern English Town." In *Christianity and Community in the West: Essays for John Bossy*, ed. Simon Ditchfield. Aldershot, UK: Ashgate, 2001: 131–147.

Corbin, Peter, and Douglas Sedge. *The Oldcastle Controversy*. Manchester, UK: Manchester University Press, 1991.

Coursen, H. R. *The Leasing Out of England: Shakespeare's Second Henriad*. Washington, DC: University Press of America, 1982.

Cressy, David. *Birth, Marriage and Death: Ritual, Religion, and the Life-Cycle in Tudor and Stuart England*. Oxford: Oxford University Press, 1997.

———. *Bonfires and Bells: National Memory and the Protestant Calendar in Elizabethan and Stuart England*. Berkeley: University of California Press, 1989.

———. "Foucault, Stone, Shakespeare and Social History." *English Literary Renaissance* 21 (1991): 121–133.

Crewe, Jonathan. "Reforming Prince Hal: The Sovereign Inheritor in 2 *Henry IV*." *Renaissance Drama*, n.s., 21 (1990): 225–242.

Curren-Aquino. Deborah T., ed. *King John: New Perspectives*. London: Associated University Presses, 1989.

Danson, Lawrence. "*Henry V*: King, Chorus, and Critics." *Shakespeare Quarterly* 34 (1983): 27–43.

de Grazia, Sebastian. *Machiavelli in Hell*. Princeton, NJ: Princeton University Press, 1989.

Derrida, Jacques. *Archive Fever: A Freudian Impression*. Trans. Eric Prenowitz. Chicago: University of Chicago Press, 1996.

———. *Mémoires: for Paul de Man*. New York: Columbia University Press, 1986.
Diehl, Huston. *Staging Reform, Reforming the Stage: Protestantism and Popular Theater in Early Modern England*. Ithaca, NY: Cornell University Press. 1997.
Ditchfield, Simon, ed. *Christianity and Community in the West: Essays for John Bossy*. Aldershot, UK: Ashgate, 2001.
Dobson, Michael, and Nicola J. Watson. *England's Elizabeth: An Afterlife in Fame and Fantasy*. Oxford: Oxford University Press, 2002.
Dollimore, Jonathan, and Alan Sinfield. "History and Ideology: The Instance of *Henry V*." In *Alternative Shakespeares*, ed. John Drakakis. London: Methuen, 1985: 206–227.
———, eds. *Political Shakespeare*. Ithaca, NY: Cornell University Press, 1985.
Döring, Tobias. *Performances of Mourning in Shakespearean Theatre and Early Modern Culture*. Basingstoke, UK: Palgrave Macmillan, 2006.
Drakakis, John, ed. *Alternative Shakespeares*. London: Methuen, 1985.
Duffy, Eamon. "Bare Ruined Choirs: Remembering Catholicism in Shakespeare's England." In *Theatre and Religion: Lancastrian Shakespeare*, ed. Richard Dutton, Alison Findlay, and Richard Wilson. Manchester, UK: Manchester University Press, 2003: 40–57.
———. "The Conservative Voice in the English Reformation." In *Christianity and Community in the West: Essays for John Bossy*, ed. Simon Ditchfield. Aldershot, UK: Ashgate, 2001: 87–105.
———. *The Stripping of the Altars: Traditional Religion in England, 1400–1580*. New Haven, CT: Yale University Press, 1992.
Dutton, Richard. *Licensing, Censorship, and Authorship in Early Modern England*. New York: Palgrave, 2000.
Dutton, Richard, Alison Findlay, and Richard Wilson, eds. *Theatre and Religion: Lancastrian Shakespeare*. Manchester, UK: Manchester University Press, 2003.
Eco, Umberto. "An *Ars Oblivionis? Forget It!*" *PMLA* 103 (1988): 254–261.
Edwards. Philip. *Threshold of a Nation: A Study in English and Irish Drama*. Cambridge: Cambridge University Press, 1979.
Ellis, Steven G. *Tudor Ireland: Crown, Community, and the Conflict of Cultures, 1470–1603*. London: Longmans, 1985.
Elton, G. R. *England under the Tudors* (3rd ed.). London: Routledge, 1991.
———. *The English*. Oxford: Blackwell, 1992.
Engel, William E. *Death and Drama in Renaissance England: Shades of Memory*. Oxford: Oxford University Press, 2002.
———. *Mapping Mortality: The Persistence of Memory and Melancholy in Early Modern England*. Amherst: University of Massachusetts Press, 1995.
Engle, Lars. *Shakespearean Pragmatism: Market of His Time*. Chicago: University of Chicago Press, 1993.
Fehrenbach, Robert J. "When Lord Cobham and Edmund Tilney 'were att odds': Oldcastle, Falstaff, and the Date of *1 Henry IV*." *Shakespeare Studies* 18 (1986): 87–101.
Fischer, Sandra K. "'He means to pay': Value and metaphor in the Lancastrian Tetralogy." *Shakespeare Quarterly* 40 (1989): 149–164.
Fitzpatrick, Joan. *Shakespeare, Spenser and the Contours of Britain: Reshaping the Atlantic Archipelago*. Hatfield, Hertfordshire: University of Hertfordshire Press, 2004.
Foner, Eric. *Who Owns History? Rethinking the Past in a Changing World*. New York: Hill and Wang, 2002.
Foucault, Michel. *Foucault Live*. Trans. John Johnston. Ed. Sylvère Lotringer. New York: Semiotext(e) Foreign Agent Series, 1989.
Fox, Adam. *Oral and Literate Culture in England 1500–1700*. Oxford: Oxford University Press, 2000.

Frow, John. *Time and Commodity Culture: Essays in Cultural Theory and Postmodernity*. Oxford: Clarendon Press, 1997.

Garber, Marjorie. *Shakespeare after All*. New York: Pantheon Books, 2004.

Gellner, Ernest. "Nationalism and the Two Forms of Cohesion in Complex Societies." In *Culture, Identity, and Politics*. Cambridge: Cambridge University Press, 1987: 6–28.

———. *Encounters with Nationalism*. Oxford: Blackwell, 1994.

———. *Nations and Nationalism*. Ithaca, NY: Cornell University Press, 1983.

Gieskes, Edward. "'He is but a bastard to the time': Status and Service in *The Troublesome Raigne of John* and Shakespeare's *King John*." *ELH* 65 (1998): 779–798.

Goldberg, Jonathan. "The Commodity of Names: 'Falstaff' and 'Oldcastle' in *1 Henry IV*." In *Reconfiguring the Renaissance: Essays in Critical Materialism*, ed. Jonathan Crewe. Lewisburg, PA: Bucknell University Press, 1992: 76–88.

Gordon, Bruce, and Peter Marshall, eds. *The Place of the Dead: Death and Remembrance in Late Medieval and Early Modern Europe*. Cambridge: Cambridge University Press, 2000.

Graham, Kenneth J. E., and Philip D. Collington, eds. *Shakespeare and Religious Change*. Basingstoke, UK: Palgrave Macmillan, 2009.

Gransden, Antonia. *Historical Writing in England ii: c. 1307 to the Early Sixteenth Century*. Ithaca, NY: Cornell University Press, 1982.

Greenblatt, Stephen. *Hamlet in Purgatory*. Princeton, NJ: Princeton University Press, 2001.

———. *Renaissance Self-Fashioning: From More to Shakespeare*. Chicago: University of Chicago Press, 1980.

———. *Shakespearean Negotiations: The Circulation of Social Energy in Renaissance England*. Berkeley: University of California Press, 1989.

———. *Will in the World: How Shakespeare Became Shakespeare*. New York: W. W. Norton, 2004.

Greenfeld, Liah. *Nationalism: Five Roads to Modernity*. Cambridge, MA: Harvard University Press, 1992.

Griffiths, Ralph A., and Roger S. Thomas. *The Making of the Tudor Dynasty*. New York: St. Martin's Press, 1985.

Groves, Beatrice. "Memory, Composition, and the Relationship of *King John* to *The Troublesome Raigne of King John*." *Comparative Drama* 38 (2004): 277–290.

———. *Texts and Traditions: Religion in Shakespeare 1592–1604*. Oxford: Clarendon Press, 2007.

Guy, John. *Tudor England*. New York: Oxford University Press, 1988.

Hadfield, Andrew. *Literature, Politics, and National Identity: Reformation to Renaissance*. Cambridge: Cambridge University Press, 1994.

Haigh, Christopher. "The Church of England, the Catholics and the People." In *The Impact of the English Reformation, 1500–1640*, ed. Peter Marshall. London: Arnold, 1997: 235–256.

———. *English Reformations: Religion, Politics, and Society under the Tudors*. Oxford: Oxford University Press, 1993.

———, ed. *The English Reformation Revised*. Cambridge: Cambridge University Press, 1987.

Harris, Tim. *Politics under the Later Stuarts: Party Conflict in a Divided Society 1660–1715*. London: Longman, 1993.

Heal, Felicity. "Appropriating History: Catholic and Protestant Polemics and the National Past." In *The Uses of History in Early Modern England*, ed. Paulina Kewes. San Marino, CA: Huntington Library, 2006: 105–128.

Heal, Felicity, and Clive Holmes. *The Gentry in England and Wales, 1500–1700*. Stanford, CA: Stanford University Press, 1994.

Helgerson, Richard. *Forms of Nationhood: The Elizabethan Writing of England*. Chicago: University of Chicago Press, 1992.

Hermassi, Karen. *Polity and Theater in Historical Perspective*. Berkeley: University of California Press, 1977.

Highley, Christopher. "Wales, Ireland, and *1 Henry IV*." *Renaissance Drama*, n.s., 21 (1990): 91–114.

———. *Shakespeare, Spenser, and the Crisis in Ireland*. Cambridge: Cambridge University Press, 1997.

Hill, Christopher. *A Nation of Change and Novelty: Radical Politics, Religion and Literature in Seventeenth-Century England*. London: Routledge, 1990.

———. "The Norman Yoke." In *Puritanism and Revolution: Studies in Interpretation of the English Revolution of the 17th Century*. London: Secker and Warburg, 1958: 50–122.

———. *Reformation to Industrial Revolution: A Social and Economic History of Britain 1530–1780*. London: Weidenfeld and Nicolson, 1967.

Hobday, Charles. "Clouted Shoon and Leather Aprons: Shakespeare and the Egalitarian Tradition." *Renaissance and Modern Studies* 23 (1979): 63–78.

Hobsbawm, E. J. *Nations and Nationalism Since 1780: Programme, Myth, Reality*. Cambridge: Cambridge University Press, 1990.

Holderness, Graham. *Shakespeare Recycled: The Making of Historical Drama*. Hemel Hempstead, UK: Harvester Wheatsheaf, 1992.

———. *Shakespeare: The Histories*. New York: St. Martin's Press, 2000.

———. *Shakespeare's History*. Dublin: Gill and Macmillan, 1985.

———. "'What ish my nation?': Shakespeare and National Identities." *Textual Practice* 5 (1991): 74–93.

Holderness, Graham, Nick Potter, and John Turner. *Shakespeare: The Play of History*. Iowa City: University of Iowa Press, 1987.

Holland, Peter, ed. *Shakespeare, Memory, and Performance*. Cambridge: Cambridge University Press, 2006.

Honigmann, E. A. J. *Shakespeare's Impact on His Contemporaries*. London: Macmillan, 1982.

———. "Sir John Oldcastle: Shakespeare's Martyr." In *"Fanned and Winnowed Opinions": Essays Presented to Harold Jenkins*, ed. John W. Mahon and Thomas A. Pendleton. London: Routledge, 1987: 118–132.

Hopkins, Lisa. "Neighborhood in *Henry V*." In *Shakespeare and Ireland: History, Politics, Culture*. Ed. Mark Thornton Burnett and Ramona Wray. London: Macmillan, 1997.

Howard, Jean E. *The Stage and Social Struggle in Early Modern England*. New York: Routledge, 1994.

———. *Theater of a City: The Places of London Comedy, 1598–1642*. Philadelphia: University of Pennsylvania Press, 2007.

Howard, Jean E., and Phyllis Rackin. *Engendering a Nation: A Feminist Account of Shakespeare's Histories*. New York: Routledge, 1997.

Hunt, Maurice. *Shakespeare's Religious Allusiveness: Its Play and Tolerance*. Aldershot, UK: Ashgate, 2004.

Hutton, Ronald. *The Rise and Fall of Merry England: The Ritual Year 1400–1700*. Oxford: Oxford University Press, 1994.

———. *The Stations of the Sun: A History of the Ritual Year in Britain*. Oxford: Oxford University Press, 1996.

Huyssen, Andreas. *Twilight Memories: Making Time in a Culture of Amnesia*. New York: Routledge, 1995.

———. *Present Pasts: Urban Palimpsests and the Politics of Memory*. Stanford, CA: Stanford University Press, 2003.

Ivic, Christopher, and Grant Williams. *Forgetting in Early Modern English Literature and Culture: Lethe's Legacies* (Routledge Studies in Renaissance Literature and Culture). London: Routledge, 2004.

Jackson, Macdonald P. "Shakespeare's *Richard II* and the Anonymous *Thomas of Woodstock*." *Medieval and Renaissance Drama in England* 14 (2001): 17–65.

Jagendorf, Zvi. "The Life of Memory: The Experience of the Past in Shakespeare's History Plays." *Hebrew University Studies in Literature and the Arts* 4.2 (Autumn 1976): 138–153.

Jensen, Phebe. *Religion and Revelry in Shakespeare's Festive World*. Cambridge: Cambridge University Press, 2008.

Johnson, Odai. "Empty Houses: The Suppression of Tate's *Richard II*." *Theatre Journal* 47 (1995): 503–516.

Jones, Robert C. *These Valiant Dead: Renewing the Past in Shakespeare's Histories*. Iowa City: University of Iowa Press, 1991.

Joughin, John J. "Shakespeare's Memorial Aesthetics." In *Shakespeare, Memory and Performance*, ed. Peter Holland. Cambridge: Cambridge University Press, 2006: 43–62.

Jump, John. "Shakespeare and History: The T. H. Searls Memorial Lecture, University of Hull, 1974." *Critical Quarterly* 17 (1975): 233–244.

Justice, Steven. *Writing and Rebellion: England in 1381* (The New Historicism: Studies in Cultural Poetics 27). Berkeley: University of California Press, 1994.

Kammen, Michael. *Mystic Chords of Memory: The Transformation of Tradition in American Culture*. New York: Knopf, 1991.

Kantorowicz, Ernst H. *The King's Two Bodies: A Study in Medieval Political Theology*. Princeton, NJ: Princeton University Press, 1957.

Karremann, Isabel. "Rites of Oblivion in Shakespearian History Plays." *Shakespeare Survey* 63 (2010): 24–36.

Kastan, David Scott. "'The King Hath Many Marching in His Coats' or What Did You Do in the War, Daddy?" In *Shakespeare Left and Right*, ed. Ivo Kamps. New York: Routledge, 1991: 241–258.

———. *Shakespeare after Theory*. New York: Routledge, 1999.

Kellner, Hans. "Ankersmit's Proposal: Let's Keep in Touch." *CLIO* 36 (2006): 85–102.

———. "Beautifying the Nightmare: The Aesthetics of Postmodern History." *Strategies: A Journal of Theory, Culture, and Politics* 4–5 (1991): 289–313.

———. "However Imperceptibly: From the Historical to the Sublime." *PMLA* 118 (2003): 591–596.

Kewes, Paulina, ed. *The Uses of History in Early Modern England*. San Marino, CA: Huntington Library, 2006.

Knapp, Jeffrey. *Shakespeare Only*. Chicago: University of Chicago Press, 2009.

Knight, G. Wilson. *The Sovereign Flower: On Shakespeare* as *the Poet of Royalism*. London: Methuen, 1958.

Kuberski, Philip. *The Persistence of Memory: Organism, Myth, Text*. Berkeley: University of California Press, 1992.

Labarge, Margaret Wade. *Henry V: The Cautious Conqueror*. London: Secker and Warburg, 1975.

Labriola, Albert C. "'This Sceptered Isle': Kingship and the Body Politic in the Lancastrian Tetralogy." In *Shakespeare and English History: Interdisciplinarv Perspectives*, ed. Ronald G. Shafer. Indiana: Indiana University of Pennsylvania Press, 1976: 45–64.

Lake, Peter, and Maria Dowling, eds. *Protestantism and the National Church in Sixteenth Century England*. London: Croom Helm, 1987.

Lake, Peter, and Michael Questier, eds. *Conformity and Orthodoxy in the English Church, c. 1560–1660* (Studies in Modern British Religious History). Woodbridge, NY: Boydell & Brewer, 2000.

Lake, Peter, with Michael Questier. *The Antichrist's Lewd Hat: Protestants, Papists and Players in Post-Reformation England*. New Haven, CT: Yale University Press, 2002.

Lander, Jesse M. *Inventing Polemic: Religion, Print, and Literary Culture in Early Modern England*. Cambridge: Cambridge University Press, 2006.

Laroque, François. "Shakespeare's Battle of Carnival and Lent: The Falstaff Scenes Reconsidered (1 & 2 Henry IV)." In *Shakespeare and Carnival: After Bakhtin*, ed. Ronald Knowles. London: Macmillan, 1998: 83–96.

———. *Shakespeare's Festive World: Elizabethan Seasonal Entertainment and the Professional Stage*. Trans. Janet Lloyd. Cambridge: Cambridge University Press, 1991.

LeGoff, Jacques. *History and Memory*. Trans. Steven Rendall and Elizabeth Claman. New York: Columbia University Press, 1992.

Lemon, Rebecca. *Treason by Words: Literature, Law, and Rebellion in Shakespeare's England*. Ithaca, NY: Cornell University Press, 2006.

Levack, Brian P. *The Formation of the British State: England, Scotland, and the Union, 1603–1707*. Oxford: Clarendon Press, 1987.

Levine, Nina. "Extending Credit in the *Henry IV* Plays." *Shakespeare Quarterly* 51 (2000): 403–431.

Levy, F. J. *Tudor Historical Thought*. San Marino, CA: The Huntington Library, 1967.

Liebler, Naomi Conn. "The Mockery King of Snow: *Richard II* and the Sacrifice of Ritual." In *True Rites and Maimed Rites: Ritual and Anti-Ritual in Shakespeare and His Age*, ed. Linda Woodbridge and Edward Berry. Urbana and Chicago: University of Illinois Press, 1992: 220–239.

Lowenthal, David. *The Heritage Crusade and the Spoils of History*. Cambridge: Cambridge University Press, 1998.

———. *The Past Is a Foreign Country*. Cambridge: Cambridge University Press, 1985.

Luis-Martinez, Zenon. "Shakespeare's Historical Drama as Trauerspiel: *Richard II* and After." *ELH* 75 (2008): 673–705.

McAlindon, Tom. *Shakespeare's Tudor History: A Study of Henry IV, Parts 1 and 2*. Aldershot, UK: Ashgate, 2001.

McCoy, Richard C. "'Thou Idol Ceremony': Elizabeth I, *The Henriad*, and the Rites of the English Monarchy." In *Urban Life in the Renaissance*, ed. Susan Zimmerman and Ronald F. E. Weissman. Newark: University of Delaware Press, 1989: 240–266.

McEachern, Claire. *The Poetics of English Nationhood, 1590–1612*. Cambridge: Cambridge University Press, 1996.

McGiffert, Michael. "God's Controversy with Jacobean England." *The American Historical Review* 88 (1983): 1151–1174.

McKeen, David. *A Memory of Honour: The Life of William Brooke, Lord Cobham*. 2 vols. Salzburg: Universität Salzburg, 1986.

Maglagan, Michael. "Genealogy and Heraldry in the Sixteenth and Seventeenth Centuries." In *English Historical Scholarship in the Sixteenth and Seventeenth Centuries*, ed. Levi Fox. London: Oxford University Press for the Dugdale Society, 1956: 31–48.

Manley, Lawrence. "Of Sites and Rites." In *The Theatrical City: Culture, Theatre and Politics in London, 1576–1649*, ed. David L Smith, Richard Strier, and David Bevington. Cambridge: Cambridge University Press, 1995: 35–54.

Marcus, Leah. *The Politics of Mirth: Jonson, Herrick, Milton, Marvell, and the Defense of Old Holiday Pastimes*. Chicago: University of Chicago Press, 1986.
Margalit, Avishai. *The Ethics of Memory*. Cambridge, MA: Harvard University Press, 2002.
Marotti, Arthur. F., ed. *Catholicism and Anti-Catholicism in Early Modern English Texts*. Basingstoke, UK: Macmillan, 1999.
———. *Religious Ideology and Cultural Fantasy: Catholic and Anti-Catholic Discourses in Early Modern England*. Notre Dame, IN: University of Notre Dame Press, 2005.
Marshall, Peter, ed. *The Impact of the English Reformation, 1500–1640*. London: Arnold, 1997.
Mayer-Schönberger, Victor. *Delete: The Virtue of Forgetting in the Digital Age*. Princeton, NJ: Princeton University Press, 2009.
Merritt, J. F., ed. *Imagining Early Modern London: Perceptions and Portrayals of the City from Stow to Strype, 1598–1720*. Cambridge: Cambridge University Press, 2001.
Mingay, G. E. *The Gentry: The Rise and Fall of a Ruling Class*. London: Longman, 1976.
Morton, A. L. "Shakespeare's Historical Outlook." *Zeitschrift fürAnglistik und Amerikanistik* 12 (1964): 229–243.
Mottram, Stewart. *Empire and Nation in Early English Renaissance Literature* (Studies in Renaissance Literature 25). Woodbridge, NY: Boydell & Brewer, 2008.
Mullaney, Steven. *The Place of the Stage: License, Play, and Power in Renaissance England*. Chicago: University of Chicago Press, 1988.
Murphy, Andrew. *But the Irish Sea Betwixt Us: Ireland, Colonialism, and Renaissance Literature*. Lexington: The University Press of Kentucky, 1999.
Mutschmann, H., and K. Wentersdorf. *Shakespeare and Catholicism*. New York: Sheed and Ward, 1952.
Neill, Michael. "Broken English and Broken Irish: Nation, Language, and the Optic of Power in Shakespeare's Histories." In *Putting History to the Question: Power, Politics, and Society in English Renaissance Drama*. New York: Columbia University Press, 2000: 339–372.
———. *Issues of Death: Mortality and Identity in English Renaissance Tragedy*. Oxford: Clarendon Press, 1997.
Norbrook, David. "'A Liberal Tongue': Language and Rebellion in *Richard II*." In *Shakespeare's Universe: Renaissance Ideas and Conventions, Essays in Honor of W. R. Elton*. Aldershot, UK: Scolar Press, 1996: 37–51.
O'Neill, Stephen. *Staging Ireland: Representations in Shakespeare and Renaissance Drama*. Dublin: Four Courts Press, 2007.
Parker, Patricia. *Literary Fat Ladies: Rhetoric, Gender, Property*. London: Methuen, 1987.
———. *Shakespeare from the Margins: Language, Culture, Context*. Chicago: University of Chicago Press, 1996.
Patterson, Annabel. *Censorship and Interpretation: The Conditions of Writing and Reading in Early Modern England*. Madison: The University of Wisconsin Press, 1984.
———. *Reading Holinshed's Chronicles*. Chicago: University of Chicago Press, 1994.
———. "Sir John Oldcastle as Symbol of Reformation Historiography." In *Religion, Literature, and Politics in Post-Reformation England, 1540–1688*, ed. Donna B. Hamilton and Richard Strier. Cambridge: Cambridge University Press, 1996: 6–26,

Poole, Adrian. "Laughter, Forgetting and Shakespeare." In *English Comedy*, ed. Michael Cordner, Peter Holland, and John Kerrigan. Cambridge: Cambridge University Press, 1994: 85–99.

Poole, Kristen. "Saints Alive!: Falstaff, Martin Marprelate, and the Staging of Puritanism." *Shakespeare Quarterly* 46 (1995): 47–75.

Pugh, T. B. *Henry V and the Southampton Plot of 1415*. Wolfboro Falls, NH: Alan Sutton, 1988.

Puterbaugh, Joseph. "'Your Selfe Be Judge and Answer Your Selfe': Formation of a Protestant Identity in Conference Betwixt a Mother and a Devout Recusant and Her Sonne a Zealous Protestant." *The Sixteenth Century Journal* 31 (2000): 419–431.

Pye, Christopher. *The Regal Phantasm: Shakespeare and the Politics of Spectacle*. London: Methuen, 1990.

———. "The Theater, The Market, and the Subject of History." *ELH* 61 (1994): 501–522.

Questier, Michael. *Conversion, Politics, and Religion in England, 1580–1624*. Cambridge: Cambridge University Press, 1996.

Quinn, David Beers. *The Elizabethans and the Irish*. Ithaca, NY: Cornell University Press, 1966.

Rackin, Phyllis. "Anti-Historians: Women's Roles in Shakespeare's Histories." *Theatre Journal* 37 (1985): 329–344.

———. "The Role of the Audience in Shakespeare's *Richard II*." *Shakespeare Quarterly* 36 (1985): 262–281.

———. *Stages of History: Shakespeare's English Chronicles*. Ithaca, NY: Cornell University Press, 1990.

Raman, Shankar. "Marking Time: Memory and Market in *The Comedy of Errors*." *Shakespeare Quarterly* 56 (2005): 176–205.

Riggs, David. *Shakespeare's Heroical Histories: Henry VI and Its Literary Tradition*. Cambridge, MA: Harvard University Press, 1971.

Rist, Thomas. *Revenge Tragedy and the Drama of Commemoration in Reforming England*. Aldershot, UK: Ashgate, 2008.

Rossiter, A. P. "Ambivalence: The Dialectic of the Histories." In *Angel with Horns*, ed. Graham Storey. London: Longmans, 1961: 40–64.

Samuel, Raphael. *Theatres of Memory*. Vol. 1: *Past and Present in Contemporary Culture*. London: Verso, 1994.

———. *Theatres of Memory*. Vol. 2: *Island Stories: Unravelling Britain*. London: Verso, 1998.

Schachter, Daniel. *Searching for Memory: The Brain, The Mind, and the Past*. New York: Basic Books, 1996.

Schafer, Ronald G., ed. *Shakespeare and English History: Interdisciplinary Perspectives*. Indiana: Indiana University of Pennsylvania, 1976.

Schwyzer, Philip. *Literature, Nationalism and Memory in Early Modern England and Wales*. Cambridge: Cambridge University Press, 2004.

Scoufos, Alice-Lyle. *Shakespeare 's Typological Satire: A Study of the Falstaff-Oldcastle Problem*. Athens: Ohio University Press, 1979.

Seward, Desmond. *Henry V: The Scourge of God. New* York: Viking Press, 1988.

Shapiro, James. "Revisiting *Tamburlaine: Henry V* as Shakespeare's Belated Armada Play." *Criticism* 31 (1989): 351–366.

———. *A Year in the Life of William Shakespeare, 1599*. New York: Harper Collins, 2005.

Sharpe, Kevin, and Stephen Zwicker, eds. *Politics of Discourse: The Literature and History of Seventeenth-century England*. Berkeley: University of California Press, 1987.

Shell, Allison. *Catholicism, Controversy and the English Literary Imagination, 1558–1660*. Cambridge: Cambridge University Press, 1999.
———. *Oral Culture and Catholicism in Early Modern England*. Cambridge: Cambridge University Press, 2007.
Shrank, Cathy. *Writing the Nation in Reformation England, 1530–1580*. Oxford: Oxford University Press, 2004.
Siemon, James R. *Shakespearean Iconoclasm*. Berkeley: University of California Press, 1985.
———. *Word Against Word: Shakespearean Utterance*. Amherst: University of Massachusetts Press, 2002.
Skinner, Quentin. *The Foundations of Modern Political Thought*. 2 vols. Cambridge: Cambridge University Press, 1978.
Smith, David L., Richard Strier, and David Bevington, eds. *The Theatrical City: Culture, Theatre and Politics in London, 1576–1649*. Cambridge: Cambridge University Press, 1995.
Spivack, Bernard. *Shakespeare and the Allegory of Evil*. New York: Columbia University Press, 1958.
Sternlicht, Sanford. "The Making of a Political Martyr-Myth: Shakespeare's Use of the Memory of Richard II in *1 & 2 Henry IV* and *Henry V*." *Ball State University Forum* 12 (1971): 26–38.
Stone, Lawrence. *The Crisis of the Aristocracy, 1558–1641*. Oxford: Clarendon Press, 1965.
Streete, Adrian. *Protestantism and Drama in Early Modern England*. Cambridge: Cambridge University Press, 2009.
Strong, Roy. *The Cult of Elizabeth: Elizabethan Portraiture and Pageantry*. Berkeley: University of California Press, 1977.
———. "The Popular Celebration of the Accession Day of Queen Elizabeth I." *Journal of the Warburg and Courtauld Institutes* 21 (1958): 86–103.
Sullivan, Jr., Garrett A. "Lethargic Corporeality On and Off the Early Modern Stage." In *Forgetting in Early Modern English Literature and Culture: Lethe's Legacies*, ed. Christopher Ivic and Grant Williams (Routledge Studies in Renaissance Literature and Culture). London: Routledge, 2004: 41–52.
———. *Memory and Forgetting in English Renaissance Drama: Shakespeare, Marlowe, Webster*. Cambridge: Cambridge University Press, 2005.
Summit, Jennifer. *Memory's Library: Medieval Books in Early Modern England*. Chicago: University of Chicago Press, 2008.
Sutton, John. *Philosophy and Memory Traces: Descartes to Connectionism*. Cambridge: Cambridge University Press, 1998.
Taylor, Gary. *Cultural Selection: Why Some Achievements Survive the Test of Time and Others Don't*. New York: Basic Books, 1996.
———. "The Fortunes of Oldcastle." *Shakespeare Survey* 38 (1985): 85–100.
———. "William Shakespeare, Richard James and the House of Cobham." *Research in English Studies*, n.s., 38 (1987): 334–354.
Tennenhouse, Leonard. "Strategies of State and Political Plays: *A Midsummer Night's Dream, Henry IV, Henry V, and Henry VIII*." In *Political Shakespeare*, ed. Jonathan Dollimore and Alan Sinfield. Ithaca, NY: Cornell University Press, 1985: 109–128
Terdiman, Richard. *Present Past: Modernity and the Memory Crisis*. Ithaca, NY: Cornell University Press, 1993.
Thomas, Keith. *The Perception of the Past in Early Modern England* (The Creighton Trust Lecture 1983). London: University of London, n.d.
———. *Religion and the Decline of Magic: Studies in Popular Beliefs in Sixteenth and Seventeenth Century England*. Oxford: Oxford University Press, 1997.
Tillyard, E. M. W. *Shakespeare's History Plays*. New York: Barnes and Noble, 1944.

Todorov, Tzvetan. *Memory as a Remedy for Evil*. Trans. Gila Walker. London: Seagull Books, 2010.

Vann, Richard T. "The Reception of Hayden White." *History and Theory* 37 (1998): 143–161.

Vaughan, Virginia Mason. "Between Tetralogies: *King John* as Transition." *Shakespeare Quarterly* 35 (1984): 407–420.

Wagner, A. R. *English Genealogy* (2nd ed.). Oxford: Oxford University Press, 1972.

Walker, Julia M. "Bones of Contention: Posthumous Images of Elizabeth and Stuart Politics." In *Dissing Elizabeth: Negative Representations of Gloriana*, ed. Julia M. Walker. Durham, NC: Duke University Press, 1992: 252–276.

———. "Reading the Tombs of Elizabeth I." *English Literary Renaissance* 26 (1996): 510–530.

Wallace, Dewey D., Jr. "George Gifford, Puritan Propaganda and Popular Religion in Elizabethan England." *The Sixteenth Century Journal* 9 (1978): 27–49.

Walsham, Alexandra. *Church Papists: Catholicism, Conformity and Confessional Polemic in Early Modern England*. Woodbridge, NY: The Boydell Press, 1993.

Warnock, Mary. *Memory*. London: Faber, 1987.

Wayland, Scott. "Religious Change and the Renaissance Elegy." *English Literary Renaissance* 39 (2009): 429–459.

Weimann, Robert. *Author's Pen and Actor's Voice: Playing and Writing in Shakespeare's Theatre*. Cambridge: Cambridge University Press, 2000.

———. *Shakespeare and the Popular Tradition in the Theater: Studies in the Social Dimension of Dramatic Form and Function*. Baltimore, MD: The Johns Hopkins University Press, 1978.

Weinrich, Harald. *Lethe: The Art and Critique of Forgetting*. Trans. Steven Rendall. Ithaca, NY: Cornell University Press, 2004.

Wentersdorf, Karl P. "The Conspiracy of Silence in *Henry V*." *Shakespeare Quarterly* 27 (1976): 264–287.

White, Hayden. *The Content of the Form: Narrative Discourse and Historical Representation*. Baltimore, MD: The Johns Hopkins University Press, 1987.

Whitehead, Anne. *Memory: The New Critical Idiom*. London: Routledge, 2009.

Wilder, Lina Perkins. *Shakespeare's Memory Theatre: Recollection, Properties, and Character*. Cambridge: Cambridge University Press, 2010.

Wilkinson, Bertie. *Constitutional History of Medieval England, 1216–1399*. 3 vols. London: Longmans, Green, 1948–1952.

Wilson, Richard. *Secret Shakespeare: Studies in Theatre, Religion and Resistance*. Manchester, UK: Manchester University Press, 2004.

Womack, Peter. Peter. "Imagining Communities: Theatres and the English Nation in the Sixteenth Century." In *Culture and History, 1350–1600*, ed. David Aers. Detroit: Wayne State University Press, 1992: 91–145.

Woolf, Daniel R. *The Idea of History in Early Stuart England: Erudition, Ideology, and the "Light of Truth" from the Accession of James I to the Civil War*. Toronto: University of Toronto Press, 1990.

———. *Reading History in Early Modern England*. Cambridge: Cambridge University Press, 2000.

———. "Two Elizabeths? James I and the Late Queen's Famous Memory." *Journal of Canadian History* 20 (1985): 167–191.

Yates, Frances A. *The Art of Memory*. London: Routledge and Kegan Paul, 1966.

———. *Astraea: The Imperial Theme in the Sixteenth Century*. London: Routledge and Kegan Paul, 1975.

———. "Elizabethan Chivalry: The Romance of the Accession Day Tilts." *Journal of the Warburg and Courtauld Institutes* 20 (1957): 4–25.

Index

L

M

N

O